Step by Step
CHINESE COOKING

Step by Step CHINESE COOKING

Lo Mei Hing, Giulia Marzotto Caotorta and Sun Tzi Hsi

CENTURY PUBLISHING

LONDON

Before you cook

You are advised to read the section on special ingredients
(pp. 298–303).
Imperial and metric measurements have been calculated
separately.
Work in either imperial or metric as they are not exact
equivalents.
All recipes serve 4 unless otherwise indicated.

Translated by Sara Harris
Copyright © 1981 Shogakukan Publishing Co. Ltd., Tokyo for the original edition.
Copyright © 1982 Arnoldo Mondadori Editore, S.p.A., Milan for the international
edition.
English translation copyright © 1983 Arnoldo Mondadori Editore, S.p.A., Milan
All rights reserved
First published in Great Britain in 1983
by Century Publishing Co. Ltd
76 Old Compton Street, London W1V 5PA

ISBN 0 7126 0192 9

Printed and bound in Italy by Arnoldo Mondadori Editore, Verona

Contents

". . . there are few who know how to distinguish the true taste of food."
—Mencius (372–289 BC)

"From the moment I awake each morning I must occupy myself with seven things: fuel, rice, oil, salt, soy sauce, vinegar, and tea."
—Lines spoken by the wife in a Chinese play dating from the Yüan dynasty (1280–1368).

Foreword

This book is both authentic and original — authentic because it successfully evokes the taste and aroma of the specialities from each region of China, and original because it is one of that rare breed of cookery books which contains illustrations not only of every stage of the recipe, but of each completed dish as well.

With Lo Mei Hing (a distant relative of mine? In classical China we believe that "all men are brothers" and all those of the same surname are blood relatives, at least in the second or third degree!) I really feel that I am entering an authentic Chinese kitchen — sparse and uncluttered. They are very different from their Western equivalents which, though full of sophisticated labour-saving devices, often lack the sense of tradition and painstaking search for excellence found in a Chinese kitchen.

In contrast to the sparseness of the kitchen, behind Chinese cooking there lies a rich knowledge of food which has been distilled from 3,000 years' experience; the result is a repertoire of dishes far exceeding that of any other national cuisine. It is only recently that Chinese food has been appreciated by the West; this recognition and appreciation has encouraged many top French chefs to make the pilgrimage to China over the last few years.

The introductory chapters to *Step by Step Chinese Cooking* are well worth reading since they touch upon many of the colourful aspects of Chinese food and cooking. The recipes themselves filled me with nostalgia for the far-off days when I was a youngster living in Foochow, Shanghai and Peking. Although nowadays I enjoy the luxury of an annual gastronomic tour of China, during which I might eat a dozen 10–15 course banquet-dinners in as many days in every culinary region of the country, these recipes were close enough to the originals to conjure up very special memories.

Among the recipes, I was particularly pleased to see Chinese cold dishes and salads. These often-neglected dishes in fact play quite an important part in the food which we Chinese prepare both for simple meals and for more formal occasions. They are usually made up with ready-prepared ingredients which need no further cooking — foods which have been spiced, salted or cooked in wine and soya sauce — which are then amalgamated to make a complete dish. Chinese charcuterie is one example, i.e. roast meats, smoked meats, "drunken meat", soya braised and spiced kidney, liver, knuckles, pork trotters and so on. When these meats are shredded or cut into strips they can be tossed with plain cooked noodles, and with a little sauce thrown over them will form another complete series of "cold-tossed noodle" dishes. Seafoods, including crab meat, served with lightly cooked vegetables (such as shredded cucumber, celery or cauliflower florets) extend the range still further. A frequently used item in these combinations is the "1,000 year old egg" (a

7

preserved egg with a distinctive cheesy flavour).

Another interesting inclusion is the plain-cooked Chinese meat dish. Western people may have gained the impression that all Chinese dishes are cooked and served in savoury sauces (and are thus a uniform brown in colour). In fact, a good percentage of Chinese dishes are plain-cooked. Plain-cooked meat dishes are served cut into slices or bite-sized chunks and are accompanied by a selection of dips made from garlic, ginger, onion, chili, mixed with different proportions of vinegar, soy sauce (dark or light), soya pastes, mustard and plum sauce and sesame oil. The advantage of this type of dish over foods cooked in sauces is that diners can choose their own sauces to dip into for every mouthful of food, and the principal ingredients of the dish – whether it's poultry, meat, fish or game – will retain the original flavour to a far greater degree.

Another attractive feature of this book is the descriptive introduction to many of the chapters. These provide a résumé of the historical and geographic background and the symbolism associated with each category of recipes. Thus for example we hear about the Chinese character for pig, "ju" (or "chu") in the introduction to the chapter about pork. As the author explains, the Chinese word "ja" or "home" consists of the radical of the word for "roof" with the radical of the word for "pig" underneath. Thus we can see that to the Chinese, the pig is a very homely animal, and pork a very domestic meat, used more frequently than any other kind.

One of the dishes which struck me most of all was "Deep-fried oysters." I can distinctly remember eating this very dish hot from the pan of a hawker one cold winter's day on a kerb-side in Shanghai, as long ago as 1922. I clearly recall the specks of seaweed amongst the oyster batter! I also welcome the mention of the usefulness of grated radish and tangerine in sauces, and the "five spice" recipe for mackerel – mackerel has such a strong fishy smell that it needs to be complemented by something which is even stronger in taste and aroma. It was also good to read about the two very different types of soup prepared in Chinese cooking, and their separate functions. Most Chinese soups are clear soups, and are often served at the end of the meal to cleanse the palate, but there are several thick soups, such as Shark's Fin Soup, which should be served near the beginning of the meal, in small bowls. Also interesting was the point made about the influence of Buddhism on Chinese vegetable cookery – in fact it seems that Buddhism's effect on Chinese vegetarian food has been rather more profound than its influence on Chinese philosophy!

All in all, I rather wish I had written the book myself!

Harmony, balance, and joy: a glimpse of Chinese philosophy through Chinese cooking

When I was a little girl in China the grown-ups used to say to me "Eat this, it's Yang and it's good for you!" or "Drink this, it will give you energy!" From then on I realised that we should no more draw a distinction between food and medicine than try to separate the body and the soul; anything which is good for the body must be both therapeutic and nourishing at one and the same time.

Eating is one of the necessities of life but it should be enjoyed and become as pleasurable as singing, talking to one another, enquiring into the meaning of life, breathing, painting ... activities which are the very stuff of being. Good nutrition consists of eating only when one is hungry, rather like writing poetry only when one is inspired; it is not healthy to stuff oneself full of food until the stomach feels as if it may burst. Likewise, we should drink only when we feel thirsty and then preferably hot or cool drinks – iced drinks are not advisable. A good general rule is always to get up from the table feeling as if one could eat a little more and never to become so hungry that one suffers from a feeling of malaise. In my youth, the grown-ups were echoing the words of the ancient philosophers when they told me: "This will keep you healthy because you will maintain the vital flow of energy and life force and the positive and negative forces of Yin and Yang will be evenly balanced."

Perhaps the best word to use when describing Chinese philosophy and the aims which it has inspired in the art of Chinese cooking would be "harmony". There are no hard and fast rules, no fixed dogma, no arbitrary categories or immutable approved methods; the aim is to achieve balance.

This means that an hors d'oeuvre can equally well serve as a side dish or as part of a main course and that a particular ingredient can form a complete meal. It is all up to the individual; the important thing to remember is not to force oneself to eat something which one doesn't want, for this will only harm the body and mind. In China, our constant endeavour is to achieve the balance between the Yin and Yang principles.

This underlying philosophy should be constantly borne in mind when learning about Chinese cooking; nor should we forget that the Chinese civilisation is over 5000 years old and yet China's population is still growing and now represents one-third of the human race. China covers vast stretches of Asia, and climate and conditions therefore vary widely from region to region. The country is surrounded from the north-east to the south-west by high mountains, fertile plains, lakes, rivers and seas and all these have inevitably made their mark on the inhabitants, determining countless different ways of living and eating.

For long periods some regions were cut off from the rest of the country by natural barriers, so that China has been influenced by many different, often alien, cultural traditions. The populations of the various regions share certain characteristics: lively imagination, creativity and the ability to make the most of what nature has provided. In central and southern China rice is the staple food; in the north, maize and cereals, depending on whether a particular region's soil and climate are more suited to growing one or the other. The variations in each region's principal crop are reflected in the thousands of local dishes which for convenience are classified under four main "schools" of cooking: the North (Hopei, Shantung and Honan); the South (Kwangtung); the East (Chekiang, Fukien and Kiangsu) and the West (Szechuan and Yunnan).

One must remember that China has always been a poor country with only a small proportion of her enormous land area suitable for agriculture. Successive invasions by barbarians, famines caused by drought or floods and the inexorably soaring population have meant that throughout her long history the problem of food has always been of crucial importance. Anything or everything which can possibly be eaten has therefore found a place in the Chinese repertoire of cooking: parts of the duck such as the beak and feet are regarded as inedible and faintly repulsive in many countries of the world; the Chinese consider them delicacies and take as much care in their preparation as a westerner would devote to the choicest ingredients at his disposal. When they do not form the basis of a meal, chicken's blood, feet and nearly every imaginable organ are used as additional ingredients in dishes, often inspired by necessity and enhanced by the imagination. An example of this is a dish which is considered by the inhabitants of Shao-hsing in the province of Chekiang to be the epitome of refined cooking and which combines the tastes of chicken skin with the wing flesh, tendons and feet – an example *par excellence* of the Chinese dictum "Everything but the feathers".

THE COOKING OF NORTHERN CHINA:
the cuisine of the Emperors

It is difficult to define the exact area represented by northern China. For simplicity's sake it can be said to be made up of the Yellow River basin, and more specifically of the provinces of Shantung and Hopei. These two provinces have played an important part in Chinese history: Shantung is the native province of the two greatest Chinese philosophers, Confucius and Mencius; Hopei is the province in which China's capital, Peking, has been situated from time immemorial. The two provinces are, in fact, so closely linked as almost to be considered

one, and as such are known as the cradle of Chinese civilisation.

Shantung can reasonably take credit as being the main source and as having the greatest influence on northern Chinese cooking, although Hopei has certainly made a considerable contribution. Hopei, more specifically Peking, has been the melting-pot of regional traditions in cooking and the focal point which attracted the best and most original cooks from all over China.

The Mongolian influence has been one of the strongest external forces; for centuries there was a steady flow of emigrants from this region southwards who came to settle in China. Later on there were several dynasties of rulers of Mongolian origin and many Mongolian dishes were adopted by the people of northern China.

The Great Wall, that monumental barrier straddling the country, had kept out the Tartar hordes for hundreds of years but eventually, in the early 13th century, China was invaded and Kubla Khan, who enjoyed a very long reign, finally ruled over all the "Sons of Han" when in 1280 he became Emperor of all China; under his reign Mongolian influence reached its highest point and left behind a legacy which survives to this day. The fact that many of the invading hordes were Moslems accounts for the relative scarcity of pork dishes in this region's cuisine and for the abundance of recipes based on mutton and goat (whose strong flavour and smell are repugnant to the Chinese from other regions).

A long succession of emperors imprinted their customs and ways of living on the country, each bringing his own native region's usages and distinctive styles to be adopted and given the seal of the imperial court's approval.

The climate in northern China is too cold for rice cultivation but the alluvial plains of the Yellow River and the windswept expanses of yellow earth in the provinces of Shansi, Shensi, Ningsia and Kansu have for thousands of years provided the fertile soil necessary for growing wheat, millet, barley and other cereals. So flour was a basic ingredient in the cooking of these regions.

Apart from limiting the choice of ingredients, the extreme cold in this region has determined the cooking techniques used. The Mongolian hot pot of today is a modest, scaled-down version of the great braziers which were once used both to cook food and warm people's homes. Oil was used a great deal for this same reason and so it was necessary to include plenty of vinegar, garlic and leeks to counteract its taste. The popularity of such starchy items as steamed breads, pancakes and dumplings of many kinds, some stuffed with finely chopped meat or vegetables, can also be explained by the need to combat the rigours of the climate.

The long duration of the Ch'ing (Qing) dynasty (1644–1911), also known as the Manchu dynasty, provided the final impetus to the establishment of what is now recognised as a separate school of cooking in the north; under the Manchu supremacy northern Chinese cuisine received its finishing touches.

Since the Manchus had no real school of cooking of their own, they were content to adopt the best of the other regions' cuisines (especially that of the south) and to absorb them into their own, less venerable culinary tradition. For this reason some purists maintain that there is no genuinely native school of northern China and that the region has simply imported what is most outstanding from the rest of the country. Be that as it may, the originality and exquisite taste of many dishes from this area, such as Peking Duck, are beyond question.

THE TASTE OF THE SOUTH: where the sun is reflected in the paddy fields

Far beyond the borders of China, in restaurants scattered all over the world, the taste of the food of Kwangtung and, to a lesser extent, of Kwangsi is certainly the most widely known and usually goes under the name of Cantonese cuisine.

The main crop of this area is rice. The sub-tropical climate makes it possible to harvest three crops a year, but apart from this an almost inexhaustible quantity and infinite variety of fruit and vegetables is produced, wide enough to satisfy the most demanding cooks. Hence the richness of taste, colour and aroma in the cuisine of this region.

From the earliest days of their ancient history the people of Kwangtung and Kwangsi have derived a large part of their food from the sea, which means that seafoods of all kinds figure largely on the menus of southern China. The most sought-after quality in these fish and shellfish is absolute freshness and to ensure this they are sold live in the markets. This does not prevent the widespread preservation of fish by drying or salting and many sauces are made with seafoods of various kinds.

As for meat, pork and chicken are the most widely consumed; beef is not particularly sought after and mutton or lamb very rarely encountered.

In spite of the fact that as far back as the Ch'in dynasty (255–207 BC) the Chinese emperors sent in troops to colonise this part of China, it became increasingly susceptible to foreign influence. The first Arab traders established trading settlements in southern China from 400 AD onwards, acting as middlemen in commerce with the West. The Portuguese were the first Europeans to trade with the Chinese and they were only to enter the scene in the 16th-century.

The 19th-century Cantonese merchants who had prospered and grown rich through commerce and trading activities with the West lived in some considerable luxury and had a taste for rare and exotic delicacies. Cantonese cooks were encouraged to create increasingly elaborate dishes, using the most costly ingredients and to this day good Cantonese cooking tends to be the most expensive; the two most extravagant dishes of Chinese cooking, Shark's Fin Soup and Bird's Nest Soup are at their most delectable in Cantonese hands. Cantonese cuisine became the favourite of the Imperial Palace, 2,000 miles away, and the Manchu court always included a stay in Canton during its travels through China, in order to taste this cooking at its best, fresh from Cantonese kitchens.

Continuous contact with foreigners meant that Cantonese cooks became masters in adapting to the tastes of the "red-haired foreign devils" as Westerners were known. Purists maintain that the tradition of sweet and sour tastes is the result of this compromise, although as early as 1700 a cookery book gives a recipe for pork in which vinegar is the predominant taste. Whether these experts are right or not, such a strong, pronounced ingredient should not be used indiscriminately or it could swamp the more delicate and candid flavours so typical of the subtle Cantonese cuisine, in which the ideal is to cook foods altering their colour or consistency as little as possible and to use accompanying ingredients as a complement and not as a disguise. Oil is used very sparingly in Cantonese kitchens. A great many dishes are steam-cooked, the most famous of these steamed foods forming a category on their own: *dim sum* or *tien hsin*, an infinite variety of mouthful-sized delicacies, which provide the equivalent of fast food for millions of Chinese.

THE COOKING OF EASTERN CHINA: the song of the carp in the Yangtze River

The coastal or eastern regions of China are so closely interlinked socially, economically and in matters of custom that they are not clearly distinguishable or separately identifiable. The climate is predominantly sub-tropical but with such a great divergence between one season and another that any number of different crops can be grown. All kinds of meat are available and there is a plentiful supply of seafood and fresh-water fish to be caught in the numerous rivers and lakes (an outstanding example being the hairy crab of Shanghai).

External influences have played their role in developing the rich and varied spectrum of dishes which are typical of these regions: in the 14th century Hangchow was chosen as the capital of the exiled Sung court. Nanking was also the capital for many years and this era left its mark on the city, not least in its cooking.

Nanking was the birthplace of pressed duck; Yangchow saw the creation of such rice, noodle and vegetable dishes as the famous Cantonese rice. Shao-hsing still produces the most highly prized rice wine while soy sauce from Amoy is considered without equal; the beautiful maidens of Suchow enjoy legendary fame: as do its *dim sum* (*tien hsin*), while Hangchow boasts superb fish in its lakes. Two of these eastern provinces have sent products all over the world for which they are justly famous: vinegar originating from Chekiang and kaolin from Kiangsi which is used in the manufacture of the world's finest porcelain.

Shanghai winters are always so bitterly cold that oil is used in abundance; a great many starchy foods are consumed such as dumplings, spring rolls stuffed with meat and vegetables, noodles in soup. For the same reason local methods of preserving food whether by salting, pickling, drying or curing have been perfected (1,000 year old eggs are a very well known example of this high level of expertise and ingenuity in preserving foodstuffs). Fukien, which was one of the last regions to come under the sway of imperial power, has not only retained its 100 dialects, some of which resemble each other very little, but also 100 distinct cooking traditions which have one aim in common: the preparation of ingredients in such a way that they retain their original flavour.

WESTERN CHINESE COOKING: the way of Buddha

Western China was politically independent for many centuries and only in 1252 did Kubla Khan manage to bring it under the sway of centralised imperial rule. Subsequently, outside influence fluctuated in strength and was seldom of lasting significance, even during the Sino–Japanese war when Chungking in the province of Szechuan was temporarily the capital of the country.

The food of western China is unique among the various schools of cooking, in that a tremendous quantity and variety of spices is used in the preparation of regional dishes. The reason for this and for the similarity between the cuisine of Szechuan and that of Thailand, Burma and India probably lies in the influence of Buddhism, introduced from India across the province of Yunnan following the path of Buddha, which moulded local habits and customs. The Buddhist monks and the merchants who followed in their footsteps brought spices and herbs together with knowledge of the art of using them for both culinary and therapeutic purposes. The fertile soil helped propagate and popularise these ingredients. Chili pepper is liberally used and is a characteristic ingredient of the cuisine of western China. The most typical method of cooking, used in particular for chicken and duck, is smoking over tea leaves and camphor wood.

The provinces of Hunan and Hopei are very like Szechuan, at least in their cooking. Yunnan, on the other hand, is a mountainous and forbidding region where the inhabitants wrest a living from the harsh terrain and whose cooking has been influenced by the Moslems sent there by Kubla Khan to colonise the land and the surrounding countries: Vietnam, Laos, Burma and, indirectly, India.

Lo Mei Hing

Chinese kitchen equipment

The range of utensils needed to cook Chinese food is relatively small. A single pan, the wok, can be used for stir-frying, sautéing, and deep-frying; it is a thoroughly versatile piece of equipment and easy to use. A sound piece of advice is to buy just a few basic utensils to begin with, making sure that they are of good quality.

Chopsticks Fingers came first ... and then came chopsticks. The Chinese first started eating with chopsticks under the Shang dynasty (1766–1123 BC). These were made of various materials, including agate, jade and even silver, valued for its imputed property of revealing the presence of poisoned food by turning black. Ivory chopsticks, however, have always been considered the best.

The ideograms or words standing for chopsticks are pronounced in almost exactly the same way as two other ideograms which are a wish for happiness and healthy children to a newly married couple and, in fact, chopsticks are often given as a wedding present.

Chopsticks come in two sizes. The shorter ones are about 10 inches (25 cm) long and are used to transfer the food from plate or bowl to mouth. They can be made of bamboo, plastic or ivory and are often lacquered and decorated with various designs. The longer size, about 14 inches (35 cm) in length, ideally made of bamboo, are for such kitchen tasks as beating eggs, mixing sauces and for transferring ingredients to and from the wok or "keeping food on the move" as the Chinese say.

Wok This is the classic Chinese cooking pan, made of iron (preferable to the cheaper metal versions) and the design is many centuries old. The wok is actually called *kuo* by the Chinese and its rounded shape is ideal for even distribution of heat – although it must be said that the wok does not function as well over an electric ring as it does over gas. Woks come in various sizes, with either two metal handles or one wooden handle.

The wok must be washed well with detergent before its first use and rinsed thoroughly, then dried with paper towels. It should then be seasoned by sprinkling the inside with oil (sunflower or sesame seed oil) and placed over a high heat for five or six minutes. Remove the wok carefully from the heat using heatproof gloves and, while it is still hot, rinse in plenty of hot water. Dry with paper towels. Repeat this operation, oiling the pan again, replacing over the heat and rinsing and drying until no more black discoloration comes off on the towels when wiped. The wok should always be dried very thoroughly to avoid rusting.

Once the wok is in use, it is better not to use detergents to wash it; always rinse well under hot running water and place over a high heat for a few seconds to dry.

Wok rings can be bought separately in speciality shops when they are not sold with the wok but they are not indispensable: their main purpose is to hold the wok steady on modern stoves, but stir-frying is best done over a flame without a ring.

For home use a wok of approximately 13–15

Strainers or skimmers

Wok

Metal ladle

Huo Kuo (Mongolian hot pot)

Chinese fish slice

Earthenware cooking pot

Chinese grater

Chinese cleavers

Chopping board

Bamboo steamer

Table chopsticks

Kitchen chopsticks

Suribachi (pestle and mortar)

inches (33–36 cm) in diameter is suitable; any smaller size would make stir-frying vegetables or cooking Cantonese rice difficult. If too large a wok is chosen, the heat from a modern burner will not be evenly distributed.

Bamboo steamer   This is set on to a wok containing boiling water (which in turn is placed on a ring for stability) and is the ideal piece of equipment for steaming food. The steamer is made of woven bamboo and since this is porous, excess moisture from the steam does not condense on the inside of the lid and drip down, spoiling the food. Bamboo steamers come in various sizes and the smaller ones are usually used for steaming *dim sum* or *tien hsin*.

How to use: fill the wok two-thirds full of water, place the bamboo steamer on top and heat the water to boiling point to produce plenty of steam which will circulate throughout the various layers of the steamer. Place the prepared food in the steamer; top up the boiling water from time to time (never add cold water as this will take time to heat and the flow of steam will be interrupted). The various layers of these steamers enable several dishes to be cooked together. The food can be placed directly on the bottom of each compartment, as in the case of steamed spring rolls; foods which release fat or juice during cooking are better placed in a heat-resistant dish (leaving enough space round the sides for the steam to circulate freely) or can be placed on a folded cloth or a cabbage or lotus leaf. Before using a new bamboo steamer for the first time, it should be simmered in gently boiling water for a minimum of ten minutes over a low heat.

Chinese cleaver   This Chinese knife brings its full weight to bear on the materials to be cut – to the uninitiated or unpractised this may seem dangerous but a Chinese cook can chop up fowl with lightning speed and efficiency and when leek or ginger has to be pounded and crushed with the flat of the knife blade, it really is revealed as a very practical tool. Furthermore, the ingredients can be scooped up on the broad blade. Chinese knives come with a very broad blade (cleaver) or with a narrower blade, when they are lighter and sharper. The latter are used for slicing or shredding meat, vegetables and fruit. The cleaver is for chopping through bone. The sharpened blade of a Chinese cleaver is the ideal tool for cutting up poultry or meat, bones and all, with sharp, decisive blows, and can also be used for chopping ingredients very finely.

Huo Kuo   This is a brass cooking pot, about 10 inches (25 cm) in diameter with a small chimney in the centre containing charcoal. As the charcoal burns, the liquid in the circular basin surrounding it is heated and comes to the boil. This method of cooking is widely used in northern China and the Huo Kuo is also known as the Mongolian Hot Pot. Meat, fish and vegetables are sliced wafer thin and each guest chooses a selection, dipping the raw ingredients (held with chopsticks) in boiling broth to cook for a minute or two; the hot pot is conveniently placed in the centre of the table.

Chopping board   A Chinese chopping board is a round, horizontally cut piece of solid wood and is usually extremely heavy. An ordinary, less cumbersome western-style chopping board can be substituted.

Metal ladle and long-handled fish slice   The Chinese ladle is made of iron or steel and is shallower than its western counterpart, adapting well to the curvature of the wok to mix and turn foods which are being stir-fried; it is also used for adding oil when frying. The Chinese fish slice is for sautéing foods which are being stir-fried with little or no liquid and is ideal for turning whole fish.

Earthenware casserole or cooking pot   This is needed for slow cooking (such as red-stewing) or braising of meat, giblets and soup. In China the *sha kwo* is used, an earthenware cooking pot with one handle. Be sure the casserole you use is flame-proof.

Strainer or skimmer   These come in various sizes. Each has a long bamboo handle and a wire mesh ladle; they are excellent for lifting deep-fried foods and the fine wire mesh ladles are efficient skimmers. It is a good idea to select a mesh ladle a little smaller than the wok so all the fried food can be removed and drained at once as soon as it is ready.

Chinese grater   A small bamboo or ceramic grater with particularly sharp teeth, usually used for grating ginger.

Suribachi (pestle and mortar)   A ceramic bowl with a ridged or striated inner surface which originated in Japan. Used as a mortar in which a wide variety of materials are pounded with a wooden pestle.

RECIPES

One of the problems confronting the Westerner who wants to try his hand at Chinese cooking can be difficulty in obtaining ingredients. Climatic conditions and other factors mean that many products cannot be grown in one's own country, making it impossible to get hold of a great many of the foodstuffs which the Chinese use in the preparation of their dishes.

These obstacles should not deter the newcomer, since the versatility of Chinese cooking has already been stressed and rarely does the success of a dish hinge solely upon one ingredient; another similar ingredient can usually be substituted. Obviously a chicken cannot be switched for the main ingredient in Peking Duck and Shark's Fin Soup cannot be counterfeited with any other type of seafood, since the taste is too distinctive; but the scope for improvisation is considerable and the final result can still be as appetising as the original dish.

Sweet and sour dishes, in which the main ingredient can equally well be pork, duck, prawns, or fish, demonstrate this flexibility. So there is no justification for giving up all thought of preparing chicken with cashew nuts because one or the other are unavailable: chicken with almonds will do equally well or pork with cashew nuts, and both are equally "genuine Chinese" dishes. Imagination is what is needed and a certain sense of what goes with what, in order to achieve the proverbial harmony of Chinese cooking.

The essence of Chinese cooking is its everyday adaptability.

The recipes given in this book are accompanied by the following symbols:

 Preparation and cooking time

 Classic Chinese dishes

 Memorable dishes for important occasions

Cooking methods

 Shallow-frying

 Stir-frying

 Steaming

 Pot roasting or casserole cooking

 Boiling and clear-simmering

 Deep-frying

 Stewing

 Mongolian hot pot cooking

HORS D'OEUVRE AND SNACKS

Chinese appetisers and first courses serve much the same purpose as in the West; they must stimulate the appetite and fill one with pleasant anticipation of the more substantial courses which are to follow. The Chinese dishes which fall into this category differ in one very important respect: they can all, without exception, be served with rice as a main course at any stage during the meal.

Besides these hors d'oeuvre there is an endless variety of little snacks which fall into a separate category. These are the famous Cantonese dim sum *or, as they are known in Mandarin* tien hsin *"the heart-touchers".* Dim sum *include dumplings of various types, spring rolls, steamed rolls filled with meat or vegetables and little dishes of duck feet or hearts and countless other ingredients cooked in every conceivable way.*

In the tea rooms of Hong Kong and southern China these fragrant and flavoursome delicacies are wheeled between the tables of the restaurant or carried on trays slung round the necks of elderly waiters or waitresses so that the clientele may pick and choose exactly what appeals and feel free to order as many and as much as they wish.

Seven-colour hors d'oeuvre

1. COLD CHICKEN SALAD WITH SWEET AND SOUR DRESSING

2 small chicken legs
1 cucumber

For the sauce:
4 tbsp light soy sauce
1½ tbsp sugar
2 tsp vinegar
½ tsp black bean paste
5 tbsp ground sesame seeds or sesame paste
1 tbsp finely chopped root ginger
½ tsp finely chopped garlic
1 tbsp sesame seed oil
½ tsp chili paste or oil
pinch monosodium glutamate
Preparation time: 40 minutes
Calories 220; protein 10.5 g; fat 17.3 g; sugar 7.5 g

1. Place the chicken legs in a pan with enough cold water to cover; bring to the boil, then lower the heat slightly and simmer for 10–15 minutes or until the juices run clear when a skewer is inserted. Remove the chicken legs and rinse under cold running water. Dry with paper towels, arrange on a plate and place in refrigerator.

2. Mix all the sauce ingredients together.

3. Wash the cucumber, slice diagonally and cut into strips about $\frac{3}{4}$ in (2 cm) long.

4. Remove the chicken flesh from the bones and cut diagonally into $\frac{1}{2}$-in (1-cm) strips. Arrange on top of the cucumber on a serving dish and sprinkle with the sauce.

2. CUTTLEFISH "FLOWERS" WITH GINGER SAUCE

10oz (300g) cuttlefish (or squid)
3–4oz (100g) celery
salt
sesame seed oil
For the sauce:
1oz (25g) root ginger
2½ tbsp light soy sauce
4 tbsp vinegar
1 tbsp sesame seed oil
pinch of monosodium glutamate
Preparation time: 40 minutes
Calories 91; protein 12g; fat 4g; sugar 1.1g

1. Hold the cuttlefish under cold running water, rub the outer skin with the fingers and pull the membrane away. Discard it. Cut off the tentacles and pull away and discard the cuttlebone, ink sac, hard mouth parts and eyes, leaving only the body of white firm meat.

2. Rinse thoroughly. Cut the bodies of the cuttlefish into strips about 2in (5cm) wide. Place the pieces on a flat surface.

3. Using a sharp knife score the pieces at an angle, in a lattice pattern, at $\frac{1}{4}$-in (5-mm) intervals, making sure that the skin is not cut through.

4. Cut the celery into matchsticks 2–2½ in (5–6cm) long, place in cold water for 10 minutes, then drain. Chop the ginger finely and mix with the other sauce ingredients.

5. Rinse the cuttlefish in cold water, place in a saucepan of boiling water and blanch for 30 seconds; the pieces of cuttlefish will curl.

6. Drain the cuttlefish and dry with paper towels, sprinkle with a pinch of salt and a little sesame seed oil.

7. Arrange the celery on a plate with the cuttlefish on top and sprinkle with the sauce.

3. MARINATED ANCHOVIES

peanut oil
1¼lb (600g) anchovies or other small fish (fresh or frozen) such as smelts or sprats
1 large leek
small piece root ginger
small piece of cinnamon stick
generous 1¼ pints (750ml) stock or water
pinch of monosodium glutamate
1 tbsp sesame seed oil
For the sauce:
4 tbsp soy sauce
4 tbsp rice wine or dry sherry
3 tbsp sugar
2 tbsp vinegar
pepper
Preparation time: 50 minutes
Calories 328; protein 26.1g; fat 17.6g; sugar 10.5g

1. Heat the oil to 350°F (180°C). Add the anchovies and fry for 2–3 minutes, remove from the oil and drain. With the oil at 325°F (170°C) fry for a second time for 4–5 minutes, or until crisp. Drain on paper towels.

2. Cut the leek into small pieces and the ginger into wafer-thin slices. Place with the cinnamon in a wok or frying pan and arrange the anchovies neatly on top.

3. Pour the stock or water into the wok. Mix the sauce ingredients and add 2 tbsp peanut oil. Skim off any scum or froth, cover and simmer for 10 minutes.

4. Remove the lid, turn up the heat and cook briskly, spooning the juices over the fish. Add 2 more tbsp peanut oil, pouring it in so that it trickles down the sides of the pan. Finally add a pinch of monosodium glutamate.

5. Continue cooking until the liquid has almost evaporated; add the sesame seed oil.

6. Arrange the fish on a serving plate, pour over the remaining sauce or juices and allow to cool.

4. SZECHUAN CUCUMBER SALAD

1 lb (500g) cucumbers
salt
small piece root ginger
2 chili peppers
2 tbsp peanut oil
2 tbsp sesame seed oil
For the sweet and sour sauce:
4 tbsp sugar
3 tbsp vinegar
Preparation time: 20 minutes
Calories 170g; protein 1.3g; fat 13.3g; sugar 12.2g

1. Wash the cucumbers, trim off ends, cut lengthways in half, and scoop out seeds. Make oblique incisions in the flesh at intervals of approx $\frac{1}{8}$ in (3mm). Cut the cucumber into 1-in (2-cm) pieces.

2. Sprinkle the pieces with $1\frac{1}{2}$ tbsp salt and then with a little water. Place in a colander with a weighted plate on top and leave for about 30 minutes.

3. Cut the ginger into very thin lengths and slice the chili peppers into fine rings. Drain the cucumber pieces, rinse under cold water and drain well. Place in a bowl.

4. Scatter the ginger and chili pepper over the cucumber. Pour on the sugar and vinegar and mix well.

5. Pour the peanut oil and the sesame seed oil into a wok and heat until the oil is just starting to smoke slightly. Pour over the cucumber mixture. Cover and leave to stand for about 30 minutes.

5. ABALONE IN OYSTER SAUCE

1$\frac{1}{4}$ lb (600g) canned abalone
$\frac{1}{4}$ leek
small piece root ginger
peanut oil
1 tbsp oyster sauce
$\frac{3}{4}$ pint (450ml) boiling stock or water
sesame seed oil
For the sauce:
1 tbsp soy sauce
1 tbsp sugar
1 tbsp rice wine or dry sherry
pinch of pepper
pinch of monosodium glutamate
Preparation time: 30 minutes
Calories 196; protein 17.9g; fat 10.9g; sugar 3.6g

1. Drain the abalone and cut the larger ones in half.

2. Slice the leek into 1-in (2-cm) lengths and pound the ginger in a mortar. Pour 2 tbsp peanut oil into a wok and stir-fry the leek and ginger.

3. Add the oyster sauce and then the abalone. Fry lightly and then pour in the hot stock; stir in the sauce ingredients.

4. Cook over a moderate heat, removing any scum from the surface. When the liquid has almost completely evaporated, add 1 tbsp sesame seed oil.

5. Discard the pieces of leek and the ginger. Turn off the heat, allow to cool and then serve.

6. VEGETARIAN "FISH" WITH SESAME SAUCE

$\frac{3}{4}$ lb (400g) bean sprouts
2 slices cooked ham
2 sweet peppers
peanut oil
salt
soy sauce
rice wine or dry sherry
pepper
2 sheets dried bean curd skin approx. 8in × 18in (20cm × 45cm)
sesame seed oil

For the sesame sauce:
3 tbsp soy sauce
2 tbsp vinegar
1 tbsp ground sesame seeds
1 tbsp sesame oil
1 tsp pepper
1 tsp chili oil
pinch of monosodium glutamate
Preparation time: 45 minutes
Calories 191; protein 7.3g; fat 16.8g; sugar 5.2g

1. Wash the bean sprouts; shred the ham and sweet peppers.

2. Heat 3 tbsp peanut oil in a wok with $\frac{1}{2}$ tsp salt; add the bean sprouts, ham and peppers and stir-fry for 1 minute.

3. Add 1 tsp each soy sauce and rice wine and a pinch of pepper; stir-fry for 1–2 minutes. When the bean sprouts are tender drain and transfer to a plate.

4. Cut the bean curd skins in three. Soak in plenty of water. Spread out flat, dab off excess moisture and arrange $\frac{1}{6}$ of the bean sprout mixture on the lower half of each sheet. Roll up securely.

5. Pour 1 tsp sesame seed oil into the wok to cover the surface with a thin film; arrange the bean curd rolls in the wok. Fry briskly until evenly browned. Allow to cool.

6. When cold, cut each roll into 6–8 portions.

7. Mix together the sesame sauce ingredients and pour over the rolls.

7. CHICKEN GIBLETS WITH SEAWEED

1$\frac{1}{4}$ lb (600g) chicken giblets
1 pre-soaked dried green seaweed leaf, approximately 12in (30cm) long
1 leek
small piece root ginger
1 small cinnamon stick
small piece dried mandarin peel
a little star anise
peanut oil
generous 1$\frac{1}{4}$ pints (750ml) hot stock or water
pinch monosodium glutamate
sesame seed oil
For the sauce:
3 tbsp soy sauce
4fl oz (125ml) rice wine or dry sherry
3oz (75g) sugar
Preparation time: 1 hour 15 minutes
Calories 373; protein 28.4g; fat 20g; sugar 14.6g

1. Wash the chicken giblets and then boil them in plenty of water for 5 minutes; refresh in cold water and trim off any fat.

2. Divide the giblets into hearts, gizzards and livers. Clean and trim the livers, removing any discoloured parts; pare away the tough outer parts of the gizzards.

3. Wash the seaweed and cut into strips about $\frac{1}{2}$ in (1 cm) wide. Slice the leek into 1$\frac{1}{4}$-in (3-cm) lengths; pound the ginger. Wrap the cinnamon stick, the dried mandarin peel and the star anise in a piece of muslin and tie to form a bag (as used for bouquet garni).

4. Pour 3 tbsp peanut oil into the wok and stir-fry the leek pieces until they start to brown; turn off the heat.

5. Add the ginger, seaweed and chicken giblets; pour in the hot stock, then add the sauce ingredients and the bag of spices and flavourings. Place over the heat.

6. As soon as the stock boils, lower the heat, remove any scum from the surface and cover. Cook for 30 minutes. As soon as the chicken giblets are tender, remove the lid and add a pinch of monosodium glutamate; increase the heat so that most of the liquid evaporates.

7. Pour in 2 tbsp peanut oil, allowing it to trickle down the side of the wok; mix and allow the liquid to reduce until 90 per cent has evaporated. Lastly, add 2 tbsp. of sesame seed oil.

Pork chitterlings with pickled vegetables

 2 h

The recipe given below can be eaten as an appetiser or as a side-dish with boiled rice. It can be prepared several days in advance.

$\frac{1}{2}$lb (250g) Chinese salted mustard greens
1–1$\frac{1}{4}$lb (500g–600g) pork chitterlings
coarse salt
small piece leek
small piece root ginger
large piece root ginger
3 tbsp peanut oil
1 tbsp rice wine or dry sherry
a few drops soy sauce (optional)
a few drops sesame seed oil
Calories 310; protein 32.2g; fat 17g; sugar 5.6g

1. If dried salted mustard greens are used, soak for 1 hour before using.

2. Rub the coarse salt well into the chitterlings; wash very well under cold running water to get rid of the mucus, paying particular attention to the inner side. Turn the chitterlings over several times and make sure they are absolutely clean.

3. Boil the chitterlings in plenty of water with a small piece of leek and ginger for 30 minutes.

4. Trim off any fat and gristle and cut the chitterlings into bite-sized pieces.

5. Rinse the salted vegetables well unless the tinned variety are used, drain; cut into pieces about the same size as the chitterlings. Cut the large piece of ginger into very small, thin strips.

6. Heat the peanut oil in the wok and sauté the ginger; when the aroma of the ginger is released, add the chitterlings and then the salted vegetables and stir-fry.

7. Add the rice wine or dry sherry, trickling it down the sides of the wok; pour in enough water to barely cover the contents of the wok and cook for 20–30 minutes.

8. If the dish needs slightly more flavour, add a few drops of soy sauce, but remember that the salted vegetables will have added a good deal of saltiness already. Lastly add a few drops of sesame seed oil.

Spring rolls

¼ lb (125 g) lean pork or chicken, cut into thin strips measuring
   ⅛ × ¾ in (3 mm × 2 cm)
2 tbsp cornflour
2 tbsp peanut oil
3½ oz (100g) bamboo shoots cut to the same size and shape as
   the meat
2 dried Chinese winter mushrooms, pre-soaked and thinly sliced
1 small leek or large spring onion including the green stem
   (finely chopped)
1 tbsp plain flour
12 Chinese pancakes (see recipe, p. 296) or bought spring roll
   skins
oil for frying
For the sauce:
1 tbsp sugar
pinch of salt
½ tsp monosodium glutamate
½ tbsp dark soy sauce
2 tsp light soy sauce
2 tbsp chicken stock (see recipe, p. 296)
1 tbsp peanut oil
a few drops sesame seed oil
Calories 320; protein 12 g; fats 25 g; sugar 20 g
Serves 6 (12 rolls)

1. Sprinkle the meat with the cornflour and mix; leave to stand for a few minutes.

2. Heat the peanut oil in the wok and stir-fry the meat for 1 minute together with the bamboo shoots and the mushrooms.

3. Add the sauce ingredients and stir-fry until the liquid has evaporated; add the finely chopped leek. Transfer to a plate and leave to cool.

4. Prepare a paste to seal the pancake rolls by dissolving the flour in 1 tbsp cold water. Add 2–3 tbsp boiling water and stir.

5. Arrange some of the filling along the lower half of each pancake; lift up the lower edge, fold it over the filling, tuck in the edges at both ends and roll up neatly, sealing the final flap with the prepared flour and water paste.

6. Fry the rolls in plenty of hot oil, 350°F (180°C), and serve while still piping hot and crisp.

Fried surprise rolls

2 leaves dried purple (nori) seaweed
3oz (75g) finely sliced belly of pork
pinch of salt
pepper
monosodium glutamate
1 slice cooked ham, cut just less than ¼ in (5mm) thick
6 bamboo shoots (boiled fresh or canned)
cornflour
2 eggs
1½oz (40g) chopped prawns
20 cashew nuts
batter (see p. 156, quantity as required)
oil for frying
Calories 389; protein 13.9g; fat 30.8g; sugar 14.8g

1. Spread one leaf of seaweed out flat and dredge the surface with cornflour.

2. Cut the belly of pork slices in half and then into rectangles; place them on the seaweed leaf; sprinkle evenly with salt, pepper and a pinch monosodium glutamate.

3. Cut the ham and bamboo shoots into very small, thin strips ⅛ in (3mm) wide. Place these on the lower half of the seaweed leaf; roll the leaf up tightly, starting from the lower edge. Sprinkle with cornflour.

4. Beat the eggs well with a pinch of salt and 1 tbsp cornflour dissolved in 1 tbsp water. Beat or mix in a blender and then use this mixture to make a very thin omelette, rather like a pancake but rectangular, measuring about 6 × 8 in (15 × 20cm).

5. Place the omelette on a board or working surface; dredge lightly with cornflour, covering the entire surface.

6. Spread the chopped prawns evenly and very delicately all over the surface of the omelette, leaving a border of ½ in (1 cm) along the lower edge. Spread the filling less thickly for a width of 1¼ in (3cm) along the upper edge of the rectangular omelette.

7. Remove the salt from the cashew nuts by rubbing with a damp cloth and arrange in a line along the lower edge of the omelette. Roll the omelette up neatly, bringing the lower edge over the cashew nuts to start with. Dredge the rolled omelette with cornflour.

8. Dip the rolls in the batter and fry in very hot oil until they are crisp and golden brown. Cut into portions as desired and serve.

Pumpkin and pork rolls

These rolls are similar to spring rolls but have a different filling, using yellow pumpkin to make a slightly sweet and floury dish which is a very appetising snack.

1¼–1½ lb (600–700 g) pumpkin
1 leek
3–4 dried black Chinese mushrooms
3 tbsp peanut oil
4 oz (125 g) lean minced or very finely chopped pork
scant ½ tsp salt
pinch of pepper
8–10 pancakes (see recipe, p. 296)
plain flour
oil for frying
Calories 339; protein 10.5 g; fat 26.7 g; sugar 18 g

1. Remove the seeds from the pumpkin, cut off the skin and slice the flesh into small pieces. Place in a bowl in the bamboo steamer. Steam the pumpkin over a moderate heat until it is tender.

2. Turn off the heat and work the pumpkin flesh through a sieve or a mouli-légumes while it is still very hot.

3. Cut the leek lengthways and then crossways so that it is chopped very finely. Place the dried mushrooms in a bowl and cover with boiling water. Allow to stand for 15–20 minutes. Squeeze to extract most of the moisture and cut off and discard the stems. Chop the mushrooms.

4. Heat the peanut oil in the wok, stir-fry the leek for a few seconds, then add the mushrooms, followed by the minced or finely chopped meat. When the meat has browned, season with salt and pepper.

5. Mix the puréed pumpkin with the meat, spread the mixture out in a shallow baking tin or plate and divide into 8–10 portions.

6. Prepare a sealing paste for the rolls: blend 1 tbsp flour in $\frac{1}{2}$–1 tbsp cold water and then add 2–3 tbsp boiling water and stir.

7. Taking the prepared pancakes one by one, spread flat on the board or working surface; place a portion of the filling on the lower half, pick up the lower edge and fold over the filling, then roll up the pancake, tucking in both ends.

8. Moisten the edge with the flour and water paste and press gently to secure. Fry the rolls until they are crisp and golden in oil heated to 325°F (160°C).

Crispy fried prawn snacks

A crunchy snack made with pounded or minced prawns. It also makes a delicious and original canapé to go with an aperitif or Chinese wine.

2oz (50g) fresh pork fat
¼lb (125g) filleted white fish (sea bass, plaice, cod, haddock etc)
¼lb (125g) peeled prawns
small piece each of leek and ginger
1 egg white
1 tbsp rice wine or dry sherry
¼ tsp salt
pinch of pepper
pinch of monosodium glutamate
2 tbsp cornflour
8 slices of bread
3oz (75g) white sesame seeds
4 hard-boiled quail's eggs
1 small slice cooked ham, finely chopped
parsley
2oz (50g) flaked almonds
oil for frying
Calories 506; protein 24g; fat 30g; sugar 35.4g

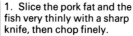

1. Slice the pork fat and the fish very thinly with a sharp knife, then chop finely.

2. Wash the prawns. Chop finely or mince. Simmer the leek and ginger together in a little water for a few minutes to obtain a lightly flavoured stock.

3. Place the chopped pork fat, fish and prawns together in a bowl; stir in 2 tbsp of the water in which the leek and ginger have simmered, add the egg white and stir in the rice wine or sherry. Mix well and stir in the salt, pepper and monosodium glutamate.

4. Beat vigorously to obtain a firm smooth paste. Finally, add the cornflour and work in.

5. Take 4 slices of bread (having removed the crusts); arrange on top of one another in two pairs, aligning the slices neatly. Cut into four and trim the corners to round them off.

6. Work half the fish and meat mixture into 8 small balls, approximately 1 in (2 cm) in diameter. Place one ball between the two halves of each little "sandwich" and press down. Smooth round the sides with a knife. Roll the sides in the sesame seeds, pressing the seeds against the sides of the sandwiches so they adhere firmly.

7. Repeat with the remaining 4 slices of bread but shape the squares into roughly oval shapes instead of the round shapes of the first batch. Spread the meat and fish paste on half the bread slices, press a hard-boiled quail's egg into the filling, cover with chopped ham and garnish with tiny sprigs of parsley. Cover the remaining small ovals of bread with meat and fish paste and then stick the flaked almonds firmly into these "open sandwiches" so that they resemble fir cones.

8. Heat the oil to 250°F (120°C), i.e. not very hot; place the prepared prawn snacks very carefully in the oil. Increase the temperature of the oil gradually until it reaches 350°F (180°C) – moderately hot. The prawn snacks should become crisp and golden. Drain well and serve immediately.

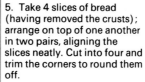

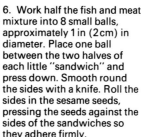

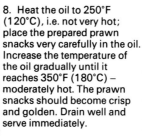

Steamed stuffed bean curd skins

Pork and transparent noodles or vermicelli wrapped in dried bean curd skins – another variation of the stuffed roll, but in this recipe the rolls are steamed.

Scant ½lb (225g) finely chopped or minced pork
2oz (50g) transparent noodles
3 large dried Chinese mushrooms
1½ tsp sugar
3 tbsp dark soy sauce
1 tbsp rice wine or dry sherry
1 tbsp cornflour
4 dried bean curd skins
a little extra dark soy sauce
Calories 208; protein 9.5g; fat 12g; sugar 14.4g

1. Spread the chopped or minced pork on the chopping board or working surface and pound with the blunt edge of the cleaver – this breaks up the fibres in the meat and makes it smoother and more tender.

2. Cook the vermicelli or noodles in boiling water for a few minutes at most; drain and cut into pieces approximately 1 in (2–3 cm) long.

3. Cover the mushrooms with boiling water and leave to stand for 15 minutes; when they have softened, squeeze free of excess water, trim off and discard the stems and slice the mushrooms in thin strips about $\frac{1}{8}$ in (3 mm) wide.

4. Place the minced pork in a bowl with the mushrooms and noodles. Add the sugar, soy sauce, rice wine or dry sherry and the cornflour, work well together by hand until a paste is formed.

5. Soak the dried bean curd skins for about 30 minutes in plenty of tepid water; spread out very carefully on the board and dab off excess water gently with a clean, dry cloth. Set the bamboo steamer over boiling water.

6. Divide the stuffing into four portions; place the first on the lower half of a bean curd skin. Fold the bottom edge over the filling and roll up.

7. Repeat the process with the other bean curd skins and remaining stuffing. Arrange carefully in a shallow dish taking care that they do not overlap. Brush sparingly with dark soy sauce.

8. Place the dish in the bamboo steamer; cover and steam over a high heat for 20 minutes; when ready, cut as desired and serve.

Roast pork appetiser

This is a spicy dish which takes very little time to prepare

approx. 10oz (300g) bean sprouts
2oz (50g) transparent noodles
½lb (250g) thinly sliced roast pork
2 tbsp sugar
3 tbsp vinegar
1 tbsp soy sauce
1 tbsp prepared mild mustard
1 tbsp sesame seed oil
Calories 245; protein 25.9g; fat 6.8g; sugar 19.3g

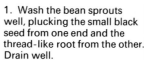

1. Wash the bean sprouts well, plucking the small black seed from one end and the thread-like root from the other. Drain well.

2. Bring plenty of water to the boil in a large pan, add the bean sprouts and boil until tender but still slightly crisp.

3. Drain the bean sprouts very well indeed.

4. Place the noodles in a bowl, cover with hot water and leave to stand for 5 minutes.

5. Drain the noodles, cut into pieces 4in (10cm) long and drain once more.

6. Place the slices of pork on top of one another and cut into strips about 3in (7–8cm) long (this gives more volume to the dish, apart from spreading the flavour evenly).

7. Make the sauce in a bowl by mixing the sugar, vinegar, soy sauce, mustard and sesame seed oil; take care to mix the mustard thoroughly with the other ingredients.

8. Place the noodles on a serving plate, cover with the bean sprouts and then the slivers of pork; pour on the sauce and mix well just before serving.

Pig's kidney salad with mustard dressing

This recipe is a good example of the many imaginative and easy Chinese methods of using offal; it is an economical dish which takes little time to prepare.

1 large pig's kidney
2 small cucumbers
½oz (15g) agar-agar
For the sauce:
2 tbsp sugar
3 tbsp vinegar
1 tbsp soy sauce
1 tbsp prepared mustard
a few drops sesame seed oil
pinch monosodium glutamate
Calories 101; protein 7.4g; fat 5.5g; sugar 8.2g
Serves 5–6

1. Cut the kidney in half horizontally; this is best done by pressing lightly down on the kidney with the flat of the left hand while slicing carefully along the centre of the kidney.

2. Remove the central core inside the kidney as neatly as possible – using the Chinese cleaver or a small pair of very sharp, pointed scissors.

3. Soak the kidney in cold water for a few minutes. Bring plenty of water to the boil and place the kidney in it to cook (but do not overcook).

4. When the kidney is just done, drop into fresh cold water in a bowl. This process rids the kidney of any excessively strong taste and firms up the flesh.

5. Drain the kidney and cut into small strips. Slice the cucumbers diagonally first, then cut the thin, slanting rounds into strips.

6. Shake out the seaweed and rinse in cold water; soak in cold water for 20 minutes, drain and squeeze gently.

7. Cut the seaweed into strips of the same size as the kidney pieces. Press a very sharp knife or cleaver down through the seaweed on to the board, do not use a sawing motion.

8. Blend all the sauce ingredients. Place the kidney, the seaweed and cucumber in a bowl, add the sauce and mix well.

Crispy chicken and beef appetisers

A dish of mixed fried meats coated in chopped nuts and sesame seeds.

$\frac{1}{4}$lb (125g) shelled walnuts
6oz (175g) boneless chicken breasts
salt
pepper
1 tbsp breadcrumbs
generous $\frac{1}{4}$lb (125g) very thinly sliced beef
6oz (175g) white sesame seeds
oil for frying
For the batter:
2 egg yolks
1 tbsp water
2 tbsp cornflour
2 tbsp plain flour
$\frac{1}{4}$ tsp salt
1 tsp sugar
Calories 521; protein 25.8g; fat 37.8g; sugar 21.6g

1. Blanch the walnuts in boiling water and peel off the thin inner skins. Chop them fairly coarsely before they have dried out completely and mix with the breadcrumbs.

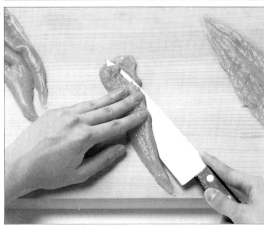

2. Trim any gristle or sinew from the chicken breasts; slit open along one side and open out; make shallow vertical and horizontal incisions in the flesh and season lightly with salt and pepper.

3. Mix the egg yolks with the other batter ingredients: water, cornflour, plain flour, salt and sugar. Beat well until smooth and creamy. Pour half the batter into a separate bowl.

4. Dip the chicken breasts in the batter; if the batter does not cling to the surface of the meat satisfactorily, mix in a little more water.

5. Place the chopped nuts and the breadcrumbs in a shallow plate and spread out so that the mixture is level; place the chicken breasts on the mixture and coat well on both sides.

6. Cut the beef into small slices; season lightly with salt and pepper; dip into the batter in the second bowl and then coat with the sesame seeds in the same way as the chicken breasts are coated with their nut and breadcrumb mixture.

7. Heat the oil until it reaches a temperature of 325°F (160°C) and fry the chicken breasts and then the small pieces of beef until crisp on the outside; the temperature of the oil should gradually be increased while the pieces of chicken and meat are cooking, to achieve a crisp outer finish, but they must not burn.

8. Both the chicken breasts and the beef will take only a short time to cook; when they are done, drain briefly on paper towels and cut into small bite-sized pieces.

Steamed chicken with mild garlic dressing

A light dish with a delicate garlic sauce which is very quick to prepare.

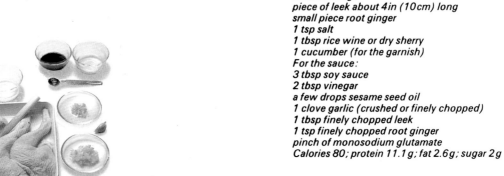

2 chicken legs
piece of leek about 4in (10cm) long
small piece root ginger
1 tsp salt
1 tbsp rice wine or dry sherry
1 cucumber (for the garnish)
For the sauce:
3 tbsp soy sauce
2 tbsp vinegar
a few drops sesame seed oil
1 clove garlic (crushed or finely chopped)
1 tbsp finely chopped leek
1 tsp finely chopped root ginger
pinch of monosodium glutamate
Calories 80; protein 11.1g; fat 2.6g; sugar 2g

1. Beat the leek and the piece of root ginger with the flat of a Chinese cleaver.

2. Wash the chicken legs; dry thoroughly; place in a dish or shallow bowl and rub with salt. Leave to stand to give the salt time to penetrate the flesh.

Set the bamboo steamer over boiling water.

3. Place the leek and the ginger on the chicken legs, sprinkle with the rice wine or dry sherry and place in the bamboo steamer; steam for 20 minutes over a high heat.

4. Meanwhile, mix all the sauce ingredients together.

5. When the chicken legs are done, remove from the steamer, allow to cool and then remove the flesh from the bones tearing it into small strips about ¼in (5mm) wide.

6. Slice the cucumber lengthways into thin strips and arrange on the serving plate. Place the small chicken pieces in the centre of the plate, pour on the garlic sauce and serve.

Steamed chicken salad with noodles

2 chicken legs
salt
1 tbsp rice wine or dry sherry
½ leek
small piece root ginger
1 packet rice noodles
2 eggs
For the sauce:
4 fl oz (125 ml) chicken stock
1 tsp soy sauce
2 tbsp vinegar
½ tsp salt
2 tbsp caster sugar
Calories 161; protein 14.4 g; fat 5.4 g; sugar 11.7 g

1. Set the bamboo steamer over boiling water. Sprinkle each chicken leg with ½ tsp salt and rub in well; place in a dish and sprinkle with rice wine or dry sherry; add the leek and ginger and place in the bamboo steamer.

2. Cook the chicken legs in the bamboo steamer for about 18–20 minutes (for longer if they are particularly cold when placed in the steamer).

3. Let the chicken legs cool a little; bend at the joint so they come apart and remove the flesh from the bones; chop the flesh finely.

4. Bring plenty of water to the boil in a large pan; add the rice noodles and stir with chopsticks so they do not stick to one another.

5. Continue to stir the noodles, keeping them as untangled as possible.

6. After cooking for 1–2 minutes, test the noodles and if they are tender, drain.

7. Mix together all the sauce ingredients. The salt and sugar should be added last and must dissolve completely.

8. Beat the eggs and make several very thin omelettes. Cut into thin strips. Arrange the noodles on a serving dish, then cover with the chicken pieces and the strips of omelette; sprinkle on the sauce just before serving.

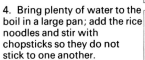

Chicken gizzard salad in spicy sesame sauce

40'

When one feels like a change from the usual dishes served with boiled rice, this original recipe offers an unusual taste. It can also be used as a quick and easy snack.

15 chicken gizzards
½ leek
root ginger
For the sauce:
3 tbsp soy sauce
1 tbsp vinegar
½ tsp sugar
1 tbsp sesame seed oil
pinch of monosodium glutamate
Calories 109; protein 13.8g; fat 5.1g; sugar 1.1g
Serves 5–6

1. Wash the chicken gizzards well; bring plenty of water to the boil in a large pan, adding the leek and a small piece of root ginger and then the gizzards.

2. Boil over a moderate heat for about 20 minutes; remove the gizzards and place in a bowl.

3. Cover the gizzards with cold water and rinse well, changing the water several times. Drain well.

4. Carefully slice off and discard the tough, muscle-like coating that covers the meaty part of the gizzards. Cut the meaty part into thin slices which should be as even in thickness as possible even if this means the shape of the slices varies.

5. Cut three fairly large slices of root ginger into fine strips and trim to an even size for good presentation.

6. Mix the sauce ingredients together, using a whisk to dissolve the sugar and blend in the sesame seed oil.

7. Add the strips of ginger to the sauce and stir, then mix in the sliced gizzards.

8. Mix the gizzards and sauce together very thoroughly, stirring and turning so that the gizzards can absorb the flavour and aroma of the ginger and sauce. Serve hot or cold.

Green bean salad

A straightforward recipe for a light and appetising first course or to serve as an effective foil for highly flavoured dishes. Best served cold.

10oz (300g) green beans
salt
small piece root ginger
For the sauce:
1 tbsp sugar
2 tbsp soy sauce
½ tsp salt
1 tbsp sesame seed oil
pinch of monosodium glutamate
Calories 67; proteins 1.6g; fat 3.4g; sugar 7.9g

1. String the beans if necessary; wash and then boil in plenty of salted water; when they are tender, refresh immediately in cold water.

2. Peel the ginger and slice into thin strips.

3. Drain the beans thoroughly and cut obliquely into 1½–2in (4–5cm) lengths.

4. Mix all the sauce ingredients together thoroughly.

5. Add the ginger and beans to the sauce, stir and leave to stand; when the beans have absorbed a good deal of the sauce and are well flavoured, serve.

Piquant cucumber salad

A chilled salad which stimulates the appetite and is particularly tempting in hot weather.

4 small or 2 large cucumbers
1 tsp salt
small piece carrot
1 small chili pepper
For the sauce:
4 tbsp vingegar
4 tbsp sugar
¼ tsp salt
pinch monosodium glutamate
a few drops of sesame seed oil
Calories 53; protein 0.9g; fat 0.2g; sugar 12.9g

1. Wash the cucumbers and drain. Cut in half lengthways and then slice diagonally. Sprinkle with salt and leave to stand for a few minutes.

2. When the cucumbers have softened slightly, rinse and drain well.

3. Cut the carrot into thin strips; remove the seeds from the chili pepper and cut into strips.

4. Mix the sauce ingredients together thoroughly in a bowl; add the cucumbers, carrot and chili pepper and leave to marinate for 30–40 minutes, turning from time to time so that the vegetables absorb the flavour of the dressing.

Bean sprout and noodle salad

🕐 30'   🍲

The subtle, almost bland taste of this side dish provides a good foil for other, more strongly seasoned or richer dishes.

1 leek
½ packet transparent noodles
¾–1 lb (400g) bean sprouts
For the sauce:
4 fl oz (125ml) vinegar
1 tbsp salt
1 tsp sugar
1 tbsp sesame seed oil
pinch monosodium glutamate
Calories 89; protein 3.2g; fat 2.7g; sugar 14.2g

1

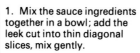

1. Mix the sauce ingredients together in a bowl; add the leek cut into thin diagonal slices, mix gently.

2. Soak the noodles in plenty of hot water until they turn completely transparent.

3. Drain the noodles and cut into 4-in (10-cm) lengths; drain again.

4. Wash the bean sprouts meticulously and remove the little black seed at one end and the thread-like root at the other. This process takes some time but the beans will taste better and the presentation of the dish will be more elegant.

5

5. Bring plenty of water to the boil in a large pan, add the bean sprouts and simmer until tender but still crisp.

6. Drain quickly and allow to cool a little.

7. Add the noodles and the warm bean sprouts to the sauce and mix.

8. Chill the salad and serve very cold for it to be at its best.

6

2

3

7

4

8

Multi-coloured vegetable salad

A cold appetiser with a delicate flavour; the medley of colours of the ingredients give it great visual appeal.

10oz (300g) celery
1 small carrot
1 small cucumber
3–4 dried Chinese mushrooms
soy sauce
sugar
1 cake fried brown bean curd
For the sauce:
1 tbsp light soy sauce
1 tbsp vinegar
1 tbsp sugar
pinch monosodium glutamate
1 tsp salt
a few drops of sesame seed oil
Calories 84; protein 5.6g; fat 32g; sugar 11g

1. Wash the celery well, pull off any strings and cut into small matchstick pieces about 2½in (6cm) long; place in a bowl, cover with cold water and when they have crisped up, drain.

2. Peel the carrot and cut into matchstick pieces the same length as the celery strips; slice the cucumber diagonally across and then cut each piece into strips.

1
2
3
4
5
6

3. Place the mushrooms in a small bowl, cover with boiling water and leave to stand for 15–30 minutes. Drain the mushrooms and discard the liquid. Cut off and discard the tough stalks. Place the mushrooms in a saucepan

with sufficient water to just cover. Season with a little soy sauce and sugar and cook; drain well and cut into thin strips.

4. Remove the excess oil from bean curd cake by pouring boiling water over it. Cut into

slices ⅛in (3mm) thick and then into very small matchstick pieces.

5. Make the sauce, mixing all the ingredients well together; add the sesame seed oil last and mix thoroughly.

6. Add the celery, carrot, mushrooms, cucumber and bean curd to the bowl containing the sauce; mix well. Leave to stand for about 20 minutes and then serve.

Fried stuffed lotus root and aubergine

½ large lotus root
cornflour
rice flour
1 large aubergine
¼ lb (125g) minced or finely chopped prawns
oil for frying
coating batter mixture (see recipe, p. 156)
For the meat filling:
¼ lb (125g) minced or finely chopped lean pork
2 tsp water taken from flavoured water in which a small piece of leek and a piece of ginger have been simmered
1 tbsp beaten egg
1 tsp rice wine or dry sherry
pinch of salt
few drops of soy sauce
pinch of pepper
pinch of monosodium glutamate
Calories 312; protein 10.8g; fat 18.9g; sugar 23.7g

1. Peel the lotus root and cut into thin rounds about ¼ in (5mm) thick. Soak in cold water for 15 minutes to get rid of any bitter taste.

2. Prepare the meat filling as directed on page 80.

3. Drain the lotus roots, pat dry and dredge with cornflour. Take half the lotus root slices, place a small quantity of the meat filling on top of each one and place the remainder of the lotus root slices on top of each "sandwich". Press down gently so the filling penetrates the inner holes of the root. Press lightly on one side so that the sandwich gapes open somewhat on the other side, making it look a little like a half-open shell.

4. Dredge thoroughly with rice flour.

5. Cut the aubergine crossways into slices ¼ in (5mm) thick; cut these slices in half horizontally, stopping ⅛ in (3mm) short of the edge so that the two halves are still attached. Soak in water to get rid of the bitter taste.

6. Dry the aubergine slices; dredge lightly inside and out with cornflour. Using a small palette knife, fill with the chopped prawns until the open edges of the aubergine are pushed ½ in (1cm) apart by the filling.

7. Heat the oil to 340°F (170°C) and lower the lotus root sandwiches carefully into the oil; reduce the heat to low. When the filled lotus roots are almost cooked, turn up the heat and finish frying at 350°F (180°C).

8. Pick up the aubergines carefully, holding by the uncut side, and dip the open edges into the batter; deep fry for a few minutes at 325°F (160°C).

Piquant turnip salad

30'

This basically simple dish owes much of its zest to the sweet and sour sauce with which it is served; the turnips should not be allowed to stand for too long in the sauce, however, or their delicate flavour will be drowned.

5–6 small turnips
1 tsp salt
½ carrot
1 chili pepper
For the sauce:
4 fl oz (125 ml) vinegar
¼ lb (125 g) sugar
a few drops of sesame seed oil
pinch of monosodium glutamate
Calories 82; protein 1.3 g; fat 0.1 g; sugar 19.3 g

1. Wash the turnips well, peel them and cut into thin slices; sprinkle with salt and allow to stand for a few minutes.

2. When the turnips have softened a little, rinse under cold running water and drain well.

3. Cut the carrot into thin strips; remove the seeds from the chili pepper and cut into thin strips.

4. Mix all the sauce ingredients together in a bowl; add the turnips, the carrot and the chili pepper; leave to stand for a little while, mixing and turning a few times before serving.

Cucumber and crisp cabbage salad in spicy dressing

1 h

This dish owes its distinctive taste to the use of spicy hot black bean paste.

2 small cucumbers
2 tsp salt
3–4 cabbage leaves
For the sauce:
1 tsp soy sauce
1 tbsp hot black bean paste
pinch of monosodium glutamate
a few drops of sesame seed oil
Calories 25; protein 1.8g; fat 0.3g; sugar 3.9g

1. Trim the ends off the cucumbers diagonally and slice diagonally into thin pieces, using the rolling oblique cutting method described on page 304. Sprinkle the slices with 1 tsp salt and leave to stand for a few minutes.

2. Cut out the hard ribs of the cabbage, wash well and then cut into small pieces 1½–2 in (4–5cm) long; sprinkle with 1 tsp salt and leave to stand.

3. When the cucumber and cabbage slices have softened a little, rinse off the salt and drain.

4. Mix all the sauce ingredients thoroughly together in a bowl, add the cucumber and cabbage pieces, stir well and leave the vegetables to absorb the sauce before serving.

Bean curd and prawn salad

A very refreshing dish, with the subtle aroma and delicate flavour of sesame seed oil.

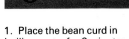

1 cake bean curd
1 tbsp dried prawns
small bunch chives
small piece salted Chinese mustard greens
For the sauce:
1 tsp sugar
1 tsp salt
pinch of monosodium glutamate
a few drops of sesame seed oil
Calories 83; protein 5.8g; fat 3g; sugar 3.4g

1. Place the bean curd in boiling water for 2 minutes; remove, cut into pieces and drain.

2. Soak the dried prawns in water until they are plumped up and tender; chop them finely; chop the chives coarsely.

3. Rinse the mustard greens thoroughly. If dried mustard greens are used, soak them in water for a while, then chop them finely.

4. Place the bean curd in a bowl and work into a paste by hand or with a wooden spoon; add the chopped prawns, the mustard greens and the sauce ingredients (which can be mixed separately before adding to the bowl). Blend all the ingredients thoroughly.

5. Arrange the mixture on a serving dish and garnish with the chopped chives.

Bean curd and turnip tops with thousand year old eggs

A recipe with a taste of spring to it which is quick and easy to prepare.

2 small cakes of bean curd
1 bunch turnip tops or broccoli
salt
4–5 slices cooked ham
2 thousand year old eggs (preserved duck eggs)
For the sauce:
2 tbsp soy sauce
1 tsp sesame seed oil
a few drops of vinegar
a few drops of chili oil
a little sugar (according to taste)
2 tsp ginger juice (obtained by crushing root ginger in a garlic press)
Calories 173; protein 13.4g; fat 12.5g; sugar 2.8g

1. Cut the bean curds in half horizontally, place in a saucepan of gently boiling water and simmer; remove carefully from the water so that they do not break up. Drain and chill in the refrigerator.

2. Wash the turnip tops or broccoli meticulously and place in boiling water, stem downwards, with a little salt and cook until the colour turns a brighter green; drain and plunge into cold water for a couple of minutes.

1

2

3

4

5

6

3. Place the thousand year old eggs in water so that the ashes and dirt clinging to their shells soften and come away easily when scraped with a knife; wash the eggs, shell them and slice them lengthwise into quarters.

4. Cut the bean curd into pieces ½ in (1 cm) wide and arrange on the serving plate, leaving spaces in between for the turnip tops or broccoli.

5. Squeeze the turnip tops or broccoli to rid them of excess moisture, cut into pieces about ¾ in (2 cm) long and arrange so that the flower heads are well-displayed.

6. Decorate the dish with the ham slices cut in half and the quartered thousand year old eggs; mix the sauce (which is handed round separately), adding the ginger juice last of all.

Chinese chicken and ham salad with noodles

A first course made with Chinese wheat-flour noodles which also makes a very good light meal or snack on hot days.

1 lb (500 g) fresh Chinese egg noodles
1 tbsp sesame seed oil
3 slices cooked ham
1 tomato
3 small cucumbers
$\frac{1}{4}$ lb (125 g) chicken breasts
salt
pepper
$\frac{1}{2}$ tbsp rice wine or dry sherry
2 large eggs
2 tbsp peanut oil
$\frac{1}{2}$ tbsp ginger juice
a little prepared mustard
For the sauce:
4 tbsp sugar
6 tbsp soy sauce
6–8 tbsp vinegar
Calories 701; protein 20.2 g; fat 23.1 g; sugar 102.3 g

1. Bring a large pan of water to the boil, throw in the noodles and stir to keep the strands separate. Cook until tender, drain and refresh by rinsing in cold water; add a few drops of sesame seed oil and stir so that the noodles do not stick.

2. Shred the ham. Blanch the tomato in boiling water, then plunge into cold water and skin; cut into semi-circular slices $\frac{1}{2}$ in (1 cm) thick. Slice the cucumbers diagonally and then cut into small strips.

3. Place the chicken breasts in a small heatproof dish, sprinkle with salt and pepper and moisten with rice wine or dry sherry. Place in a bamboo steamer which is already hot and full of steam and cook for 8 minutes.

4. When the chicken is completely cooked, remove from the steamer and cut into very small strips; strain the chicken juices produced during cooking.

5. Beat the eggs, add $\frac{1}{4}$ tsp salt and mix well. Heat the peanut oil in the wok, pour in the beaten egg and beat with a fork briskly, over a high heat.

6. Add water or, preferably, stock to the juices from the chicken to make up a quantity of 12 fl oz (350ml) liquid; add the sauce ingredients and boil gently.

7. Add the ginger juice and then pour the mixture into a bowl and allow to cool.

8. Arrange the noodles in a serving dish and place the cucumbers, tomato, ham, chicken and the egg on top, finally pour over plenty of the cold sauce; serve with a little mustard.

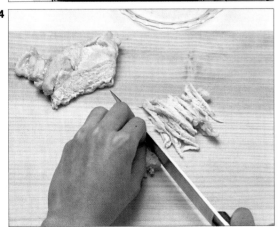

Steamed rice-coated pork balls

Pork rissoles covered in glutinous rice, this dish must be served piping hot or the rice will start to harden.

5 oz (150 g) glutinous rice
1 lb (500 g) lean pork, minced or very finely chopped
1 egg white
3 tbsp soy sauce
2 tsp sugar
1 tbsp rice wine or dry sherry
peanut oil
Calories 406; protein 23.1 g; fat 26.1 g; sugar 17.7 g

1. Rinse the rice in cold water and leave to stand overnight in cold water. Drain the following day. If the pork has not already been minced chop it finely with a Chinese cleaver.

2. Place the meat in a basin, add the egg white, the soy sauce, sugar and rice wine or sherry; work lightly but thoroughly together with the hands until well blended; do not pack the meat together too tightly or the balls will be heavy.

1

2

3

4

5

6

3. Oil the hands lightly and, taking a small handful of the mixture, force it out from the closed hand so that it comes out of the opening made by the forefinger and thumb, in a ball shape.

4. Spread out the drained rice in a large flat plate and roll the meat balls in the rice so they are covered all over; make sure the rice sticks by pressing gently.

5. Brush a thin film of peanut oil over the bottom of the bamboo steamer in which the meat balls are to be cooked or cover the bottom with a dampened but well wrung out cloth.

6. Place the rice-covered meat balls in the steamer, leaving a little space between each one; place over the wok in which the water should already be boiling, cover and cook over a moderate heat for about 30 minutes.

Chiao tzu (steamed or boiled stuffed dumplings)

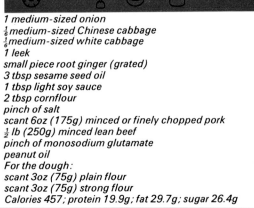

1 medium-sized onion
⅙ medium-sized Chinese cabbage
⅙ medium-sized white cabbage
1 leek
small piece root ginger (grated)
3 tbsp sesame seed oil
1 tbsp light soy sauce
2 tbsp cornflour
pinch of salt
scant 6oz (175g) minced or finely chopped pork
½ lb (250g) minced lean beef
pinch of monosodium glutamate
peanut oil
For the dough:
scant 3oz (75g) plain flour
scant 3oz (75g) strong flour
Calories 457; protein 19.9g; fat 29.7g; sugar 26.4g

1. Sift the flours, gradually add ½ pint (300ml) warm water and work into a firm dough.

2. Place the pastry dough in a bowl, cover with a damp cloth and leave to rest for 2 hours, then knead well again, place in the bowl, cover and leave to rest for a further 2 hours. Finally, knead once more and then leave to stand in the bowl covered with the cloth overnight. Knead yet again the following day.

3. Dredge a large pastry board or working surface lightly with flour and roll out the pastry into as thin a sheet as possible, dredging very lightly with a little flour.

4. Cut the pastry into rounds with a pastry cutter of about 4in (10cm) diameter.

5. The sign of good "chiao tzu" is the excellence of the pastry which should be smooth and very thin; this thin, silk-like texture can only be achieved if the dough is kneaded and rested in the manner indicated above.

6. Prepare the filling by chopping the onion very finely, together with the Chinese cabbage, the white cabbage and the leek, and then chop lightly with the blunt side of the cleaver.

(Continued overleaf.)

7. Wrap the chopped vegetables in a cloth; twist and squeeze tightly to get rid of excess moisture.

8. Place the vegetables in a bowl and, mixing with the hands, add the grated ginger, the sesame seed oil, soy sauce, the cornflour and salt and then the chopped meat and monosodium glutamate. Work together until all the ingredients are blended into a smooth mixture.

9. Prepare the chiao tzu for steaming or frying: moisten the edges of the circles of pastry, place a little stuffing slightly off-centre on each circle and fold the pastry in half so that one side is longer than the other; pinch the ends together, make two pleats and close the edges firmly together.

10. In order to prepare the dumplings for boiling they must be shaped somewhat differently. Proceed as directed above until the top edges of the semi-circle have been pinched firmly together and then bring up the edges from either side, forming an inverted pleat on each side and pinch the overlapping layers firmly together to seal.

11. To cook the dumplings in a frying pan, pour a layer of oil into the pan and when it is hot place the dumplings, arranged neatly, broad side down, in the oil. Fry for about 2 minutes or until golden brown on the bottom. Water should then be poured all around the dumplings and the pan covered as tightly as possible with the lid. Cook over a high heat until the water boils away – about 5–10 minutes.

12. To steam the dumplings, spread a damp cloth over the bottom of the perforated steamer and set over boiling water; when the steamer is full of steam, arrange the dumplings neatly on the cloth and steam over a moderate heat until the pastry has become almost transparent.

13. To boil the dumplings, bring a large pan of water to the boil and add the dumplings. Remove as they rise to the surface.

Crab and cauliflower salad

 20'

The attractive colours of this salad are matched by its flavour.

1¼ lb (600 g) crab, or ¾ lb (350 g) canned or frozen crab meat
1 medium-sized cauliflower
salt
vinegar
½ onion
bunch of radishes
2 small cucumbers
For the sauce:
4 tbsp vinegar
2 tbsp sugar
3 tbsp peanut oil
1 tsp salt
Calories 208; protein 16.3 g; fat 10.8 g; sugar 12.5 g

1. Wash the crab, place in a saucepan with plenty of cold water. Cover and bring slowly to the boil. Cook for 10–15 minutes. Remove the meat from the shell and break up into small pieces. If canned or frozen, drain the crab meat and break into medium-sized pieces.

2. Cut the cauliflower into small florets, soak in salted water and then rinse. Boil briskly in water acidulated with a few drops of vinegar until just tender. Refresh in cold water and drain.

3. Cut the onion into thin slices, rub a little salt into the slices, and wrap in a kitchen cloth. Rinse in cold water and then squeeze tightly, twisting the cloth, to get rid of all excess moisture.

4. Trim the radishes and cut into quarters.

5. Place the cucumbers on a chopping board or work surface, sprinkle with salt and roll against the board, pressing them so that the salt penetrates; rinse in cold water and cut lengthways in half and then diagonally in pieces about ⅛ in (3 mm) thick.

6. Mix the sauce in a large dish; add the prepared salad ingredients, mix and serve.

Five-colour hsao mai (steamed dumplings)

These tempting little dumplings form part of the range of *dim sum* served in Canton tea rooms and are called *hsao mai*. They should be served piping hot straight from the bamboo steamer.

¾lb (350g) onions
generous 2oz (50g) cornflour
14oz (400g) minced lean pork
20 hsao mai dough sheets (see recipe, p. 296)
peanut oil
Seasonings:
2 tbsp rice wine or dry sherry
½ tsp salt
½ tsp sugar
1 tbsp soy sauce
small pinch monosodium glutamate
1 tbsp sesame seed oil
pinch of pepper
½ tsp chopped root ginger
For the toppings:
peanut oil
2–3 egg yolks, beaten
seaweed as required
3 slices cooked ham
1 small can crab meat
3 dried Chinese winter mushrooms, pre-soaked and chopped
Calories 539; protein 26.5g; fat 29g; sugar 41g

1. To prepare the scrambled eggs for the topping, heat a little peanut oil in the wok, pour in the beaten egg yolks and cook over a gentle heat, breaking up the egg yolks as they set into small pieces.

2. Prepare the filling: chop the onions finely, add the cornflour and mix well by hand so that the flour is evenly distributed over the chopped onion.

3. Mix all the seasonings together. Place the minced pork in a bowl, add the seasoning mixture and mix well until smooth.

4. Add the floured onion to the meat mixture; mix well by hand.

5. Make a loose fist, thumb upwards, with one hand, and stretch a hsao mai sheet over the hole formed by thumb and forefinger. Place some filling in the centre of the dough sheet and push down into the hole, supporting the bottom of the little "bag" as it is filled with the meat stuffing with the little finger of the same hand.

6. When all the dough sheets are filled in this way, decorate the tops with a selection of seaweed, chopped ham, scrambled egg, crab meat and the chopped Chinese mushrooms.

7. Brush the bottom of the bamboo steamer with a thin film of oil, arrange the hsao mai carefully in the steamer and place over boiling water. Cover and steam for 9–12 minutes over boiling water.

Hsiao lung pao (steamed dumplings with meat stuffing)

For the dough:
generous 2 oz (50 g) sugar
¾ pint (450 ml) hot water
1 tbsp dried yeast
1½ lb (700 g) plain flour
2 tbsp margarine or lard
For the filling:
10 oz (300 g) minced lean pork
½ tbsp soy sauce
1 tsp salt
1 tsp monosodium glutamate
1 tbsp sesame seed oil
1 tbsp finely chopped leek
½ tbsp grated or finely chopped root ginger
4 fl oz (125 ml) water
Calories 380; protein 17.5 g; fat 23 g; sugar 25 g
Makes 24 dumplings

1. To make the dough, dissolve the sugar in the hot water, add the yeast and allow to stand for 10 minutes.

2. Sift the flour, work in the fat, then add the yeast mixture. Knead, adding more flour if necessary. Cover with a damp cloth and leave to rise away from draughts for 3–4 hours in a warm place.

3. To prepare the filling: mix the minced pork well with the other filling ingredients until thoroughly amalgamated.

4. Roll the risen dough into a long cylindrical sausage. Cut into 24 pieces and roll each piece into a circle with the rolling pin; each disc should measure about 4 in (10 cm) in diameter.

5. Place some filling in the centre of each circle of dough and enclose, forming a small ball as shown in the illustration.

6. Arrange the hsiao lung pao in the bamboo steamer on lettuce leaves and steam for 8 minutes over a moderate heat. Serve very hot.

Cha shao (roast pork)

 2 h 45'

This is a Cantonese dish which can be served as a first course, as a main dish or can be chopped up and used as a filling for hot dumplings (cha shao pao).

$3\frac{1}{2}$ lb (1.5 kg) loin of pork
6 tbsp honey
For the sauce:
5 tbsp sugar
1 tbsp salt
8 fl oz (scant 250 ml) soy sauce
1 tbsp rice wine or dry sherry
1 tbsp ginger juice
pinch of red food colouring ("red rice") or 1 tsp liquid food
    colouring
Calories 510; protein 26.3 g; fat 38.5 g; sugar 12.3 g
Serves 12

1. Bone the loin of pork and prick the meat all over with the point of a sharp knife. Cut into strips about $1\frac{1}{2}$ in (4 cm) thick.

2. Mix all the sauce ingredients together with the red food colouring and sprinkle over the meat. Leave to marinate for $1\frac{1}{2}$ hours.

3. Thread one end of each strip of meat onto a metal skewer and hang the meat to dry for 45 minutes.

4. Roast in the oven at 350°F (180°C) gas 4 for 20–25 minutes, basting from time to time with some of the honey.

5. When the pork is done (russet brown on the outside, almost white inside), brush with the remaining honey and leave so that the honey dries.

6. Serve hot or cold.

Cha shao pao (dumplings stuffed with roast pork)

For the dough:
1¼lb (600g) strong flour
2oz (50g) sugar
1 tbsp dried yeast
2 tbsp melted margarine or lard
For the filling:
1 tbsp peanut oil
10oz (300g) cha shao (see recipe, p. 67), cut into small dice
1 slice root ginger
1 small leek
For the sauce:
2 tsp sugar
pinch of salt
½ tsp monosodium glutamate
1 tbsp dark soy sauce
2 tsp light soy sauce
1 tbsp oyster sauce
4floz (125ml) chicken stock
1 tsp sesame seed oil
pinch of red food colouring
1 tbsp cornflour
Calories 490; protein 24.3g; fat 36.3g; sugar 25g
Makes 24 dumplings

1. Sift the flour into a large mixing bowl.

2. Dissolve the sugar in 8floz (225ml) hot water, add the yeast and mix well; leave to stand for 10 minutes.

3. Add to the flour and mix in the melted margarine or lard. Mix well, remove from the bowl and knead for about 3 minutes; shape into a long sausage and cover with a cloth.

4. Blend the sauce ingredients together (except the cornflour) and set aside.

5. To make the filling, heat the oil in the wok and fry the diced cha shao over a high heat for a minute, together with the leek and ginger. Remove the leek and ginger and discard; pour in the sauce.

Dissolve the cornflour in 1 tbsp water and add to the wok. Stir and cook until the mixture is smooth and well blended. Leave to cool.

6. Cut the length of dough into 24 pieces, flattening each piece with the fingers and shaping into a disc.

7. Place 1 tbsp filling in the centre of each round of dough and enclose, pinching the dough closed with the fingers. Place a small circle of greaseproof paper or foil under each dumpling. Leave to rise for 10 minutes.

8. Cook in the bamboo steamer for about 10 minutes, leaving each dumpling enough space to expand. Do not open the steamer while the dumplings are cooking.

PORK DISHES

The widely varying climate of China means that there are few basic foodstuffs which are not cultivated or raised. The very wide range of dishes seems to include every taste imaginable, but everything is a matter of balance, with no one aspect overshadowing another.

Pork is usually tender and can be cooked in a hundred different ways. This quality, combined with the fact that it goes well with almost any accompaniment, means that seven out of ten Chinese meat dishes include pork. So important is pork in Chinese cuisine that, whereas other meats are each called by their separate names, pork is referred to simply by the generic term, "meat".

As an intriguing note, the Chinese ideogram which stands for "house" is made up of the basic sign meaning "roof" positioned over the ideogram meaning "pig".

Twice-cooked pork and green peppers Szechuan style

A famous Szechuan dish in which the pork is stir-fried twice in the wok and flavoured with black bean paste.

small piece root ginger
1 leek approx 4in (10cm) long
1¼lb (600g) leg of pork
1 tbsp rice wine or dry sherry
5 green peppers
2 small chili peppers
oil for frying
1 clove garlic, finely chopped
cornflour or potato flour
For the sauce:
2 tbsp stock
2 tbsp sugar
2 tbsp black bean paste
¼ tsp salt
1 tbsp rice wine or dry sherry
Calories 520; protein 26.7g; fat 39.8g; sugar 10.2g

1. Peel the ginger and crush it slightly with the flat of the cleaver blade; flatten the leek with the flat of the blade to release the flavour.

2. Bring a large pan of water to the boil and place the whole piece of pork in it, followed by the ginger and the leek; cook for 20 minutes. Remove the pork from the water and leave to cool.

3. When the pork has cooled, cut into cubes approximately $1\frac{1}{2}$ in (4cm) square and then into very thin slices; place in a bowl and sprinkle with the rice wine.

4. Cut the green peppers in half lengthways, remove the seeds and pith, then wash and chop into pieces slightly smaller than the meat. Remove the seeds from the chili peppers and cut into rings about $\frac{1}{8}$ in (3mm) thick.

5. For the sauce, use a whisk to blend the stock, sugar, black bean paste and the salt.

6. Heat the wok over a high heat, pour in 2–3 tbsp oil and when it is very hot, add the chopped garlic, the green peppers and the chili peppers.

7. When the green peppers are tender (but still quite crisp) add the pieces of pork and sprinkle with 1 tablespoon rice wine, followed by the blended sauce ingredients.

8. Fry over a high heat, mixing and turning; add 2 tsp cornflour or potato flour dissolved in 4 tsp water and stir; this will give the dish body and gloss.

Sweet and sour pork

🕐 25'

A Cantonese dish which has become a favourite world-wide. Very good with boiled rice.

¾lb (350g) leg of pork (boned)
1 hot red chili pepper
2 leeks
1 tsp finely chopped garlic
½ small can pineapple
4 green peppers
1 beaten egg
cornflour
oil for frying
1 tbsp rice wine or dry sherry
For the sauce:
3floz (75ml) vinegar
1 tbsp soy sauce
4½ tbsp sugar
1 tbsp tomato ketchup
2 tbsp Worcestershire sauce
½ tsp salt
Calories 536; protein 17.2g; fat 37g; sugar 33.9g

1

5

1. Cut the pork into slices $\frac{1}{4}$–$\frac{1}{2}$ in (1 cm) thick and beat lightly with the blunt edge of the cleaver on both sides of each piece to tenderise. Then cut into bite-sized portions.

2. Remove the seeds from the chili pepper and cut into rings about $\frac{1}{8}$ in (3 mm) thick. Slice the leeks into $\frac{3}{4}$-in (1-cm) lengths and chop the garlic very finely.

3. Drain the canned pineapple and cut into small pieces; slice the green peppers lengthways, remove the seeds, pith and stalk and cut into portions the same size as the pieces of pork.

4. Mix the sauce ingredients together. In a separate small bowl or cup dissolve 2 tsp cornflour in 4 tsp cold water.

5. Dip the pork pieces into the beaten egg and then coat with cornflour. Heat 2 tbsp oil over a medium heat in the wok and fry the pork until cooked through. Set aside.

6. Heat 2 tablespoons more oil in the wok and stir-fry the chopped garlic; as soon as this releases its aroma, add the leeks followed by the green peppers.

7. When the green peppers are tender, add the chili pepper, the pineapple and the pork and stir-fry, mixing and turning all the ingredients briskly; moisten with the rice wine or dry sherry to add flavour.

8. Finally, add the sweet and sour sauce, followed by the cornflour dissolved in water and mix thoroughly. Turn off the heat and serve.

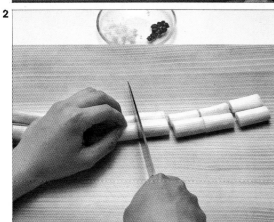

2

6

3

7

4

8

Stir-fried belly of pork in sweet and sour sauce

20'

A fuller-flavoured version of the classic sweet and sour pork using the more robust-tasting cut of belly of pork

1 lb (500 g) belly of pork
1 tbsp soy sauce
1 egg
cornflour
oil for frying
For the sauce:
2 fl oz (50 ml) stock
4½ tbsp sugar
2 tbsp vinegar
1 tbsp soy sauce
1 tsp salt
1 tbsp rice wine or dry sherry
Calories 421; protein 22.5 g; fat 40.1 g; sugar 21.8 g
Serves 4–5

1

2

3

4

5

6

1. Cut the belly of pork into slices approx. ⅛ in (3 mm) thick; place in a dish and sprinkle with the soy sauce, coating the strips of meat evenly.

2. Beat the egg and pour over the meat; dip each piece of meat in cornflour, shake off the excess and stir-fry in very hot oil. When done, drain and set aside.

3. Mix the sauce ingredients together until thoroughly blended.

4. Place the wok on the heat, pour in the sauce and cook over a fairly high heat. While the sauce is heating, dissolve 1 tsp cornflour in 2 tsp water.

5. When the sauce comes to the boil, add the fried pork and cook over a high heat, mixing and turning so that the pork slices absorb the sauce.

6. Use a Chinese scoop or slice for easy turning and mixing of the pork slices so that they are evenly flavoured; reduce the heat and stir in the cornflour mixture for a thick and glossy coating sauce.

Fried pork fillet

A savoury-sweet dish eaten with boiled rice or with Chinese noodles in broth.

1¼lb (600g) sliced fillet of pork
oil for frying
1 egg
cornflour
1 tsp finely chopped garlic
1 tbsp rice wine or dry sherry
For the sauce:
4floz (125ml) stock
2oz (50g) sugar
2½ tbsp soy sauce
Calories 737; protein 22.8g; fat 65.2g; sugar 12.8g

1. Pound the meat lightly on both sides with the back of a cleaver and cut into small pieces.

2. Heat plenty of oil in the wok; dip the pork into the beaten egg and coat with the cornflour. Fry until the coating is crisp and golden brown. Remove from the wok and drain off the oil. Wipe out the wok.

3. Mix the sauce ingredients together, combining the stock, sugar and soy sauce.

4. Heat 2 tbsp oil in the wok, stir-fry the chopped garlic and as it begins to release its flavour, add the fried pieces of pork and stir-fry.

5. Sprinkle with rice wine or dry sherry and the prepared sauce and cook over a high heat; if the sauce is too thin, stir in an extra 1 tsp cornflour dissolved in 2 tsp water.

Belly of pork with bamboo shoots

A very good example of the Chinese flair for combining complementary ingredients; the bamboo shoots balance and highlight the stronger taste of the pork.

1¼lb (600g) belly of pork in one piece
¾lb (approx. 400g) tender winter bamboo shoots, unsalted
   canned or fresh, parboiled
2 tbsp oil
small piece peeled root ginger, finely sliced
To flavour:
4 tbsp soy sauce
2 tbsp sugar
1 tbsp rice wine or dry sherry
Calories 630; protein 26g; fat 52.6g; sugar 12.3g

1. Cut the belly of pork into 1¼-in (3-cm) cubes.

2. Cut the bamboo shoots crosswise into pieces the same size as the pork.

3. Heat 2 tbsp oil in the wok, and stir-fry the slices of ginger. Add the cubed belly of pork and fry over a high heat, mixing and turning so that the pork browns evenly all over.

4. Place the pork in a heavy saucepan or flameproof casserole; stir in the bamboo shoots and the flavouring of soy sauce, sugar and rice wine or sherry. Add enough water to just cover the meat, mix and place over the heat.

5. Cook over a high heat until the water comes to the boil; turn the heat down to very low, cover and cook for about 1 hour. When nearly all the liquid has reduced or been absorbed, the dish is ready to serve.

Stir-fried pork with black bean paste

A highly-flavoured dish, best served with a light broth.

½–¾lb (approx. 300g) piece of boned leg of pork
1 egg white
1 tsp cornflour
oil for frying
½–¾lb (approx. 300g) fresh spinach, well washed and trimmed, but left attached to the root tops
1 tsp salt
1½ tbsp black bean paste
1 tbsp sugar
1 tbsp soy sauce
a few drops of sesame seed oil
pinch of monosodium glutamate
Calories 391; protein 16.4g; fat 32.7g; sugar 7.6g
Serves 4–5

1. Slice the pork thinly and then cut into matchstick pieces about ¼in (5mm) wide. Mix the pork strips with the egg white to cover thoroughly and then dredge with cornflour.

2. Heat 2in (5cm) oil in the wok to about 200°F (90°C) or until it sizzles when the first piece of meat is added. Fry briskly, taking care that the pork strips do not stick together as they fry; as soon

1

2

3

4

5

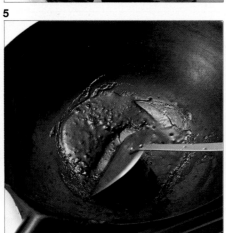

6

as the meat turns from pink to white on the outside, remove from the wok and drain on paper towels. Drain off the oil.

3. Heat 2 tbsp fresh oil in the wok, add the spinach (dried with paper towels) and stir-fry over a high heat.

4. As soon as the spinach has softened, add the salt and 8floz (250ml) water; cover and cook until tender; drain and keep warm.

5. Tip the cooking water from the wok and dry; heat 1 tbsp more oil and pour in the black bean paste, sugar and soy sauce and adding a few drops sesame seed oil and a pinch of monosodium glutamate.

6. As soon as the sauce comes to the boil, add the meat and cook briefly over a high heat, mixing and turning so that the pork is evenly flavoured with the sauce. Serve the meat on the bed of hot spinach as illustrated.

Fried pork balls

Little meat balls which can be dipped in a variety of sauces, according to taste.

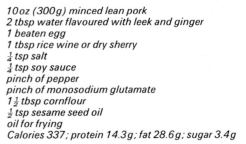

10oz (300g) minced lean pork
2 tbsp water flavoured with leek and ginger
1 beaten egg
1 tbsp rice wine or dry sherry
$\frac{1}{4}$ tsp salt
$\frac{1}{4}$ tsp soy sauce
pinch of pepper
pinch of monosodium glutamate
$1\frac{1}{2}$ tbsp cornflour
$\frac{1}{2}$ tsp sesame seed oil
oil for frying
Calories 337; protein 14.3g; fat 28.6g; sugar 3.4g

1. Put the minced pork in a bowl; add the water flavoured with leek and ginger and work into the meat by hand until the meat is softened and has formed a smooth paste. Add the beaten egg and the rice wine and mix well.

2. Add the salt, soy sauce, pepper and the monosodium glutamate, mixing in the same way until well blended.

3. Add the cornflour, stir well and add the sesame seed oil to give more flavour.

4. Shape the pork balls by taking a small quantity of the meat mixture in the left hand; form a fist, enclosing the meat, and then squeeze the meat out through the hole formed by thumb and forefinger, producing a small ball.

5. Heat 2in (5cm) oil in the wok. Fry half the pork balls, drain and set aside; fry the other half in their turn and drain. Re-heat the oil in the wok to 350°F (180°C) and fry the first batch of pork balls again until they are crisp and crunchy on the outside. Repeat with second batch.

6. Sweet and sour sauce is optional: make about one-third quantity of the recipe given on p. 132. Add 2 tbsp chopped leek and $\frac{1}{2}$ tsp finely chopped fresh ginger and cook as directed.

Thrice-cooked pork

4-5 h

A dish which is cooked in three stages; first
boiled, then fried and finally steamed.

1¾ lb (800g) belly of pork in one piece
1 leek
small piece root ginger
oil for frying
1 star anise
½ tbsp cornflour
For the sauce:
4–6 tbsp soy sauce
1 tbsp sugar
1 tbsp rice wine or dry sherry
4 fl oz (125 ml) stock from cooking the pork
Calories 662; protein 33.5 g; fat 55.8 g; sugar 4.3 g
Serves 4–6

1. Bring plenty of water to the boil in a large pan; place the belly of pork in the boiling water for a few minutes. Take out the pork and place in a fresh pan of boiling water, together with a whole leek and the ginger, sliced wafer thin. Cover and cook for 30–40 minutes.

2. Mix the sauce ingredients together.

3. When the pork is done, allow to cool slightly, drain and dry with paper towels. Heat 2 in (5 cm) oil in the wok to 350°F (180°C) and fry the pork until it is well-coloured all over.

4. Remove the pork from the wok and refresh in cold water; once it is cold enough to handle, cut down at right angles to the grain of the meat into rectangular pieces about ¼ in (5 mm) thick.

5. Place the sliced pork in a heatproof dish, fat part downwards; add the star anise and the sauce, sprinkling it evenly over the meat.

6. Place the dish in the bamboo steamer, over boiling water producing plenty of steam. Cook over a moderate heat for about 2 hours, continually topping up the boiling water with hot water whenever needed, to avoid burning the steamer.

7. Remove the dish from the steamer and allow to cool. Place in the refrigerator and remove the layer of fat which will form on the surface. Return the dish to the steamer and cook for a further 1–2 hours, or until the pork is very tender. Transfer to a hot serving dish.

8. Pour the juices which have been produced during cooking into a saucepan, heat until boiling and then stir in the cornflour dissolved in 1 tbsp cold water. Cook briefly until thickened and then pour over the pork.

Casseroled shizitou (braised pork balls)

Large pork rissoles which are first fried and then braised with Chinese cabbage. A hearty dish for cold days.

14oz (400g) minced lean pork
1 tbsp finely chopped leek
½ tsp ginger juice
¼ tsp salt
1 tbsp rice wine or dry sherry
pinch of pepper
1 egg
½ tbsp sesame seed oil
2 tbsp cornflour
oil for frying
5–6 leaves Chinese cabbage
3floz (75ml) soy sauce
1 tbsp rice wine or dry sherry
Calories 381; protein 19g; fat 28.7g; sugar 9.2g

1. Spread the minced pork out on the chopping board and chop even more finely with the cleaver in both directions to make sure that the consistency is very soft and no lumps of meat remain.

2. Place the pork in a bowl, add the finely chopped leek, the ginger juice, salt, rice wine and pepper; work together well by hand.

3. Add the egg to the mixture, and stir in the sesame seed oil and cornflour; continue kneading until smooth and well blended. If the mixture is too firm, add a little water.

4. Divide the mixture in four; oil the palms of the hands lightly and shape four large balls. Slap the balls sharply from one hand to the other to help firm them up.

5. Heat 2 in (5 cm) oil in the wok, lower the pork balls into the hot oil and fry over a high heat until the outside of the pork is crisp and sealed. Lower the heat and continue cooking until they are golden-brown. Drain and set aside.

6. Wash and drain the Chinese cabbage leaves; cut into pieces 2–2½ in (5–6 cm) long. Fry in the oil until they are tender. Drain on paper towels.

7. Line the bottom of a flameproof casserole with some of the cabbage leaves, place the pork balls on the bed of leaves and top with the rest of the cabbage. Sprinkle with soy sauce and rice wine.

8. Add approx. 1¾ pints (1 litre) water, enough to just cover the contents of the casserole; bring to the boil over a high heat, reduce the heat, cover and cook slowly for about 1 hour.

Boiled pork with garlic sauce

A simple dish, made original and appetising by the subtle garlic sauce.

1¼lb (600g) boned shoulder or loin of pork
small piece root ginger
½ leek
1 tbsp rice wine or dry sherry
1 large clove garlic
1 tsp sugar
For the garlic sauce:
1 large clove garlic
1 tsp sugar
1 tbsp soy sauce
a few drops of sesame seed oil
pinch of monosodium glutamate
Calories 281; protein 30.8g; fat 15g; sugar 2.7g

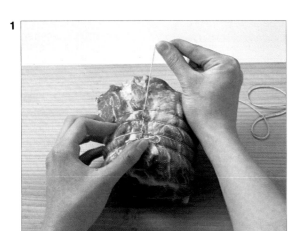

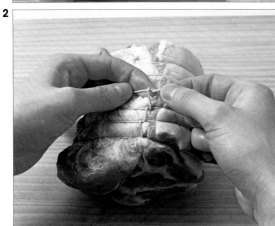

1. Tie up the boned shoulder or loin of pork securely as shown in the illustration, leaving intervals of $\frac{1}{2}$—$\frac{3}{4}$ in ($1\frac{1}{2}$ cm) between each piece of string.

2. Make a very compactly tied joint; knot the ends of the string tightly.

3. Peel the ginger; crush with a sharp blow from the flat of the cleaver blade and do the same with the leek.

4. Bring plenty of water to the boil in a saucepan large enough to take the pork; place the ginger, leek and the pork in the boiling water, sprinkle with the rice wine and cook over a moderate heat for about 45 minutes. Do not add salt.

5. To test whether the meat is cooked right through, pierce deeply with a skewer; if the juice runs clear, the meat is done; if the juice is still pink, continue cooking and test again later.

6. When the pork is cooked remove from the pan, leave to cool to room temperature, untie and carve into thin, even slices.

7. Peel the garlic and crush in a garlic press; place in a bowl.

8. Stir in the sauce ingredients. Arrange the sliced meat on a serving plate and sprinkle with the garlic sauce.

Fried pork Shanghai style

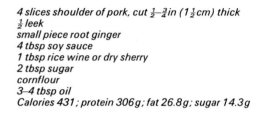

The rich flavour and colour of this dish are typical of Shanghai cuisine.

4 slices shoulder of pork, cut ½–¾in (1½cm) thick
½ leek
small piece root ginger
4 tbsp soy sauce
1 tbsp rice wine or dry sherry
2 tbsp sugar
cornflour
3–4 tbsp oil
Calories 431; protein 306g; fat 26.8g; sugar 14.3g

1. Beat first one side of the pork slices and then the other with the blunt edge of the cleaver – the ideal tool to use since it tenderises the meat and also breaks up the fibres somewhat so that the flavourings can penetrate easily.

2. Bring the flat of the cleaver down on the leek in one sharp blow; repeat this with the ginger, having first peeled it: this will help to release the flavour.

3. Lay the pork slices out flat in a dish, place the leek and ginger on top. Mix the soy sauce with the rice wine or sherry and the sugar and sprinkle all over the meat. Leave to stand for 20–30 minutes to allow the meat to absorb all the flavours.

4. Coat the pork slices lightly with cornflour. Heat the oil in the wok and stir-fry the leek and ginger.

5. Fry the pork, keeping it as flat as possible, in the flavoured oil, two slices at a time.

6. Fry over a high heat until browned on one side, turn, and when both sides have browned, lower the heat and cover the wok.

7. Cook until the pork is tender and well-coloured all over. Remove from the wok and cook the remaining slices in the same way.

8. When all the pork is cooked, cut into strips about $\frac{1}{2}-\frac{3}{4}$ in ($1\frac{1}{2}$–2cm) wide and arrange on the serving dish. The slices are best cut with a very sharp cleaver; cut straight down through the meat without a sawing motion which would break up the meat, pressing firmly down on the cleaver.

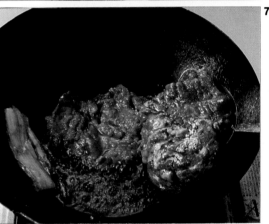

Stir-fried pork and potatoes

The soft consistency of potato absorbs and subtly changes the taste of the pork. Best served with slow-cooked Congee rice (see recipe, page 260).

(see recipe, page 260)

7oz (200g) sliced leg of pork
10oz (300g) potatoes
¼lb (100g) carrots
4 tbsp oil
For the marinade:
1 tsp soy sauce
½ tsp sugar
1 tsp cornflour
1 tbsp peanut oil
For the sauce:
1 tbsp soy sauce
1 tsp sugar
1 tbsp rice wine or dry sherry
½ tsp salt
pinch of monosodium glutamate
Calories 250; protein 12.6g; fat 14.5g; sugar 16.3g

1. Cut the pork slices into thin strips, place in a bowl and add the marinade of soy sauce, sugar, cornflour and peanut oil. Mix well by hand and leave to stand for a little while for the flavouring to penetrate the meat.

2. Peel the potatoes and cut to the same size as the pork. Bring a large pan of water to the boil; parboil the potato strips and drain.

3. Peel the carrots and cut into thin strips the same size as the pork and potatoes.

4. Heat 2 tbsp oil in the wok; fry the pork lightly, keeping the strips as separate as possible. When just cooked, remove from the wok and set aside.

5. Wipe the wok clean, heat 2 tbsp fresh oil and stir-fry the carrots and parboiled potatoes; when they are just tender, add the pork and stir-fry all the ingredients together briefly.

6. Mix the sauce ingredients and pour into the wok; mix quickly but thoroughly and serve at once.

Stir-fried pork and celery

20'

The crisp, crunchy consistency of the celery contrasts agreeably with the tender pork.

½–¾lb (300g) celery
a small piece of leek
small piece root ginger
oil for frying
¼lb (125g) finely chopped or minced pork
cornflour
For the sauce:
1 tsp soy sauce
1 tbsp rice wine or dry sherry
2 tsp sugar
1 tbsp black bean paste
pinch of monosodium glutamate
cornflour
Calories 77; protein 5.8g; fat 11.5g; sugar 4.2g

1. Wash the celery thoroughly, remove any strings and cut into ½-in (1-cm) dice.

2. Bring a large saucepan of water to the boil and parboil the diced celery. Drain and set aside.

3. Finely chop enough leek to yield 1 tbsp; peel the ginger and chop very finely, enough to give 1 tsp.

4. Prepare the sauce by mixing all the ingredients together, making sure the black bean paste is smoothly blended.

5. Heat 2 tbsp oil in the wok and lightly stir-fry the chopped leek and ginger; once they have started to release their aroma, add the pork and fry, stirring to prevent it sticking or forming lumps; mix in the celery and keep turning to ensure even cooking.

6. Pour in the sauce and cook briskly, stirring to ensure that the sauce is absorbed evenly.

7. If the liquid seems too thin, dissolve a small quantity of cornflour in a double quantity of water, and stir into the wok.

Small green chili peppers stuffed with pork

A full-flavoured dish; the brilliant green of the peppers makes for attractive presentation.

5oz (150g) finely chopped or minced pork
20 small green chili peppers
oil for frying
For the flavouring and seasoning:
$\frac{1}{4}$ tsp salt
2 tsp soy sauce
1 tsp sugar
2 tbsp rice wine or dry sherry
a few drops sesame seed oil
pinch of monosodium glutamate
Calories 256; protein 10.4g; fat 17.8g; sugar 6.9g

1. Spread the minced meat out on the chopping board and, using the sharp edge of the cleaver, go over the meat chopping in both directions to help soften the pork further and avoid the formation of lumps in the stuffing mixture.

2. Place the meat in a bowl, add the seasonings and flavourings as listed, working in well with the hands until a smooth paste is obtained.

3. Wash the chilis, slit carefully down one side, stopping short of both ends so that they do not open into two halves.

4. Remove the seeds delicately, using a chopstick or small spoon handle.

5. To avoid splattering when the peppers are fried in oil, dry thoroughly with paper towels or a dry cloth.

6. Prise open the slits in the chilis carefully and fill with the stuffing, adding a little at a time, until the chilis are full of firmly packed meat, bulging out of the opening.

7. Heat 2 tbsp oil in the wok; place the filled chilis, meat side downwards, to fry over a medium heat until the meat is browned.

8. Turn the chilis with a spatula, cover and turn down the heat, leaving to cook through. Check every so often to make sure they do not stick and burn.

Szechuan minced pork and transparent noodles

A robust, peppery dish, typical of Szechuan

2oz (50–60g) transparent noodles
oil for frying
2 tbsp leek, ginger and garlic, finely chopped together
1 tsp black bean paste
7oz (200g) minced pork
1 tbsp rice wine or dry sherry
generous 1¼ pints (¾ litre) stock
soy sauce
pinch of salt
1 tbsp cornflour
a few drops of sesame seed oil
2–3 aubergines
Calories 364; protein 9.1g; fat 29.1g; sugar 15.7g

1. Wash the noodles, cook in boiling water until they are tender, drain and cut into 1½–2-in (4–5-cm) lengths with scissors.

2. Heat 3 tbsp oil in the wok; add the chopped mixture of leek, ginger and garlic and stir-fry; do not allow to colour. When they have started to give off their aroma add the black bean paste.

3. Stir-fry for a little longer and then add the minced pork; stir-fry, mixing well to avoid lumps forming; add the rice wine or dry sherry, pouring it in down the side of the wok, and cook until the meat has coloured.

4. Add the stock, season with soy sauce and salt and cook slowly.

5. Add the noodles, followed by the cornflour dissolved in 2 tbsp water; add a few drops sesame seed oil for extra flavour.

6. Wash the aubergines well and slice crossways into rounds.

7. Heat some oil in the wok and fry the aubergine slices briskly; when tender, remove with a slotted spoon and allow to drain.

8. Serve the pork and noodles in a deep serving dish with the fried aubergine slices arranged in the centre.

BEEF DISHES

The Chinese have never been great eaters of beef, as cattle are raised and kept for other purposes. Since time immemorial, oxen and water buffalo have been the faithful servants and friends of the Chinese, useful beasts of burden and working animals. The time finally comes, however, when these animals can no longer work; few of their owners can afford to be sentimental and allow them to pass an idle retirement, and so they usually end up in the cooking pot.

The relative scarcity of recipes for beef in Chinese cooking can be explained by the fact that the beef is usually from old animals and is therefore tough, or by the dislike of many Chinese for red meat (more marked in previous centuries). What beef dishes there are can usually be found in the north and west of China, where Islam has made a greater impact, reducing the consumption of pork.

Beef is usually cut into very thin slices, across the grain, or minced and used as a stuffing for dumplings, when it is flavoured with ginger and spring onions.

Thin slices of beef are also treated with spices and dried, to be eaten as snacks.

Szechuan beef with ginger and green peppers

This dish is a good example of the strong flavours of Szechuan cooking and should be accompanied by rice.

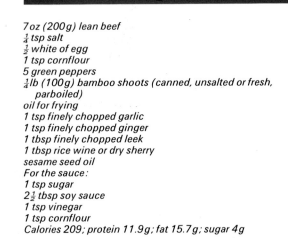

7 oz (200 g) lean beef
¼ tsp salt
½ white of egg
1 tsp cornflour
5 green peppers
¼ lb (100 g) bamboo shoots (canned, unsalted or fresh, parboiled)
oil for frying
1 tsp finely chopped garlic
1 tsp finely chopped ginger
1 tbsp finely chopped leek
1 tbsp rice wine or dry sherry
sesame seed oil
For the sauce:
1 tsp sugar
2½ tbsp soy sauce
1 tsp vinegar
1 tsp cornflour
Calories 209; protein 11.9 g; fat 15.7 g; sugar 4 g

1. Cut the beef into thin slices across the grain and then into thin strips $\frac{1}{4}$ in (5 mm) wide, season with salt. Dip the strips in the white of egg and then sprinkle with the cornflour, mixing well by hand.

2. Cut the green peppers lengthways in half, remove the seeds and pith and shred into thin strips, less than $\frac{1}{8}$ in (3 mm) wide. Cut the bamboo shoots into strips the same size.

3. Heat 2 tbsp oil in the wok and stir-fry the strips of beef, taking care that they do not stick to one another; remove as soon as they have turned a whitish colour on the outside.

4. Heat a further 2 tbsp oil and stir-fry the chopped garlic, ginger and leek briskly over a high heat.

5. Once the ginger has turned golden-brown and has started to release its aroma, add the shredded green peppers and the bamboo shoots. Stir-fry briefly over a high heat.

6. When the peppers and bamboo shoots are nearly tender add the beef and sprinkle with the rice wine or dry sherry; stir-fry all the ingredients together.

7. Pour in the sauce ingredients and stir-fry rapidly to allow the beef and vegetables to absorb the flavours evenly.

8. Finish by adding a few drops of sesame seed oil to give the dish extra flavour; if the sauce is too thin, stir in 1 tsp cornflour dissolved in 2 tsp water.

Beef and Chinese white radish in soy sauce

A Szechuan speciality which involves long, slow cooking and has a spicy flavour.

1 lb (500 g) shin of beef
1 tbsp rice wine or dry sherry
½ tbsp soy sauce
1 tbsp cornflour
oil for frying
a 4-in (10-cm) length of leek
4–5 slivers of root ginger
1 star anise
5–7 tbsp soy sauce
2 lb (1 kg) Chinese white radish
Calories 348; protein 29.2 g; fat 17.9 g; sugar 14.8 g

1. Cut the beef into 1–1½-in (3–4-cm) cubes; place in a bowl and sprinkle with rice wine and soy sauce. Add the cornflour and mix well by hand.

2. Heat plenty of oil in the wok, add the meat and fry quickly over a high heat until the beef is well browned. If desired, the beef can be given more colour by shallow-frying. Drain.

3. Place the meat in a heavy saucepan together with the leek, sliced diagonally into thin rounds, and the slightly crushed ginger. Cover with 2¾–3¼ pints (1½–1¾ litres) water.

4. Add the star anise and about 2 tbsp soy sauce; bring to the boil over a high heat, skim, cover the pan and turn the heat down to low. Simmer for about 2 hours.

5. The remaining soy sauce will be added to the beef later on if the flavour needs strengthening.

6. Peel the Chinese radishes and slice into pieces about 1½–2in (4–5cm) long; cut these pieces lengthways in half or in quarters if they are very large. Trim the edges to round them off.

7. When the beef is very tender, add the radish pieces and continue cooking over a low heat.

8. When the liquid in the saucepan has reduced by half during this long, slow cooking process, taste and add the reserved soy sauce if needed. Continue cooking until the radish has reached a really tender, almost buttery, consistency.

Stir-fried beef with green beans

An appetising dish which is easy to prepare.

5oz (150g) thinly sliced lean beef
1 tsp sugar
2 tbsp soy sauce
1 tsp cornflour
1 tsp peanut oil
7oz (200g) green beans
oil for frying
1 tsp salt
1 tbsp finely chopped leek
½ can of straw mushrooms
1 tsp sugar
1 tbsp rice wine or dry sherry
pinch of monosodium glutamate
a few drops of sesame seed oil
Calories 170; protein 9.4g; fat 12.5g; sugar 6.1g

1. Cut the slices of beef into pieces about ¾–1 in (2–3cm) long and place in a bowl or deep dish. Add the sugar, 1 tbsp soy sauce, cornflour and peanut oil; mix well and leave to marinate.

2. String the beans if necessary, wash and cut into 1¾–2-in (4–5-cm) lengths.

3. Heat the wok, pour in 2 tbsp oil and stir-fry the beans lightly; add the salt and 8floz (225ml) water, cover and simmer until tender. Remove from the wok and drain. Discard the cooling liquid.

4. Heat 2 tbsp oil in the wok, add the marinated beef and stir-fry lightly, until browned on the outside but still a little pink inside.

5. In another frying pan, heat 2 tbsp oil and stir-fry the chopped leek; when the leek starts to release its aroma, add the drained straw mushrooms and the beans.

6. Stir-fry these briefly and then add the meat, the sugar, 1 tbsp soy sauce, the rice wine or dry sherry and the monosodium glutamate. Stir-fry over a high heat, and add a few drops of sesame seed oil to add more flavour to the dish.

Stir-fried beef and onions

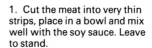

Western cooks have followed the Chinese in combining beef with onions. This is a mouth-watering dish which is no trouble to prepare.

7oz (200g) thinly sliced lean beef
1 tbsp soy sauce
10oz (300g) onions
oil for frying
½ egg white
1 tsp cornflour
For the sauce:
1 tbsp rice wine or dry sherry
1 tbsp sugar
2 tbsp soy sauce
pinch of monosodium glutamate
Calories 277; protein 13.4g; fat 17.6g; sugar 12.3g

1. Cut the meat into very thin strips, place in a bowl and mix well with the soy sauce. Leave to stand.

2. Peel the onions; cut lengthways in two and then across the layers into slices ¼ in (5mm) thick.

3. Heat 3 tbsp oil in the wok and stir-fry the onions until light golden-brown. Do not allow to burn or crisp at all. Set aside.

4. Mix the beef with the egg white and then the cornflour by hand. Heat 2 tbsp oil in a separate wok or frying pan and stir-fry the beef gently over a fairly low heat, using chopsticks to separate the shreds of beef. As soon as the beef is done, remove the whole lot at once, using a mesh ladle. Drain.

5. Replace the wok containing the onions over a fairly low heat, add the cooked beef and stir in the sauce ingredients: rice wine or dry sherry, sugar, soy sauce and monosodium glutamate. Stir-fry briefly and then serve.

Szechuan braised shin of beef with Chinese cabbage

A spicy dish from Szechuan which needs long, slow cooking.

1½ lb (700 g) shin of beef in one piece
5 tbsp peanut oil
½ Chinese cabbage
2 tbsp rice wine or dry sherry
1 tsp black bean paste
3–4 fl oz (100–125 ml) soy sauce
1 tsp sesame seed oil
1 tbsp cornflour
Calories 467; protein 38.6 g; fat 30.8 g; sugar 6 g

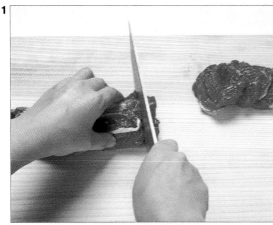

1. Cut the shin of beef into pieces about 2 in (5 cm) wide and ¾ in (2 cm) thick; it is best not to cut the pieces too small or they will become dry and tasteless during the lengthy cooking process.

2. Heat the peanut oil in the wok and fry the beef over a high heat until well-browned on all sides.

3. Wash the Chinese cabbage, place in a large saucepan of boiling water and simmer until just tender. Refresh in cold water, drain and cut lengthwise into strips ¾ in (2 cm) wide. Squeeze gently to get rid of excess liquid.

4. Place the meat in a saucepan, add the rice wine, 2½ pints (1½ litres) water and the black bean paste; bring to the boil quickly over a high heat, leaving the pan uncovered.

5. As soon as the water comes to the boil, turn down the heat; remove any scum from the surface with a skimmer. Cover and simmer slowly for about 1½ hours.

6. When the beef is quite tender, place the Chinese cabbage strips on top of it and stir half the soy sauce into the liquid.

7. Cook for another 30 minutes, after which time the flavouring should have been absorbed by the meat and vegetable. Add some or all of the remaining soy sauce, depending on how pronounced a taste you prefer; add a little sesame seed oil for extra flavour.

8. Mix the cornflour with 2 tbsp water, draw aside the cabbage and pour in. Stir in and bring to the boil; once the sauce has thickened the dish is ready to serve.

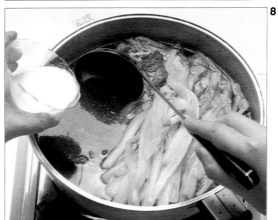

Sweet and sour beef rissoles

When made with beef, this recipe is less rich and more digestible than the pork version.

¾lb (350g) finely chopped or minced beef
½ beaten egg
½ tsp salt
2 tbsp cornflour
oil for frying
1 onion
4 green peppers
4 slices canned pineapple
1 chili pepper
small piece garlic
For the sauce:
2 fl oz (50ml) stock
4½ oz (135g) sugar
1 tbsp soy sauce
2 tbsp vinegar
1 tsp salt
1 tsp rice wine or dry sherry
Calories 526; protein 17.3g; fat 31.1g; sugar 20.7g

1. Spread the minced beef out on a chopping board and, using the cleaver, chop it in both directions to make it absolutely smooth. Place in a bowl and add the beaten egg, salt, 1 tbsp cornflour and 2 tbsp water. Knead well.

2. When the mixture forms a smooth paste, shape into balls about 1 in (2.5cm) in diameter. To make well shaped rissoles, take a small amount of mixture in one hand and close the hand to make a fist; squeeze the meat out through the hole formed by thumb and forefinger, forming a small ball.

3. Heat plenty of oil to medium hot in the wok, and fry the beef balls until they are well browned all over. Use chopsticks to keep them from sticking to each other while cooking; drain and set aside. Discard the oil.

4. Cut the onion in half across and then slice thinly lengthways. Cut the green peppers in half, remove the seeds and pith. Drain the juice from the pineapple slices and cut both the peppers and the pineapple into pieces.

5. Remove the seeds from the chili pepper and cut into $\frac{1}{4}$-in (5-mm) thick rings; finely chop enough garlic to yield 1 tsp. Mix all the sauce ingredients together.

6. Heat 2 tbsp oil in the wok, stir-fry the garlic and as soon as it starts to release its aroma, add the peppers, onion and the pineapple.

7. When these are tender, add the beef balls and stir-fry; sprinkle with the chili pepper rings. Finally, pour in the sauce and mix quickly.

8. When the sauce has started to bubble dissolve 1 tbsp cornflour in 2 tbsp water; add to the sauce and stir quickly to thicken it evenly.

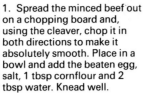

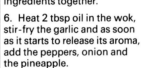

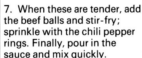

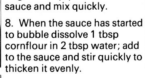

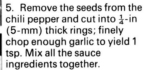

Cantonese beef with oyster sauce

A famous dish from Canton. The contrasting flavour of the oyster sauce heightens and enhances the taste of the beef.

1 lb (450 g) thinly sliced lean beef
½ egg white
1 tsp cornflour
small clove garlic
3 fl oz (75 ml) oyster sauce
1 tsp sugar
2 tbsp stock
oil for deep-frying
2 tbsp peanut oil
1 tbsp rice wine or dry sherry
1 tsp cornflour
Calories 343; protein 26.4 g; fat 21.8; sugar 8.2 g

1. Cut the beef into bite-sized pieces, place in a bowl and mix well with the white of egg and the cornflour.

2. Chop enough garlic to yield 1 tsp. Mix the oyster sauce, sugar and stock and set aside.

3. Heat the deep-frying oil until moderately hot, add the beef and fry lightly; separate the pieces as they cook with chopsticks. Drain and set aside.

4. Heat the wok; when it is hot pour in the peanut oil and stir-fry the finely chopped garlic. When the garlic starts to give off its aroma, add the beef and sprinkle with the rice wine.

5. Add the oyster sauce mixture, mixing and turning well to make sure the meat is evenly covered. Dissolve the cornflour in 2 tsp water and stir in to thicken and glaze the sauce.

CHICKEN AND DUCK

In its own way chicken is as versatile as pork in Chinese cooking, and can be considered as its domestic equivalent, providing another source of delicately flavoured, tender meat which presents few problems, even for the inexperienced cook. The eating of its flesh is not proscribed by any religion, another reason for its widespread popularity. It must be said, however, that the fowl so beloved of the Chinese is not the watery, almost tasteless product of factory farming which all too often we in the West have to eat, but a very different bird which has grown to early maturity scratching around in farmyards and courtyards, nourished on a wide variety of foods and living a normal life. The Chinese also eat their chickens extremely fresh – as soon after they have been killed as possible – and for this reason the birds are usually bought at street markets and taken home alive.

Duck demands a little more skill for successful preparation. If inexpertly cooked it can be fatty and indigestible or tough and rubbery; if overdone, the flesh is dry. The flesh has a distinctive taste and consistency, with a lower ratio of meat to bone than chicken. It is also less versatile and combines well with a narrower range of ingredients.

It is difficult to assign a particular rôle to duck in Chinese cuisine. Its pronounced flavour precludes it from being an everyday food, and its lower meat yield means it can be quite expensive, but with a little care duck can be a delectable treat, and in Chinese hands it has become a delicacy known all over the world, as anyone who has tasted Peking Duck would agree.

Stir-fried chicken and cucumbers

A light, low-calorie dish with a delicate flavour.

7 oz (200 g) chicken breasts
½ egg white
1 tsp cornflour
2 small cucumbers
oil for frying
small slice root ginger
1 tbsp rice wine or dry sherry
a few drops of sesame seed oil
For the sauce:
1 tbsp soy sauce
1 tsp sugar
½ tsp salt
pinch of monosodium glutamate
pinch of pepper
Calories 219; protein 11.4 g; fat 17.6 g; sugar 2.8 g

1. Cut the chicken breasts into thin, diagonal slices. (Hold the chicken breast firmly with the left hand and cut carefully with the knife at 45° to the chopping board, working from right to left). Dip the slices in the egg white and then in the cornflour.

2. Cut the cucumbers in half lengthways and then slice diagonally into ¼-in (5-mm) thick pieces.

3. In a deep pan, over a low heat, heat enough oil for deep-frying. Add the chicken and fry gently. Remove the chicken and drain.

4. Heat the wok and when hot pour in 2 tbsp oil; stir-fry the ginger and once it has started to give off its aroma, add the cucumbers.

5. Add the chicken, sprinkle with the rice wine and the sauce ingredients. Stir-fry quickly over a high heat.

6. Finish the dish by adding a few drops of sesame seed oil.

Chicken and cashew nuts Szechuan style

7oz (200g) chicken breasts
½ white of egg
1 tsp cornflour
pinch of salt
oil for frying
3 green peppers
3½oz (100g) bamboo shoots (canned or parboiled)
2oz (50g) cashew nuts
1 tsp finely chopped garlic
1 tbsp rice wine or dry sherry
monosodium glutamate
For the sauce:
1 tbsp black bean paste
1 tbsp soy sauce
2 tsp sugar
½ tbsp vinegar
¼ tsp salt
Calories 317; protein 14.8g; fat 23.7g; sugar 11.5g

1. Cut the chicken breasts into ½-in (1-cm) dice; dip in the egg white and then in the cornflour, adding a pinch of salt.

2. In a large pan, heat enough oil for deep-frying until fairly hot. Fry the diced chicken. Drain.

3. Slice the peppers in half lengthways, remove the seeds, stalks and pith; cut into ½-in (1-cm) squares.

4. Cut the bamboo shoots to the same size as the peppers. Mix the sauce ingredients together in a bowl.

5. Fry the cashew nuts in moderately hot oil until they are lightly browned and crunchy.

6. Heat 2 tbsp oil in the wok and stir-fry the garlic until it starts to release its aroma; add the bamboo shoots and the peppers and stir-fry.

7. Add the chicken and cashew nuts, sprinkle with rice wine and pour in the sauce. Stir-fry all the ingredients briefly over a high heat and add a pinch of monosodium glutamate to heighten the flavour.

Stir-fried chicken with ginger

This is a seasonal dish with a pleasant piquant taste of root ginger.

10 oz (300 g) chicken breasts
1 tbsp rice wine or dry sherry
salt
2–4 oz (50–100 g) root ginger
4 green peppers
1 egg white
1 tbsp cornflour
oil for frying
1 tsp finely chopped garlic
1 tbsp rice wine
For the sauce:
$\frac{1}{2}$ tsp salt
$2\frac{1}{2}$ tbsp vinegar
3 tbsp sugar
1 tbsp tomato ketchup
1 tsp cornflour, if required
Calories 303; protein 17.2 g; fat 18.9 g; sugar 13.6 g

1. Slice the chicken diagonally into bite-sized pieces; hold the chicken breast firmly with the left hand and with the knife at 45° to the chopping board, slice across the grain of the meat; begin from the right hand end and work to the left. Place the meat in a bowl and mix with the rice wine and ½ tsp salt.

2. Peel the ginger and slice lengthways wafer-thin. Sprinkle with a pinch of salt and leave to stand.

3. Cut the peppers lengthways in half; remove the seeds, stalks and pith and cut into even-sized triangular pieces.

4. Place all the sauce ingredients (except the cornflour) in a small saucepan and heat, mixing well. As soon as the liquid comes to the boil, remove from heat and set aside to cool.

5. Squeeze out the ginger, which will have been softened by the salt, add to the tepid or cold sauce and leave to stand.

6. Mix the chicken with the egg white and then with the cornflour. Heat enough oil for deep-frying until fairly hot, add the chicken and fry, stirring and turning to prevent crisping or browning.

7. Heat 2 tbsp oil in the wok and stir-fry the finely chopped garlic until it starts to give off its scent. Drain the peppers and the ginger from the sauce and add to the garlic.

8. When the peppers are tender, add the chicken; sprinkle with rice wine, pour in the sauce and stir-fry over a high heat. If the sauce is too thin, stir in the cornflour dissolved in 2 tsp water.

111

Chinese fried chicken

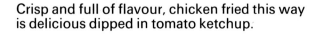

Crisp and full of flavour, chicken fried this way is delicious dipped in tomato ketchup.

2 chicken legs
½ beaten egg
4 tbsp cornflour
a few drops of sesame seed oil (optional)
oil for frying
1 tbsp finely chopped leek (optional)
For the flavouring:
¼ tsp salt
2–3 drops soy sauce
1 tsp rice wine or dry sherry
pinch of pepper
pinch of monosodium glutamate
Calories 255; protein 25.7 g; fat 12.4 g; sugar 8.3 g
Serves 2–3

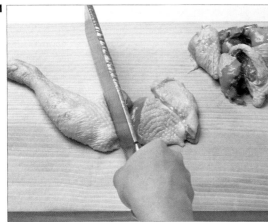

1

2

3

4

1. Wash and trim the chicken legs, dry with a cloth or paper towels; use a cleaver to chop through the bone into triangular, bite-sized pieces.

2. Gently mix the beaten egg and the flavouring ingredients together in a bowl and add the chicken pieces.

3. Sprinkle with cornflour and mix well by hand. Leave to stand for 5 minutes. If a slightly stronger flavour is preferred, add a few drops sesame seed oil.

4. Heat plenty of oil in the wok or in a deep-fryer to 350°F (180°C). If a wok is used, test to see whether the oil is hot enough by dropping in a little coarsely chopped leek; if the leek travels to the edge of the pan and browns quickly, the temperature should be hot enough.

5. Lower the chicken pieces into the oil one by one, working as quickly as possible to ensure even cooking; if the skin of the chicken flaps loose, press it back into place to neaten the portions.

6. Adding the chicken to the oil will have lowered the temperature to about 300°F (150°C). Maintain this lower temperature by turning down the heat; when the chicken is half done, remove it from the wok and prick the pieces with a skewer to enable them to cook through more quickly. Lower into the oil once more.

7. When the chicken is nearly cooked, increase the heat so that the oil is really hot; this will make it easier to drain the chicken so that it does not taste oily.

8. If desired, the flavour can be heightened by stir-frying the drained chicken pieces briefly in another skillet with a few drops of sesame seed oil and 1 tbsp finely chopped leek.

5

6

7

8

Chicken and pork in savoury batter

Fritters encased in an extra-light batter made with oil and baking powder and seasoned with sesame seeds and seaweed.

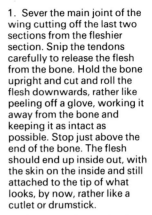

3 chicken wings
3oz (75g) tenderloin of pork
pinch of salt
pinch of pepper
pinch of monosodium glutamate
cornflour
batter (see recipe, p. 156)
pinch of black sesame seeds
1 leaf purple seaweed (nori), pre-soaked and shredded
oil for frying
Calories 345; protein 12g; fat 21.3g; sugar 25.6g
Serves 3–4

1. Sever the main joint of the wing cutting off the last two sections from the fleshier section. Snip the tendons carefully to release the flesh from the bone. Hold the bone upright and cut and roll the flesh downwards, rather like peeling off a glove, working it away from the bone and keeping it as intact as possible. Stop just above the end of the bone. The flesh should end up inside out, with the skin on the inside and still attached to the tip of what looks, by now, rather like a cutlet or drumstick.

2. Cut the pork into chunks.

3. Season the chicken with salt, pepper and monosodium glutamate and dredge lightly with cornflour.

4. Season the pork with salt, pepper and monosodium glutamate and coat with cornflour.

5. Make the batter and pour slightly less than half into a separate bowl. Stir the sesame seeds into the smaller quantity and the seaweed into the larger bowl, mixing well.

6. Heat plenty of oil to medium hot in a deep-fryer or wok; dip the chicken wings into the sesame seed batter and the pork into the seaweed batter.

7. Fry the coated portions at a medium-hot temperature until almost cooked; turn up the heat so that the oil reaches a temperature of 350°F (180°C) and finish frying.

Sweet and sour chicken legs

4 plump chicken legs
2 tsp salt
pepper
small quantity chopped leek and ginger
1 tbsp rice wine or dry sherry
cornflour
oil for frying
For the sweet and sour sauce:
2 oz (50 g) leek
1 oz (25 g) root ginger
small bunch parsley
4 tbsp soy sauce
4 tbsp sugar
4 tbsp vinegar
3 tbsp stock or hot water
pinch of monosodium glutamate
1 tbsp sesame seed oil
Calories 299; protein 25.3 g; fat 14.3 g; sugar 15.7 g

1. Allowing $\frac{1}{2}$ tsp salt and a pinch of pepper for each leg, rub these seasonings well into the chicken flesh. Pound the chopped leek and ginger briefly and mix with the chicken legs and rice wine. Leave for 30 minutes to absorb the flavours.

2. Bring a large saucepan of water to the boil, add the chicken legs one at a time. Allow to come back to the boil, turning the legs every now and then. Draw aside from heat; remove the chicken legs from the saucepan, tie a piece of string round each drumstick end and hang up to dry for 1–2 hours.

3. Start to prepare the sweet-sour sauce by cutting the leek into tiny dice and chop the ginger and the parsley very finely. Set plenty of oil to heat.

4. Untie the chicken legs and coat with cornflour, rubbing it well into the flesh. Lower the legs carefully into the hot oil; reduce the heat and fry for 5–6 minutes. Increase the temperature of the oil and continue cooking until the chicken is golden-brown and the coating is crisp.

5. Meanwhile, mix all the sauce ingredients with the leek, ginger and the parsley.

6. Chop each chicken leg cleanly (ideally with a cleaver) into 5–6 pieces and place on a warmed serving dish. Cover with the sweet and sour sauce.

Chicken with Chinese white radish

A homely, satisfying dish which needs painstaking preparation.

2 boned chicken legs
4-in (10-cm) length of leek cut into thin rings
1 small piece root ginger, sliced wafer-thin and lightly beaten
2 tbsp soy sauce
1 tbsp rice wine or dry sherry
cornflour
oil for frying
1 small Chinese white radish
a few drops of soy sauce
1 tsp salt
If desired:
1 star anise
a little sugar
a few drops of sesame seed oil
Calories 227; protein 10.4g; fat 12.5g; sugar 17g

1. Cut the boned chicken legs into pieces 2–2½ in (5–6 cm) wide and place in a bowl; marinate with the sliced leek and the lightly-beaten slices of ginger, the soy sauce and the rice wine.

2. Leave the chicken to absorb the flavours for 1–2 hours, turning every now and then. Remove the portions from the marinade, pat dry with a cloth or paper towels and coat with cornflour.

3. Heat the oil for deep-frying in the wok and fry the chicken (having shaken off any excess cornflour). Turn the pieces regularly with a Chinese scoop or spatula so that they brown well all over.

4. Cut the Chinese white radish into 1½–2-in (4–5-cm) lengths, peel and pare the sharp edges, rounding off the corners.

5. Place the chicken, radish pieces, rice wine, a few drops soy sauce and the salt in a saucepan, pour in enough water to just cover and place over the heat.

6. At this point add the star anise, a very little sugar and a few drops of sesame seed oil if a stronger, more robust, flavour is required.

7. Turn on the heat and when the water comes to the boil, carefully skim off any scum. Have a bowl of water standing near the pan in which the mesh ladle or skimmer can be rinsed between uses.

8. Cover the saucepan and lower the heat; shake the pan gently from time to time to prevent the contents sticking and burning; simmer for 1 hour, until the radish is tender.

Simmered chicken giblets

A tasty and frugal dish, the chicken giblets are cooked and then allowed to stand in their juice to absorb all the flavour.

10 oz (300 g) chicken gizzards
10 oz (300 g) chicken livers
1 large leek
small piece root ginger, sliced wafer-thin
1 tbsp rice wine or dry sherry
scant 1 tbsp sugar
3–4 fl oz (100–125 ml) soy sauce
1 star anise
Calories 344; protein 26.8 g; fat 23.5 g; sugar 3.8 g

1. Wash the chicken livers well and trim away the bile ducts and discoloured portions; trim the gristle and white parts from the gizzards.

2. Place the giblets in a bowl or colander and wash under running water until completely clean.

3. Bring a saucepan of water to the boil and add the giblets; turn down the heat and simmer gently; remove from the pan as soon as they have changed colour, and refresh in cold water.

4. Wash well again in several changes of cold water; if this procedure is not followed thoroughly enough, the giblets will still have a rather strong taste.

5. Place the giblets in a saucepan with the leek (cut in two or more pieces) and the sliced ginger; add enough water to cover.

6. Add the rice wine, sugar, soy sauce and the star anise and bring quickly to the boil.

7. Once the liquid has boiled, lower the heat and simmer very gently; skim off any scum, cover and cook slowly for about 30 minutes.

8. Turn off the heat and leave the giblets to cool in the liquid and absorb the full flavour. Once cold, drain and slice thinly.

Szechuan chicken with chestnuts

1 h 30'

In this Szechuan dish the sweet taste of the chestnuts marries well with the flavour of chicken.

3 chicken legs
1 leek
small piece root ginger
2 tbsp soy sauce
1 tsp rice wine or dry sherry
pinch of salt
pinch of pepper
cornflour
oil for frying
scant 1 pint ($\frac{1}{2}$ litre) stock
15 dried water chestnuts (soaked overnight)
Calories 256; protein 11.4g; fat 12.7g; sugar 22.9g

1. Chop the chicken legs into pieces with a cleaver.

2. Slice the leek and ginger very thinly.

3. Place the chicken, leek and ginger in a bowl, add the soy sauce, the rice wine, salt and pepper. Mix well and leave to marinate for about 30 minutes.

4. Wipe the chicken with paper towels and coat with cornflour. Heat enough oil for deep-frying until very hot and fry the chicken until crisp on the outside and golden-brown.

5. Pour the stock into a saucepan add the marinade in which the chicken was left to stand, followed by the fried chicken. Bring to the boil over a high heat and then lower the heat. Cook over a medium heat for about 20–30 minutes.

6. Remove the leek and ginger from the saucepan and discard; add the pre-soaked water chestnuts and cook for about 10 minutes or until they have absorbed the flavours and juices.

Empress chicken wings

This recipe was named after one of the wives of the Emperor Hsuan Tsung of the Tang dynasty.

12 chicken wings
½ leek
small piece root ginger
2 tbsp rice wine or dry sherry
2 tbsp soy sauce
cornflour
oil for frying
1 tsp sugar
½lb (250g) spinach
2 tbsp peanut oil
pinch of salt
Calories 346; protein 21.4g; fat 22.3g; sugar 13.4g
Serves 4–6

1. Wash the chicken wings well, cut off the tips and reserve for use in making the stock; slice the leek and the ginger finely.

2. Place the chicken wings, leek and ginger in a bowl and add a marinade made with 1 tbsp rice wine and 1 tbsp soy sauce; mix and leave to stand for 30 minutes.

3. Remove the chicken wings from the marinade and pat dry with paper towels or a clean cloth; coat evenly with cornflour and fry lightly in plenty of hot oil.

4. Pour the scant 1½ pints (¾ litre) water into a saucepan, add 1 tbsp soy sauce, 1½ tbsp rice wine, the sugar, the leek and ginger from the marinade and the wing tips.

5. Add the fried chicken wings and bring to the boil over a high heat; once it has come to the boil, lower the heat and leave to cook for about 40 minutes.

6. Wash and dry the spinach thoroughly and stir-fry lightly in the peanut oil; season with a pinch of salt and 1 tbsp rice wine. Add 8 fl oz (225 ml) boiling water; as soon as this comes back to the boil, remove the spinach and drain.

7. Arrange the chicken wings on a serving dish together with the spinach, chopping the latter in half if too long.

Paper-wrapped Cantonese chicken

An elegant Cantonese dish in which the chicken is cooked "en papillote" and keeps all its flavour – and is a good conversation piece for a dinner party. Beef, fish fillets or prawns can be cooked in the same way.

5oz (150g) chicken breasts
3 pre-soaked Chinese dried mushrooms
small piece root ginger
2oz (50g) parboiled fresh or canned bamboo shoots
small bunch chives
2 tbsp shelled peas
12 squares greaseproof or waxed paper 6 × 6in (16 × 16cm)
oil for frying
For the marinade:
1 tsp soy sauce
½ tsp salt
1 tbsp rice wine or dry sherry
pinch of pepper
a few drops of sesame seed oil
pinch of monosodium glutamate
1 tsp cornflour
Calories 174; protein 10.2g; fat 13.4g; sugar 3.3g

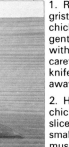

1. Remove the strip of white gristle on the inside of each chicken breast, pulling it gently away from the flesh with one hand while cutting carefully with a very sharp knife; pull the last few inches away with a sharp tug.

2. Having trimmed all the chicken breasts in this way, slice them diagonally into small pieces. Drain the mushrooms.

3. Squeeze the mushrooms gently to get rid of excess moisture, remove the stalks and slice into thin strips. Peel the ginger, cut into 2–3 thin slices and then into strips.

4. Shred the bamboo shoots and snip the chives into very short lengths. If fresh peas are used, boil until tender in salted water; if frozen, place in a bowl, cover with boiling water and leave to stand for a few minutes.

5. Place the chicken breasts in a deep dish or bowl together with the mushrooms, ginger bamboo shoots, chives and peas. Sprinkle with the marinade ingredients and mix well with chopsticks to make sure it is absorbed evenly.

6. Spread the greaseproof or waxed paper squares on a working surface, brush the centre of each square with a little oil and place a portion of the chicken and vegetable mixture on the oiled patch.

7. Take the lower corner and fold over the chicken to meet the opposite, top corner, forming a triangle. Fold back the apex of the triangle of the top layer of wrapping; bring first the right hand point and then the left of the base of the triangle into the centre, folding them neatly. By now the package should look rather like an open envelope; fold the remaining apex of the triangle down towards you, over the folded-in sides and tuck neatly underneath the fold.

8. Heat plenty of oil in the wok until it is fairly hot; fry the rectangular packages gently, turning carefully. When the flesh of the chicken has turned a whiteish colour, it is ready to be served. Each guest unwraps his or her own package with chopsticks.

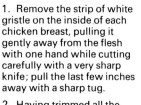

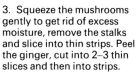

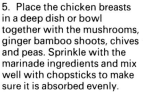

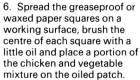

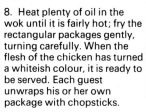

Fried chicken with curry seasoning

The unmistakable flavour of Chinese curry powder seasons the chicken and the turmeric in the curry gives it an appetising colour.

a 1¾lb (800g) chicken, chopped into small portions
1 tsp salt
1 tbsp rice wine or dry sherry
oil for frying
For the sauce:
1½ tsp Chinese curry powder
1 tsp sugar
½ tsp salt
1 tbsp soy sauce
1 tbsp rice wine or dry sherry
Calories 447; protein 26.3g; fat 36.2g; sugar 0.8g

1. Spread the chicken portions in a single layer in a deep-sided heatproof dish which can fit into the bamboo steamer; sprinkle with the salt and the rice wine and rub these into the flesh so that the flavour penetrates. Use two dishes and two steamers if necessary.

2. Place the dish in the steamer, which should already be hot and full of steam. Cover and steam for about 20 minutes over rapidly boiling water. Meanwhile mix together the ingredients for the sauce.

1

2

3

4

5

6

3. When the chicken is cooked through, remove from the steamer; drain off and reserve the juices produced during cooking.

4. Place the chicken in another dish and mix well with the curry sauce. Leave to stand so that the chicken pieces absorb the flavours.

5. Heat plenty of oil in the wok. Drain the chicken portions and pat with paper towels to remove any excess moisture and fry them one by one until well browned.

6. Mix the curry sauce remaining from marinating the chicken with the reserved steaming juices, heat in a small saucepan and serve with the chicken.

Chicken with green peppers and bamboo shoots

7oz (200g) chicken breasts
½ egg white
1 tsp cornflour
3–4 green peppers
5oz (150g) boiled fresh or canned bamboo shoots
oil for frying
2 tbsp peanut oil
For the sauce:
1 tbsp rice wine or dry sherry
½ tsp salt
½ tsp sugar
pinch of monosodium glutamate
Calories 194; protein 13.7g; fat 12.9g; sugar 3.2g

1. Cut the chicken breasts into fine strips, place in a bowl and mix well with the egg white and cornflour.

2. Cut the green peppers lengthways in half; remove the seeds, stalks and pith and shred, cutting along the grain of the flesh.

3. Cut the bamboo shoots into strips the same size as the peppers.

4. Heat plenty of oil until fairly hot and deep-fry the shredded chicken using chopsticks to keep the strips separate. Drain well.

5. Heat 2 tbsp peanut oil in the wok and stir-fry the chopped leek and ginger. Add the peppers and bamboo shoots and when these are tender stir in the chicken. Moisten with the rice wine and then mix in the salt, sugar and monosodium glutamate.

Simmered chicken livers

A highly economical recipe made more exotic by the flavour of star anise.

8 chicken livers (or 4 livers and 4 hearts)
½ leek
small piece root ginger, peeled
1 star anise
1 tbsp sugar
1 tbsp rice wine or dry sherry
3 tbsp soy sauce
Calories 239; protein 37.9g; fat 6.2g; sugar 4.3g
Serves 5–6

1. Wash the chicken livers under cold, running water. Snip away the bile duct and any discoloured parts. If chicken hearts are also used, cut them open, wash and trim.

2. Beat the leek and the ginger once or twice with the flat of the cleaver blade; flavour will then be released more readily when they are simmered with the chicken livers.

3. Place the livers (and the hearts if used) in a flameproof casserole, add the leek, ginger, star anise, sugar, rice wine, soy sauce and 8 fl oz (225 ml) water; stir and place over a high heat.

4. As soon as the water comes to the boil, lower the heat so that the contents of the casserole simmer very gently indeed. Cook until all the liquid is absorbed, stirring and turning every now and then. Do not allow to dry out, the livers should be very moist.

5. Slice the chicken livers in half and arrange on a serving dish.

Peking duck

Tradition has it that the technique for preparing Peking duck was invented by a cook to one of the emperors of the Ming dynasty (1368–1644). In those days ducks raised in the Yangtze River valley were used for this recipe. In the 16th century the Ming emperors made Peking their capital and the technique of preparing ducks spread to all the popular eating houses of the city, since many of their owners had once been cooks at the Imperial Palace. Many years later, in 1866, in the fourth year of the reign of the Emperor T'ung Chih of the Ch'ing dynasty, a certain Yang Quan-ren opened an eating house outside the Qianmen gate of Peking. The speciality of the "Quanjude" restaurant was duck, prepared according to the original, classic recipe of the Imperial Palace. Towards the end of the Ch'ing dynasty, breeding experiments with ducks led to a new strain, a white Peking duck raised for its extremely tender flesh and delicate skin. As the years went by this technique of cooking duck was perfected still further and the restaurant became very famous.

1 whole duck, plucked but undrawn and with the head and feet left on, weighing about 6½lb (3kg)
2 tbsp molasses or black treacle
12 spring onions or leeks (about 2in [5cm] of the white part)
24 pancakes, about 4in (10cm) in diameter (see recipe, p. 296)
For the sauce:
4 tbsp sugar
4 tbsp sweet yellow bean paste
2 tbsp sesame seed oil
(This sauce can be replaced by hoisin sauce which is readily available from oriental stores.)
Calories 490; protein 24.5g; fat 42g; sugar 13g
Serves 10–12

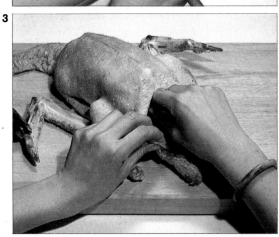

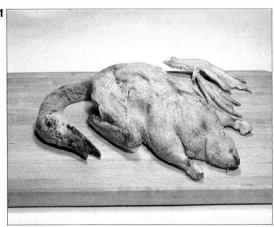

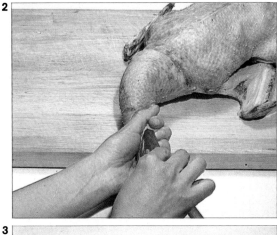

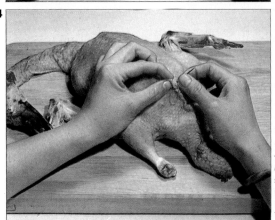

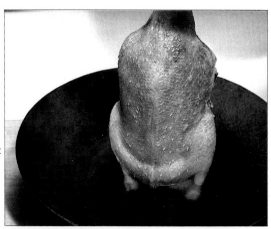

1. Wash the duck and cut off the feet.

2. With a small, sharp knife pierce the duck's neck in the front below the head, making a cut just large enough to insert a straw between the skin and the flesh; blow air between the skin and flesh until the whole duck is expanded.

3. Make a small slit in the vent end and draw the duck. Do not worry about air escaping, enough will remain between skin and flesh.

4. Wash the duck inside and out and sew up the slit tightly.

5. Trim off the wings and hang the duck up by the neck over a basin.

6. Pour about 1¾ pints (1 litre) boiling water over the duck, then leave to dry a little. Discard the water. Combine the molasses with 8 fl oz (¼ litre) boiling water and pour evenly all over the bird, catching the liquid in the basin. Baste well with the molasses mixture and repeat the process several times. Leave the bird hung up in a warm dry place for up to 4 hours or until the skin is completely dry.

7. Make sharp notches all round the ends of the spring onions along the grain of the stem. Place in a bowl of iced water for 1–2 hours so that the ends curl outwards.

8. Cut off the head of the duck, place breast downwards in a large roasting tin and roast in a preheated oven at 400°F (200°C) gas mark 6 for 20 minutes. Turn and continue cooking for a further 20 minutes. Place the roasting tin in another, larger, tin containing hot water and simmer for a few minutes over a low heat, then return to the oven for a final 20 minutes' roasting, turning again half way through this time.

9. Remove the duck from the oven and carve off thin horizontal slices of skin and meat; place on a serving dish. Prepare the sauce: mix the sugar with the sweet bean paste and 4½ fl oz (135 ml) water. Heat the wok and pour in the sesame seed oil, add the sauce and cook until thickened.

10. Each person helps himself to a pancake, takes some duck, and dips the ends of a spring onion in the sauce, placing it on the duck. The pancake is then rolled round the duck and eaten.

Hsiang su fei ya (classic spiced duck)

A dish for very special occasions when the duck would be accompanied by sweet and fairly strong Chinese wines and such condiments as chiao yen (roasted salt and pepper) or sweet bean paste.

1 duck weighing about 4½lb (2kg)
1 tbsp freshly ground black pepper
1 tbsp salt
1½ tsp five-spice powder
½ tsp monosodium glutamate
1 tsp rice wine or dry sherry
2 slices root ginger, finely chopped
1 small leek or shallot, finely chopped
2 tbsp dark soy sauce
oil for frying
Calories 470; protein 22g; fat 38.5g; sugar 8g
Serves 12

1. Clean the duck, and remove the oil sacs above the tail; wash and dry thoroughly.

2. Toast the fresh, coarsely ground pepper in the wok without any oil for 2 minutes over a moderate heat. Add the salt and draw aside from heat. Mix the five-spice powder, monosodium glutamate and rice wine together and add to the wok, followed by the ginger, leek and the dark soy sauce. Rub the duck all over, inside and out, with this mixture, working it well into the skin and then leave to marinate for 6 hours.

3. Place the duck on a heatproof dish in the bamboo steamer and steam for about 2½ hours, until it is very tender. Remove from steamer and pat dry with paper towels, tipping any liquid out of its cavity. Leave to cool.

4. Heat plenty of oil in the wok over a high heat and fry the duck until the skin is brown and very crisp. Baste constantly with the oil.

5. Remove the duck from the wok and leave to drain on paper towels.

6. Cut into fairly small, thickish pieces and arrange on a serving dish.

FISH AND SHELLFISH

Outside in the moonlit garden,
our servant sets about his task of cleaning a golden carp
with such dispatch that the scales fly far and wide,
high enough to reach the sky; perhaps the stars up there in
the heavens are the carp's golden scales.

—*From an old Chinese poem dedicated to the carp of the Yellow River*

The ideogram which stands for fish is pronounced in the same way as the word for prosperity and plenty, an indication of the importance of fish and shellfish in the Chinese diet.

Carp is the most highly prized of all the fish. Apart from being valued as a delicacy, it has a special significance for the Chinese. An old legend appears in Chinese literature which tells of a carp which swam against the current of the river in the hope of becoming a powerful dragon; the fish therefore became a synonym for the perseverance and driving ambition required of any young student who strove to qualify for a coveted position in the Mandarin hierarchy, a goal not easily attained and one which would require great courage and self-sacrifice. Fish are the most popular motif used for the decoration of buildings and especially for people's homes, since it is a traditional belief that the fishes' habit of swimming in pairs symbolises happiness in marriage.

Crispy fish in sweet and sour sauce

2 whole fish (whiting, sea bream or similar)
1 egg white
½ tsp salt
1 tbsp rice wine or dry sherry
pinch of pepper
cornflour
oil for frying
¼ carrot
1 small bamboo shoot
1 green pepper
¼ leek
2 dried Chinese mushrooms, pre-soaked
small piece root ginger
For the sweet and sour sauce:
5 tbsp sugar
4 tbsp vinegar
1 tsp soy sauce
½ tsp salt
3 tbsp tomato ketchup
½ tsp cornflour
Calories 376; protein 14.4g; fat 13.5g; sugar 50g

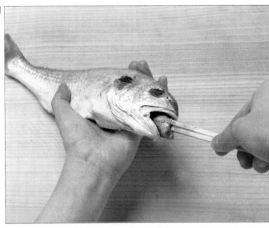

1. Clean the fish, trim the fins and make a very small incision by the ventral fin, just big enough to draw out the intestine. Draw out the remaining innards through the fish's mouth using chopsticks.

2. Cut out the gills (the red, spongy matter in the head) and wash the fish well. Slash the sides of the fish diagonally about 1 in (2.5cm) apart, cutting through to the bone and rotating the blade from right to left to lift the flesh partly away from the bone, but not completely severing it.

3. Mix the egg white with the salt, rice wine, pepper, 1 tbsp water and 3 tbsp cornflour. Coat the fish with this mixture, rubbing it well into the fish and into the diagonal slashes.

4. Dredge the fish all over, inside and out, with about 4oz (125g) cornflour. Hold them by their tails and shake or knock to remove excess.

5. Heat plenty of oil to 350°F (180°C) in a wok or deep-fryer. Grasp each fish firmly by its tail and hold over the hot oil; spoon the hot oil very carefully over the slashes two or three times to open them up. Then deep-fry the whole fish. Discard the frying oil and wipe out the wok.

6. Remove the fish when they are crisp and place them belly downwards, covered with a clean cloth, on a wire rack; press gently to soften (the flesh will "give" slightly and absorb more of the sauce).

7. Cut the carrot, bamboo shoot, green pepper, leek, mushrooms and ginger into matchstick strips. Heat 2 tbsp oil in the wok and stir-fry the vegetables, adding them to the oil in the order listed. When they are all lightly browned and tender, set aside.

8. Heat 3 tbsp oil with the sweet and sour sauce ingredients and $2\frac{1}{2}$ fl oz (75ml) water; then add another 1 tbsp oil, tricking it down the side of the wok, and as soon as the mixture comes to the boil, add the vegetables, stir and pour over the fish.

Fried fish in egg batter

The batter used for this recipe is delicate and melts in the mouth but care must be taken to have the oil at the correct temperature or it will burn.

20 small fresh white fish fillets (such as sole, plaice, striped bass or sea bass)
½ tsp salt
pinch of pepper
1 tsp rice wine or dry sherry
1 tbsp cornflour
oil for frying
For the batter:
2 egg whites
2 tbsp cornflour
2 tbsp plain flour
pinch of salt
pinch of monosodium glutamate
Calories 263; protein 26.7g; fat 12g; sugar 10.4g

1. Use only the freshest fish fillets. Lay the fillets flat on a plate and season with salt, pepper and rice wine, leave for a few minutes and then mix with the cornflour.

2. For the batter, whisk the egg whites until stiff but not dry, add the cornflour, the sifted plain flour, salt and monosodium glutamate; mix gently with a metal spoon, taking care not to stir too much or the egg whites will release too much air and the batter will not be light enough.

3. Heat plenty of oil to 275°F (140°C); dip the fish in the batter and fry a few at a time.

4. Turn the fish while deep-frying and gradually increase the temperature to 335°F (170°C), remove the fish and drain when only pale gold or the batter will lose its delicate texture and be too crisp.

Braised fish and bean curd

A very hot and spicy dish braised in an earthenware cooking pot.

4 steaks of firm-fleshed fish (bream, bass, cod or fresh tuna)
2 cakes bean curd
1 leek
small piece root ginger
3–5 tbsp peanut oil
1–2 chili peppers
For the sauce:
4 fl oz (125 ml) soy sauce
1 tbsp rice wine or dry sherry
1 tbsp sugar
$\frac{1}{4}$–$\frac{1}{2}$ tsp black bean paste
Calories 328; protein 27.1 g; fat 21.1 g; sugar 8.2 g

1. Rinse and dry the fish steaks; cut the bean curd into small squares (about 8 squares per cake); cut the leek into thin, diagonal slices and the ginger into wafer-thin shreds.

2. Heat the peanut oil in the wok; brown the fish steaks well on both sides over a high heat.

3. Line the bottom of a flameproof casserole with a layer of leek slices, place the fish steaks on top, surrounded by the bean curd squares and top with the ginger shreds and chili peppers.

4. Mix the sauce ingredients and pour over the fish. Cover and cook over a moderate heat for 20–25 minutes; from time to time tip up the casserole collect the juices and sauce in a ladle and moisten the top of the fish and bean curd.

Steamed fish

The classic Cantonese way of steaming a whole fish, combining simplicity with elegance. A good dish to serve when entertaining.

1 whole very fresh white fish (such as bass, carp, mullet or bream) weighing approx. 1¼lb (600g)
2–3 dried Chinese mushrooms, pre-soaked
2 slices root ginger
2 slices ham
1 leek
1 tbsp rice wine or dry sherry
a few drops sesame seed oil
2 tbsp soy sauce
Calories 190; protein 28.8g; fat 6.3g; sugar 1.6g

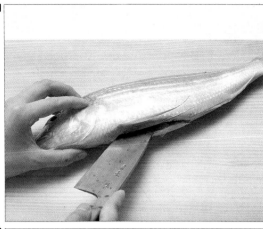

1. Always use the freshest fish for this recipe; slit the fish's belly and remove the guts. (Cut the fish open slightly to one side and serve, when the time comes, with the slit out of sight.)

2. Remove the scales from the fish with a sharp knife, wash well in cold running water inside and out and pat dry.

3. Remove the stalks from the Chinese mushrooms and slice the caps into thin strips about $\frac{1}{8}$ in (3 mm) wide.

4. Pound one slice of ginger with the blunt edge of the cleaver; cut the second slice into thin strips.

5. Shred the ham and cut the leek into two pieces, each 4 in (10 cm) long.

6. Place the pounded slice of ginger in the stomach of the fish; lay the fish on its side in a heatproof dish, resting on one piece of leek near its head and with the other under the tail. Sprinkle the shredded ginger, ham and mushrooms over the top of the fish.

7. Moisten the fish with the rice wine and a few drops of sesame seed oil to flavour; place the dish in the bamboo steamer which should be already full of steam.

8. Steam the fish over rapidly boiling water for 15–20 minutes without opening the steamer; when the fish is done, remove the slice of ginger from the inside of the fish. Place the fish on a heated serving dish and sprinkle with soy sauce while still hot.

Mackerel in sweet and sour sauce

The best accompaniment to complement the fish in its sweet and sour sauce (made with plenty of tomato ketchup) is boiled rice.

4 medium-sized mackerel
2 tbsp fresh ginger juice
1 tbsp rice wine or dry sherry
1 onion
2 sweet peppers
peanut oil for frying
1½–2 oz (40–50 g) cornflour
1 clove garlic
For the sauce:
4 tbsp tomato ketchup
1 tbsp sugar
1 tbsp soy sauce
2 tsp Worcestershire sauce
4 fl oz (125 ml) stock
cornflour
Calories 314; protein 15.8 g; fat 15.7 g; sugar 26.5 g

1. Choose the freshest fish available. Using a very sharp knife, cut away the line of spines, working from the tail towards the head. Cut off the head and gut; wash the fish in cold running water and drain.

2. Lay the fish on a working surface and fillet by inserting a very sharp knife between the backbone and the flesh and by cutting along the top of the backbone. Turn the fish over on its other side and repeat.

3. Cut the fillets into bite-sized pieces; sprinkle with ginger juice and rice wine and mix. Leave to stand for 5–6 minutes.

4. Peel the onion, cut lengthways in half and then into $\frac{3}{4}$-in (2-cm) slices. Cut the green peppers in half lengthways, remove the seeds and pith and cut into $\frac{3}{4}$-in (2-cm) slices.

5. Heat $1\frac{1}{4}$ pints (750 ml) peanut oil to 300°F (150°C); fry the onions (adding these first as they will take longer) and the green peppers until they are lightly browned; remove with a perforated ladle or spoon and drain.

6. Dry the pieces of fish fillet with paper towels, coat with cornflour and shake free of excess. Increase the temperature of the oil left over from step 5 to 335°F (170°C) and fry the fish until crisp.

7. Heat 1 tbsp oil in the wok and stir-fry the finely chopped garlic. As soon as this starts to release its aroma, add the onion and green pepper. Stir-fry over a high heat and add the tomato ketchup, sugar, soy sauce, Worcestershire sauce and stock.

8. When the sauce comes to the boil, add the fried fish pieces and cook for a minute or so. Thicken the sauce by stirring in 2 tsp cornflour mixed with 4 tsp water.

Cantonese pickled salmon mould

2 pickled salmon steaks (or cod or halibut plus 2 tsp chopped
    snow pickles)
14 oz (400 g) finely chopped or minced pork
peanut oil
2 eggs
½ egg white
½ tsp sugar
pinch of salt
lard or shortening
For the sauce:
2 tbsp stock
pinch of salt
pinch of monosodium glutamate
1 tsp cornflour
Calories 388; protein 28.5 g; fat 27.5 g; sugar 5.1 g

1. Hard-boil the eggs, stirring constantly so that the yolks remain in the centre, surrounded by egg white. Shell and slice into rings.

2. Heat 2 tbsp oil in the wok and fry the salmon steaks until they are golden-brown. Remove the skin and the bones. Flake carefully.

3. Chop or beat the minced pork with the blunt edge of the cleaver to soften the meat and get rid of any remaining lumps. Place in a bowl and add the salmon, egg white, sugar and salt. Mix very thoroughly.

4. Heat the bamboo steamer over boiling water until it is full of steam. Grease the inside of a heatproof bowl with the lard. Line the bowl with the sliced hard-boiled eggs and fill with the salmon and pork mixture.

5. Place the bowl in the bamboo steamer and cook over fast-boiling water for 20 minutes.

6. Drain off the juice produced during steaming and mix with the broth or stock in a small saucepan. Heat, adding the salt and monosodium glutamate, followed by the cornflour mixed with water to thicken the sauce.

7. Put a round serving plate on top of the bowl and turn the bowl upside down with a sharp jerk, releasing the mould onto the dish. Coat with the sauce.

Mackerel with five-spice seasoning

Five-spice powder is used to flavour fried mackerel. Equally good hot or cold.

1 large mackerel
2⅓ tbsp soy sauce
1½ tbsp rice wine or dry sherry
⅓ leek
root ginger
½ tsp five-spice powder
generous 2oz (50g) cornflour
1¾ pints (1 litre) oil for frying
For the sauce:
4 tbsp soy sauce
1 tbsp sugar
Calories 335; protein 16g; fat 23.2g; sugar 13g

1. Cut off the head of the mackerel and remove the guts; wash under cold running water and dry well. Lay the mackerel out flat on a working surface or chopping board and fillet as directed on page 139, running the knife blade along the backbone and cutting away the flesh on both sides.

2. Slice the fillets diagonally into bite-sized pieces; place in a deep-sided dish or bowl and sprinkle with the soy sauce and rice wine. Leave to marinate for 15 minutes.

3. Chop the leek and the ginger very finely and mix with the five-spice powder.

4. Mix the sauce ingredients together, combining the soy sauce, sugar and 4 fl oz (125ml) water and heat in a saucepan to boiling point. As soon as the sauce has boiled, pour into a bowl and stir in the ginger, leek and the five-spice powder.

5. Dry the marinated pieces of fish with paper towels, coat with cornflour and shake gently to remove excess.

6. Heat the oil to 340°–350°F (175°–180°C) and fry the pieces of mackerel until they are well browned and crisp, remove and drain.

7. Place the fried fish in the bowl containing the sauce and leave for 20 minutes to absorb the flavour before serving.

Fried fillets of fish mimosa

Egg yolks and whites are fried separately to make a decorative addition to the fish. A light and delicately flavoured dish which lends itself to a menu for entertaining.

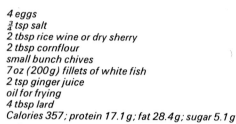

4 eggs
¾ tsp salt
2 tbsp rice wine or dry sherry
2 tbsp cornflour
small bunch chives
7 oz (200 g) fillets of white fish
2 tsp ginger juice
oil for frying
4 tbsp lard
Calories 357; protein 17.1 g; fat 28.4 g; sugar 5.1 g

1. Separate the egg yolks and whites; reserve 2 tbsp of the egg whites for later use. Add ¼ tsp salt to the remainder of the egg white and mix well. Stir ¼ tsp salt and 2 tbsp rice wine into the egg yolks.

2. Run the reserved egg white (2 tbsp) through the fingers to mix well. Add the cornflour and blend. Snip the chives into small pieces.

1

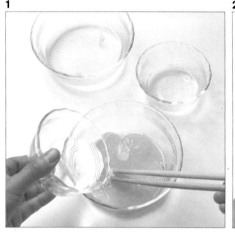

2

3

4

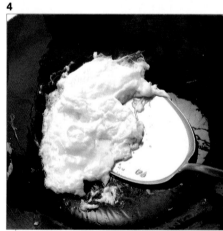

5

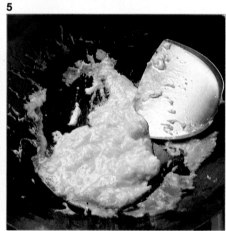

6

3. Cut the fish fillets into small, diagonal pieces, season with ¼ tsp salt and the ginger juice and coat with the egg white and cornflour mixture. Fry briskly in plenty of oil heated to 300°F (150°C).

4. Heat the wok, add 2 tbsp lard and when the fat is hot, pour in the mixture of egg white and salt prepared in step 1. Mix and turn quickly, scraping away from the wok, until the mixture has set but is still soft and light.

5. Transfer the cooked egg white to a warm dish; heat the remaining lard in the wok and pour in the egg yolk, salt and rice wine mixture and cook as for scrambled egg; when the yolks are half-cooked, return the egg whites to the wok.

6. Mix and turn the scrambled egg yolks and whites briskly; add the fried fish, scooping and turning quickly and incorporating the chopped chives.

Mackerel and mixed vegetables in black bean sauce

1 large mackerel
4 tsp ginger juice
1 tbsp soy sauce
2 tbsp finely chopped leek
2 potatoes
1 carrot
1 clove garlic
2 small leeks
3–4 Chinese mushrooms, pre-soaked
8 mange-tout
scant 1½ pints (¾ litre oil for frying)
approx. 2 oz (50 g) cornflour
2 tbsp lard
For the sauce:
3 tbsp black bean paste
3 tbsp soy sauce
2 tbsp sugar
½ tbsp sesame seed oil
Calories 465; protein 19.6 g; fat 31.5 g; sugar 25.3 g

1. Cut off the head of the mackerel and gut; wash well. Place the mackerel on a chopping board or working surface and carefully cut along the top of the backbone; turn the fish over and repeat the operation on the other side, producing two fillets.

2. Cut the fillets into sections 1 in (2.5cm) wide and mix well in a dish or bowl with the ginger juice, the soy sauce and the chopped leek. Marinate in this mixture for about 10 minutes.

3. Peel the potatoes and the carrot, cut diagonally into uneven shapes and boil until they are just tender. Chop the garlic finely.

4. Slice the leeks into ¾-in (2-cm) sections; drain the soaked Chinese mushrooms; remove the stalks and quarter the caps. Boil the mange-tout in lightly salted water until tender but still crisp; cut each pod into two or three pieces.

5. Heat plenty of oil to 350°F (180°C) and fry the potatoes until golden-brown; drain. Keep the oil at the same temperature.

6. Coat the pieces of mackerel with cornflour, shake off the excess and fry the fish in the oil until well-browned. Remove and drain on paper towels.

7. Heat the lard in the wok and stir-fry the garlic and leek; as soon as they have started to release their aroma, add the Chinese mushrooms and carrot and stir-fry. Pour in the sauce ingredients.

8. Pour in 1½ pints (¾ litre) water and bring to the boil; add the mackerel and the potatoes and cook for 3–4 minutes so they can absorb some of the sauce. Finally, stir in the mange-tout quickly and serve.

Steamed fish and lotus root

A very subtle flavour for a digestible dish of flaked fish and grated lotus root.

1 lb (500 g) lotus root
vinegar
7 oz (200 g) white fish such as cod
2 oz (50 g) pork back fat
2 tsp rice wine or dry sherry
¾ tsp salt
1 tsp cornflour
lard as required
1 large piece root ginger
a little parsley
Calories 249; protein 12.3 g; fat 14.4 g; sugar 20 g

1. Peel the lotus roots and immediately place in a bowl of water acidulated with a few drops of vinegar. Leave for 3 minutes and then dry with paper towels. Grate finely.

2. Skin and bone the fish and chop the flesh very finely with a large kitchen knife or cleaver. Place the chopped fish in a mortar and pound well.

3. Cut the pork fat into thin slices and then chop the slices finely; add to the pounded fish in the mortar and mix and pound together until well blended.

4. Add the rice wine, the salt and the cornflour and mix well. Incorporate the grated lotus root together with any juice produced during grating.

5. Grease a heatproof flat plate with plenty of lard. Transfer the mixture of fish and lotus root to the plate, smoothing the surface and rounding off the top and sides with a palette knife.

6. Place the bamboo steamer over boiling water in the wok and allow time for it to fill with steam. Keeping the heat high, place the plate in the steamer and cook for about 8 minutes over rapidly boiling water.

7. While the fish is steaming, peel the ginger; cut into slivers and then into thin strips. Soak in water.

8. Once the fish is cooked, remove from steamer, sprinkle with the ginger slices (drained and dried in paper towels) and decorate with chopped parsley.

Bream fried in noodles

Portions of fish are coated with transparent noodles which puff up and become crisp and light when deep-fried. Sole can be used instead of bream.

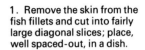

10oz (300g) fillets of bream or sole
a little salt
2 tbsp rice wine or dry sherry
2 tsp ginger juice
a small packet Chinese transparent noodles
5 tbsp cornflour
1 beaten egg
1¾ pints (1 litre) peanut oil for frying
For the sauce:
3oz (75g) Chinese white radish, grated
1½ tbsp soy sauce
1½ tbsp vinegar
small piece mandarin peel or dried mandarin peel, pre-soaked
Calories 261; protein 17.4g; fat 13.9g; sugar 14.1g

1. Remove the skin from the fish fillets and cut into fairly large diagonal slices; place, well spaced-out, in a dish.

2. Add the salt and the rice wine and ginger juice. Leave to stand for 5 minutes; this will get rid of any fishy smell and flavour the fish.

1

2

3

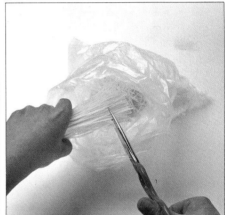

4

5

6

3. Take a polythene or plastic bag and, using scissors, cut the noodles into ¾-in (2-cm) lengths inside the bag. This will prevent the noodles scattering as you cut.

4. Coat the pieces of fish with cornflour, dip in the beaten egg and cover with noodles, pressing them onto the fish so that they adhere.

5. Heat plenty of oil in a wok or deep fryer to 340°F (175°C) and lower the coated fish pieces one by one into the hot oil; fry until crisp, but do not allow to become darker than pale gold.

6. Make the sauce by mixing the grated white radish with the soy sauce and vinegar and a little grated mandarin peel to add more flavour. Each person helps himself to some of this sauce as an accompaniment to the fish.

Saury with vegetables in sweet and sour sauce

40'

4 saury or garfish
1 tbsp soy sauce
1 tbsp rice wine or dry sherry
3 dried Chinese mushrooms, pre-soaked
3oz (75g) boiled fresh or canned bamboo shoots
⅓ leek
small piece root ginger
1 chili pepper
2oz (50g) lard
2 tbsp oil
For the sauce:
3 tbsp soy sauce
1 generous tbsp sugar
2 tbsp rice wine or dry sherry
Calories 434; protein 21.7g; fat 35g; sugar 5.9g

1. Cut off the head and tail of the fish and gut. Wash well in salted water and dry. Cut each fish in half, place in a dish and sprinkle with the soy sauce and the rice wine; leave to stand for about 15 minutes.

2. Drain the soaked mushrooms, remove the stalks and slice the caps into rectangular pieces; cut the bamboo shoots into rectangles, about 1½ in (4cm) long.

3. Remove the seeds from the chili pepper and chop coarsely with the leek and peeled ginger.

4. Mix the sauce ingredients with 6½ fl oz (185ml) water.

5. Heat the lard in the wok; dry the fish with paper towels and fry in the hot lard over a high heat until the pieces are golden-brown.

6. Remove the fish from the wok and set aside. Clean the wok and heat 2 tbsp oil; stir-fry the leek, ginger and chili pepper and as soon as they start to release their aroma add the Chinese mushrooms and the bamboo shoots, stir-frying over a high heat.

7. Return the fish to the wok; pour in the sauce while stirring and immediately it comes to the boil, lower the heat and simmer for about 15 minutes.

Cod in spicy sauce

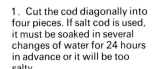

A delicious, peppery dish which should be served with plain boiled rice.

4 steaks fresh cod or well soaked salt cod
1 egg white
2 tbsp cornflour
scant 1 pint (½ litre) oil for frying
1 small clove garlic
½ leek
7–8 chives or spring onion stems (green part)
1 cake bean curd
2 tbsp peanut oil
4oz (125g) finely chopped or minced pork
2 tbsp soy sauce
¾ pint (450ml) hot stock (see recipe, p. 296)
2 tbsp rice wine or dry sherry
1 tbsp cornflour
½ tsp chili powder
2 tsp sesame seed oil
Calories 313; protein 23.6g; fat 21.6g; sugar 5.1g

1. Cut the cod diagonally into four pieces. If salt cod is used, it must be soaked in several changes of water for 24 hours in advance or it will be too salty.

2. Lightly beat the egg white and press between the fingers so that it is evenly blended. Dip the fish in the egg white and then coat with cornflour. Heat the oil to about 300°F (150°C) and fry the fish lightly.

3. Chop the garlic and leek finely. Chop the chives into 1-in (approx. 2.5-cm) lengths. Remove excess moisture from the bean curd by cutting and wrapping the squares gently in a clean, dry cloth.

4. Heat the wok and add the peanut oil; stir-fry the minced pork until it is well cooked and forms even, separate 'grains'. Add 1 tbsp soy sauce, stir and then pour in the hot stock.

5. Add the fried cod, followed by the rice wine and the remaining soy sauce, and cook for about 5–6 minutes.

6. Add the curd and cook for a further 3–4 minutes, then stir in the cornflour mixed with 2 tbsp water. Stir very carefully to thicken the sauce (the bean curd will break up if mixed too vigorously). Add the chili powder, chives and a few drops of sesame seed oil to give the dish its finishing touch.

Fried fish with peanuts

4 pieces filleted white fish
1 tbsp rice wine or dry sherry
2 tsp ginger juice
small piece root ginger
1 clove garlic
1 chili pepper
½ leek
3½ oz (100 g) shelled unsalted peanuts
½ leek for decoration
1 head broccoli
salt
4 tbsp cornflour
2 tbsp oil
For the sauce:
4 tbsp sweet red bean paste
3 tbsp rice wine or dry sherry
2 tbsp sugar
1 tsp sesame seed oil
8 fl oz (225 ml) stock (see recipe, p. 296)
Calories 450; protein 23.5 g; fat 29 g; sugar 21.6 g

1. Cut each piece of fish diagonally into three portions; place in a dish and sprinkle with the rice wine and the ginger juice; leave to marinate for 5 minutes.

2. Peel the ginger and the garlic; remove the seeds of the chili pepper, wash the half leek and chop all these ingredients finely.

3. Peel off the thin brown papery skins from the peanuts spread the nuts on a piece of paper covering the chopping board and chop coarsely.

4. Mix the sauce ingredients together until the bean paste and the sugar are well blended and dissolved; add the chopped peanuts and stir.

5. Cut the remaining half leek into thin, feathery strips ready to garnish, and place in a bowl of cold water. Boil the broccoli in salted water until tender and divide into florets.

6. Coat the pieces of fish with cornflour. Heat the oil in the wok and fry the fish quickly over a high heat. Add the finely chopped ginger, garlic, chili pepper and leek mixture. Stir and turn so that they release their flavour; pour in the sauce and cook over a moderate heat for about 10 minutes.

7. Transfer the fish to a heated serving platter once it has absorbed most of the sauce, sprinkle with the shredded leek and garnish with the broccoli florets.

Stir-fried prawns with broad beans

12 large prawns
2 tbsp rice wine or dry sherry
salt
1 tsp ginger juice
5 oz (150 g) fresh shelled broad beans
2 chili peppers
1 clove garlic
small piece root ginger
2 tbsp lard
For the sauce:
2 tbsp sugar
2 tbsp rice wine or dry sherry
2½ tbsp soy sauce
¼ tsp salt
2 tbsp tomato ketchup
Calories 390; protein 42 g; fat 16.4 g; sugar 12.9 g

1. Remove the shells of the prawns and, if they are very large, the black vein which runs down their backs (a cocktail stick is useful for this). Mix with the rice wine, ½ tsp salt and ginger juice and leave to marinate.

2. Wash the shelled broad beans and mix with a little salt, rubbing it into their skins. Boil until just tender and remove the pale, loose skins.

3. Remove the seeds from the chili pepper and chop finely with the garlic and ginger.

4. Mix the sauce ingredients thoroughly together in a bowl with 4 fl oz (125 ml) of water, making sure that the sugar dissolves completely.

5. Heat the wok and add the lard; when the fat is hot add the drained prawns. If the prawns are raw, stir-fry for a few minutes until they change colour, then add the ginger, garlic and chili pepper. If cooked prawns are used, add to the fat only just before the garlic and other seasonings. Stir-fry briefly over a high heat then set aside on a plate.

6. Fry the beans in the fat remaining in the wok over a high heat; when the beans are thoroughly coated and impregnated with the fat, return the prawns to the pan, pour in the sauce and mix quickly before serving.

Szechuan fried prawns and peas

1 lb (450 g) prawns
1 egg white
1 tsp cornflour
peanut oil
½ lb (250 g) shelled peas
1 thin slice root ginger
1 tbsp rice wine or dry sherry
1 tsp salt
½ tsp sugar
pepper
monosodium glutamate
Calories 276; protein 17.8 g; fat 16.1 g; sugar 13.5 g

1. Peel the prawns and if they are very large remove the black vein that runs down their backs using a cocktail stick. Wash and drain. If cooked prawns are used (preferably bought with their shells on as these have more flavour) there is no need to wash.

2. Dry the prawns and mix with the white of egg and cornflour in a bowl, using your hands.

3. Heat enough oil for deep-frying to 325°F (160°C) and fry the prawns making sure they do not stick to one another; remove with a mesh ladle or perforated spoon so that they drain properly. Drain off the oil and wipe the wok.

4. If frozen peas are used, place in a bowl and cover with boiling water; when they have completely unfrozen, drain. If fresh peas are used, boil until just tender, drain.

5. Heat the wok; pour in 2 tbsp oil and when very hot add the lightly-pounded ginger slice to flavour.

6. Once the ginger has started to release its aroma, add the peas and just allow to heat through; add the prawns and stir-fry.

7. Pour in the rice wine and add the salt and sugar; season with a pinch of pepper and monosodium glutamate.

8. Remove the slice of ginger and stir all the ingredients to ensure even flavouring. Do not overcook or the prawns will begin to lose their flavour.

155

Cantonese fried scampi

 40'

A very digestible way of frying shellfish in a light, melting batter.

8 scampi or Dublin Bay prawns (with or without the heads on)
pinch of salt
1 tsp rice wine or dry sherry
pinch of pepper
4-in (10-cm) length of leek
small piece root ginger
1 tbsp cornflour
oil for frying
For the batter:
1 large egg, beaten
1 tbsp cornflour
4oz (125g) plain flour
1 tsp baking powder
1 tbsp oil or melted lard
Calories 381; protein 29.4g; fat 16.7g; sugar 26.1g

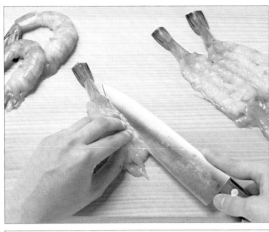

1. Shell the scampi, remove the heads but leave on the tails; slit down the back without cutting right through the shellfish and splay, opening them out flat. Make two lengthways incisions on each side of the scampi and some shallow slashes across them.

2. Place the scampi in a shallow dish and add a marinade of salt, rice wine and pepper. Chop the leek and pound the ginger and add to the marinade. Rub this mixture gently into the scampi so that the flavour penetrates the flesh.

3. Prepare the batter: using a whisk, beat together the egg, 4 fl oz (125 ml) water and the cornflour in a bowl; sift the flour and place ready for use.

4. Add nine-tenths of the flour to the egg, water and cornflour mixture and mix quickly; do not pay too much attention to the smoothness of the batter at this stage, but adjust the consistency by adding some or all of the remaining flour if needed.

5. Beat the batter until smooth; it should not be too thick, the right consistency is indicated if a ribbon of mixture falls from the whisk when this is lifted.

6. Add the baking powder and allow to stand for 1–2 minutes, until the mixture bubbles and expands slightly.

7. For a really melting crisp batter which will dissolve in the mouth, add the oil and whisk in lightly and quickly.

8. Working quickly, remove the leek and ginger from the scampi. Coat each scampi with cornflour and dip in the batter, frying a few at a time until the batter is crisp, light and golden.

Prawns in savoury tomato sauce

The varied flavours combine to make this a tempting dish.

7 oz (200 g) large prawns
1 tbsp rice wine or dry sherry
salt
pinch of pepper
⅓ egg white
cornflour
oil for frying
1 large, ripe tomato
1–2 cloves garlic
2–3 tbsp peanut oil
4 fl oz (125 ml) stock
1 tsp soy sauce
a few drops of sesame seed oil
Calories 243; protein 7.3 g; fat 20.5 g; sugar 8.8 g

1. Whether raw prawns or cooked are used, shell, remove the black vein running down the backs (with a cocktail stick) and place in a dish with ½ tbsp rice wine and a pinch of salt and pepper.

2. Add the egg white to the prawns and mix with the fingers, then add 2 tbsp cornflour and mix well.

3. Pour about ½–¾ pint (¼–½ litre) oil into the wok and heat to 260°F–300°F (130°C–150°C); stir-fry the prawns until they turn pink if they are raw and for only 1–2 minutes if they are cooked. Drain on paper towels.

4. Blanch the tomato for a few seconds in boiling water, rinse in the cold water and peel. Quarter, remove the seeds and slice thinly. Chop the garlic very finely.

5. Heat the peanut oil in the wok and stir-fry the garlic. When it starts to release its aroma, add the tomato and fry quickly; pour in the stock.

6. Season with 1 tsp each salt, soy sauce and rice wine. Add the cooked prawns and then thicken the sauce by adding a little cornflour mixed with water. Add a few drops sesame seed oil (approx. ½ tsp) for extra flavour.

Chili fried scampi

Deep-fried scampi served with a savoury piquant sauce made with tomato ketchup and Tabasco.

15 scampi or Dublin Bay prawns, preferably raw
oil for frying
1 tsp finely chopped garlic
1 tbsp chopped leek
1 tsp finely chopped root ginger
1 tbsp rice wine or dry sherry
1 tsp cornflour
For the sauce:
4 fl oz (125 ml) chicken stock
4 fl oz (125 ml) tomato ketchup
1 tsp salt
½ tbsp sugar
1 tsp Tabasco sauce
Calories 258; protein 18.6 g; fat 8.8 g; sugar 24.3 g

1

2

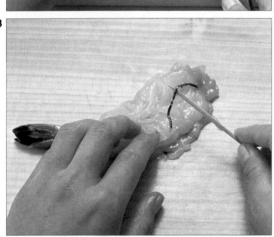

3

4

1. Rinse and drain the scampi; remove the heads by bending them over and inwards, toward the legs and tail. Remove the shells, leaving the tails on.

2. Slit the scampi down their backs with a sharp knife, stopping short of the second to last joint nearest the tail and being careful not to cut through or the scampi will separate into two halves.

3. Remove the dark vein from down the backs of the scampi using a cocktail stick (this black vein is actually the alimentary tract).

4. Rinse the scampi, dry with paper towels or a clean cloth. Trim the tail flippers with scissors.

5. Spread the scampi out and force out the excess moisture pressing and squeezing with the knife by the tail joint.

6. Heat plenty of oil in the wok or deep fryer to 340°F (170°C) and lower the scampi carefully into the hot oil; stir with chopsticks or tongs; remove and drain.

7. Heat 2 tbsp fresh oil in the wok and stir-fry the garlic, leek and ginger; when these start to release their aroma, add the scampi.

8. Pour in the rice wine, and all the ingredients for the sauce, stir-fry to make sure the scampi are well flavoured and then stir in the cornflour dissolved in 1 tsp water to thicken the sauce so that it will coat the scampi.

5

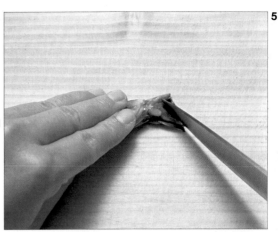

6

7

8

Prawns in fluffy batter

14oz (400g) prawns in their shells
1 tsp rice wine or dry sherry
1 tsp ginger juice
3 tbsp cornflour
oil for frying
For the batter:
2 egg whites
2 tbsp cornflour
pinch of salt
Seasoning:
chili sauce
salt and pepper
Calories 179; protein 10.6g; fat 10.5g; sugar 9.6g

1. Wash the prawns if they are raw; remove their shells and heads and the thin black vein running down their backs, using a cocktail stick. Leave their tails in place.

2. Place the prawns in a dish and sprinkle with the rice wine and ginger juice, leaving them to stand for 5–6 minutes; this will remove any strong smell without impairing the taste.

1

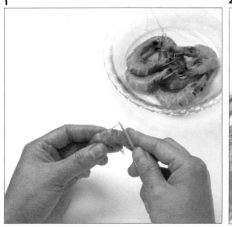

2

3

4

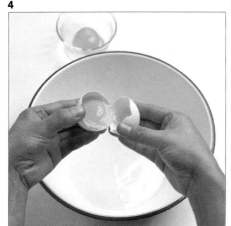

5

6

3. Drain the prawns and, holding them by the tail, dip them one by one in the cornflour to coat thoroughly. Shake off excess.

4. For the batter, separate the egg yolks from the whites.

Mix the whites gently to obtain an even consistency.

5. Whisk the egg whites until stiff but not too dry. Fold in the cornflour and a pinch of salt gently but thoroughly.

6. Cover each prawn with the batter; use a teaspoon to heap the light mixture onto the prawns as it does not always cling when dipped. Heat enough oil for deep-frying to 345°F (175°C) and lower the prawns in one by one, holding them by the tail. Fry until pale golden. Hand round chili sauce and freshly ground pepper and salt.

Szechuan prawns with chili peppers

20'

12 very large prawns
1 tbsp rice wine or dry sherry
1 tbsp soy sauce
½ leek
small piece root ginger
1 clove garlic
2 chili peppers
4 tbsp oil
½ tsp cornflour
For the sauce:
1½ tbsp soy sauce
1½ tbsp sugar
2 tbsp rice wine or dry sherry
2 tbsp tomato ketchup
Calories 270; protein 26.2 g; fat 13.4 g; sugar 9.1 g

1. Rinse the prawns and remove the black vein running down their backs by inserting a cocktail stick between the second and third joint from the head and drawing it out between the joints of the shell. Use a pair of scissors to cut off the feelers and legs. Sprinkle them with rice wine and soy sauce and leave to stand.

2. Coarsely chop the leek, ginger and garlic. Remove the seeds from the chili peppers, and chop the peppers.

3. Mix all the sauce ingredients and 2½ fl oz (80 ml) water together in a bowl.

4. Heat the wok and pour in the oil; when it is hot, fry the prawns over a high heat, and as soon as they change colour (if pre-cooked prawns are used, fry for 1–2 minutes at most) add the leek, garlic, ginger and chili peppers and continue frying, stirring and turning so that the flavours blend evenly.

5. Pour in the sauce and continue cooking over a high heat. Mix for 1–2 minutes, by which time the liquid should have been partly absorbed by the prawns; thicken by stirring in the cornflour mixed with 1 tsp water.

Fried crab claws

12 crab claws
7oz (200g) prawns
¾oz (20g) pork fat
1 egg
½ tsp salt
2 tsp ginger juice
1 tbsp rice wine or dry sherry
plain flour
2oz (50g) fine fresh breadcrumbs
approx. 1½ pints (scant 1 litre) oil for frying
1 lemon
parsley to garnish
Seasoning:
pepper
tomato ketchup
Calories 287; protein 213g; fat 17.1g; sugar 10.5g

1. Remove the flesh from either side of the thin cartilage on each claw and flake very finely.

2. Rinse the prawns if raw; de-vein with a cocktail stick, peel and chop the flesh very finely with a sharp, heavy knife.

3. Chop the pork fat very finely indeed and mix with the chopped prawns; chop both together to make a smooth, well blended mixture and transfer to a bowl.

4. Separate the egg whites from the yolks and add the whites to the prawn and pork fat mixture; add the salt, ginger juice and the rice wine and stir well. Blend in the crab flesh. Divide the mixture into 12 equal portions and shape into small balls.

5. Press each little ball on to the base of a crab claw and coat with flour.

6. Mix 1 tbsp water with the egg yolk; hold the claws and dip the crab and prawn mixture into the egg yolk; then coat with the breadcrumbs.

7. Heat the oil to 345°F (175°C) and lower the crab claws into the oil; fry until well browned. Remove carefully with a slotted spoon or mesh ladle and drain.

8. Arrange on a serving platter with the sharp claws pointing inwards towards the centre; arrange the parsley in the middle to form a bed for the claws and garnish with lemon wedges. Hand round freshly ground pepper or tomato ketchup for each person to season as desired.

Scallops with Chinese cabbage in creamy sauce

6 scallops
1 tsp ginger juice
2 tsp rice wine or dry sherry
6 large Chinese cabbage leaves
8 mange-tout
$\frac{1}{3}$ carrot
$\frac{1}{4}$ leek
7 oz (200 g) honey fungus or button mushrooms
4 tbsp cornflour
oil for frying
12 fl oz (350 ml) stock (see recipe, p. 296)
$\frac{3}{4}$ tsp salt
$\frac{1}{2}$ tsp sugar
1 tbsp rice wine or dry sherry
4 fl oz (125 ml) unsweetened evaporated milk
2 tsp cornflour
1 tbsp melted chicken fat
Calories 267; protein 14.5 g; fat 16.5 g; sugar 14.4 g

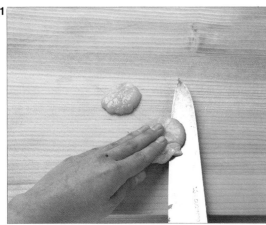

1. Rinse and dry the scallops and snip off the thin band of rather tough skin surrounding them. Slice diagonally into small pieces and leave to stand in a dish with the ginger juice and the rice wine for about 5 minutes.

2. Cut the stalks of the Chinese cabbage into triangular shaped pieces, measuring about 1½ in (4 cm) from base to apex and about ¾ in (2 cm) wide at their base. Cut the green leafy part into small pieces.

3. Peel the carrot and cut in half lengthwise. Cut down one side of each half carrot, making a series of shallow vertical incisions; in between each of these cuts, make another incision, this time holding the knife obliquely so as to cut towards the adjoining incision; when the two cuts meet in each case a small triangular section will be detached, leaving the carrot portions with a 'stepped' appearance. Cut horizontally, producing several ladder-shaped thin slices of carrot. Boil until tender. Chop the leek, wash and slice the mushrooms.

4. Coat the scallops one at a time with cornflour and shake off the excess. Heat enough oil for deep-frying to 300°F (150°C) and fry the scallops briefly.

5. Heat 2 tbsp oil in the wok and stir-fry the leek; when it starts to release its aroma, add the harder, white parts of the Chinese cabbage, then the mange-tout, mushrooms, the green leafy parts of the cabbage and the carrots.

6. Pour in the stock and cook for 5–7 minutes; as soon as the vegetables are tender, add the scallops; season with salt, sugar and the rice wine.

7. To make the sauce rich and creamy, add the evaporated milk, cook for a minute or two and then stir in the cornflour mixed with 4 tsp water to thicken.

8. If wished, the flavour can be enhanced by trickling melted rendered chicken fat down the sides of the wok and cooking briefly before serving.

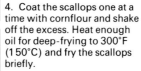

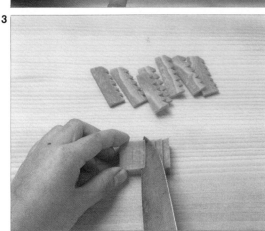

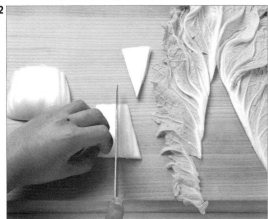

Fried sea cucumber with okra

Most Western palates will find that a taste for sea cucumber is an acquired one, but this is an important dish in Chinese cookery. Long soaking is part of the protracted process which produces a gelatinous consistency.

2 oz (50g) dried sea cucumber
2 oz (50g) Chinese transparent noodles
4 okra
small piece root ginger
¼ pint (150ml) stock
2 tbsp rice wine or dry sherry
3 tbsp sweet rice wine
2 tbsp soy sauce
salt
straw ties or raffia
Calories 113; protein 0.7g; fat 3.8g; sugar 15.5g

1. Select black, evenly coloured dried sea cucumbers (some are large in which case only one would be needed). Wash thoroughly in plenty of water removing any mud or dirt from between the spines.

2. Leave the sea cucumber in a bowl of cold water with the twist of straw ties or raffia for 3 days to soften and plump up.

3. Squeeze the sea cucumber to see whether it is soft enough to cut; when it is, cut between the spines, lengthwise, where the skin is relatively smooth.

4. Open up the slit and remove the innards. Wash the inside carefully.

5. Continue the softening process by placing the sea cucumber in a saucepan of cold water and bring to the boil. While the sea cucumber is cooking (this can be for as long as $1\frac{1}{2}$ hours, simmering) pour boiling water into a bowl containing the noodles; leave to soften for a few minutes, then drain and cut into $1\frac{1}{4}$-in (3-cm) lengths.

6. Rub the okra with the salt; cover with boiling water, leave to stand for a few minutes, then drain and cut into small pieces. When the sea cucumber is tender, drain and slice thinly.

7. Peel the ginger and cut into thin strips; stir-fry in a little oil over a medium heat until it releases its aroma.

8. Add the sea cucumber to the ginger in the pan and fry; pour in the stock, rice wine, soy sauce and the sweet rice wine. Add the noodles, cook for a few minutes and finally stir in the okra.

Abalone in soy sauce

Richly contrasting ingredients are blended perfectly in this dish.

15 oz (400–450 g) of canned abalone
5–6 dried Chinese mushrooms, pre-soaked
2 tbsp peanut oil
$\frac{1}{4}$ tsp salt
$\frac{1}{2}$ tsp soy sauce
generous tbsp vinegar
1 $\frac{1}{2}$ tsp sugar
cornflour
a few drops of sesame seed oil
Calories 133; protein 9.5 g; fat 7.7 g; sugar 8.9 g

1. Drain the canned abalone, reserving the liquid. Hold the abalone firmly with the left hand and slice them diagonally, one by one, cutting from right to left.

2. Drain the Chinese mushrooms and remove the stalks. Cut any large mushrooms in half.

3. Make up 8 fl oz (225 ml) liquid by combining water with the liquid from the abalone.

4. Heat the peanut oil in the wok; fry the Chinese mushrooms, and once they are heated through, pour in the liquid.

5. Add the salt, soy sauce, vinegar and the sugar. As soon as the liquid boils, stir in 1 tsp cornflour mixed with 2 tsp water to thicken.

6. Add the abalone and cook very briefly and gently, just enough to heat through. Sprinkle with a few drops sesame seed oil to add flavour.

Squid "flowers" with leek

The flavour of garlic and leek brings out the delicate taste of the squid and the subtle colour scheme of ivory and green makes a very attractive dish.

1 squid
1 small leek
3 tbsp oil
1 tsp finely chopped garlic
1 tbsp rice wine or dry sherry
1 tsp Tabasco sauce
¾ tsp salt
½ tsp sugar
4 fl oz (125 ml) stock
1 tsp cornflour
Calories 120; protein 8.8 g; fat 8 g; sugar 3.6 g

1. Cut off the squid's tentacles, wash the body well and cut into ½–¾-in (1–2-cm) pieces. Rub the thin outer skin from the body of the squid under running water; pull away and discard the centre bone, ink sac, head and inner organs. Rinse thoroughly, dry and cut down one side to open out.

2. Place the squid, inner side up, on a working surface or board; using a sharp knife, lightly score the squid at ¼-in (5-mm) intervals; score to form a lattice pattern, making sure the skin is not cut through. Then cut the squid into rectangles about ¾ in (½ cm) long.

3. Slice the leek into ¾-in (2-cm) pieces.

4. Heat 1 tbsp oil in the wok; add the squid, stir-fry lightly and then set aside on a plate.

5. Heat 2 tbsp oil in the wok; stir-fry the chopped garlic and leek, add the squid and sprinkle with rice wine; stir-fry briefly.

6. Add the seasoning of Tabasco, salt, sugar and the stock; cook over a high heat until the squid has curled well. Thicken the sauce with 1 tsp cornflour dissolved in 2 tsp water.

Fried squid with jellyfish

Squid:
2 dried squid
1 tsp bicarbonate of soda
3–4 dried Chinese mushrooms
4oz (125g) carrot
1 stick celery
4oz (125g) mange-tout
oil for frying
salt

For the sauce:
2 tsp sugar
1 tbsp soy sauce
½ tsp salt
1 tbsp rice wine or dry sherry

Calories 198; protein 28.6g; fat 5g; sugar 8.9g
Jellyfish:
4oz (125g) dried jellyfish
1¼lb (600g) baby turnips
1 tsp salt
4oz (125g) sugar
4floz (125ml) vinegar
a few drops sesame seed oil
Calories 148; protein 3g; fat 5.2g; sugar 22.6g

Squid (main dish)

1. Soak the dried squid overnight in water; then boil in water with 1 tsp bicarbonate of soda until tender. Drain and score in a lattice pattern (see page 171) and cut into pieces. Cut the tentacles into 1½-in (4-cm) lengths.

2. Soak the Chinese mushrooms in water for 20 minutes; remove the stalks and cut the mushrooms in half. Cut the carrot into ¼-in (5-mm) thick slices; cut the celery obliquely into thin slices.

3. Remove strings from the mange-tout and stir-fry very lightly in 2 tbsp oil; add 1 tsp salt and 8floz (225ml) water, cover and cook until tender but still crisp.

4. Stir-fry the carrot and celery in 2 tbsp oil; add the mushrooms and the squid and, lastly, the mange-tout. Pour in the sauce mixture of sugar, soy sauce, salt and rice wine. Stir-fry for a minute or two more before serving, to blend the seasoning.

Jellyfish (side dish)

1. Peel the turnips and cut into 2–2½-in (5–6-cm) strips; sprinkle with the salt and leave for 30 minutes.

2. Soak the dried jellyfish in hot water, about 125°F (55°C) for about 30 seconds; (dried jellyfish comes in 1-lb (500-g) slabs; what is not used for this recipe will keep well). The jellyfish should curl up when soaked; drain and refresh immediately in cold water.

3. Mix the sugar, vinegar and the sesame seed oil in a bowl and stir in the jellyfish.

4. Add the rinsed and drained turnips; mix well and serve cold.

Cantonese fried squid

2 large squid
1 tsp rice wine or dry sherry
1 tsp ginger juice
1 tbsp cornflour
1 medium-sized onion
4 large canned Chinese mushrooms or dried Chinese
   mushrooms, pre-soaked
3oz (75g) boiled fresh or canned bamboo shoots
4-in (10-cm) length of carrot
2oz (50g) mange-tout
1½oz (40g) lard or shortening
1 tsp cornflour
For the sauce:
1 tbsp rice wine or dry sherry
1 tsp sugar
1 tsp salt
Calories 249; protein 25.2g; fat 11.7g; sugar 9.1g

1. Cut away the tentacles of the squid, carefully draw out the ink sac, inner organs and central bone; peel off the thin outer skin. Rinse thoroughly and dry. Slit the bodies of the squid and open them out flat.

Holding the knife at an angle of 45° to the work surface, score a lattice pattern, cutting fairly deeply into the flesh at an oblique angle. Cut the squid into pieces 1 in (3cm) square.

2. Flavour the squid by sprinkling with the rice wine and the ginger juice; coat lightly with cornflour and drop into briskly boiling water to blanch. Remove after a few seconds; drain thoroughly.

3. Cut the onion lengthways into 8 segments and separate the various layers. Remove the mushroom stalks and cut the caps in four; cut the bamboo shoots into small rectangular pieces.

4. Use a canelle knife or a table fork to score grooves along the length of the carrot so that when it is sliced the sections look like flowers or scalloped circles. These slices should be about ¼ in (5mm) thick. Boil for a very few minutes and drain. Trim the mange-tout and remove the strings, cut in half diagonally and boil in salted water until they turn a vivid green.

5. Mix together the sauce ingredients, the rice wine, sugar, salt and 4 fl oz (125ml) water.

6. Heat the wok; add the lard and when it is hot (never overheat lard or it will acquire an unpleasant taste) add the vegetables in the following order: onions, Chinese mushrooms, bamboo shoots and carrot rounds. Pour in the sauce.

7. Add the pieces of squid and stir-fry over a high heat; add the cornflour dissolved in 2 tsp water and finally add the mange-tout.

Squid balls

Crisply fried squid balls which melt in the mouth.

3 large squid
$\frac{1}{3}$ leek
small piece root ginger
2 tbsp cornflour
1$\frac{3}{4}$ pints (1 litre) oil for frying
1 tbsp peanut oil
1 tbsp sugar
1 tbsp soy sauce
For the batter:
1 egg white
2 tbsp cornflour
Calories 277; protein 24.4g; fat 14.8g; sugar 10.5g

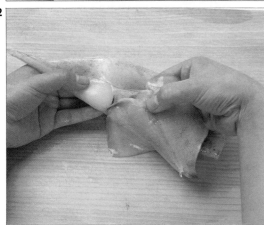

1. Place the squid in a large bowl of water. Remove the central bone and the tentacles together with the innards of the squid, keeping them intact.

2. Pull the thin outer skin off the squid; trim off or pull away the cartilaginous tips on either side and slit the body of the squid open.

3. Cut the thick band of flesh to which the tentacles are attached and open them out; trim off the hard, inedible parts and discard. Blanch the tentacles in boiling water. Scrape off the suckers by running the back of a knife down the tentacles. Rub off the skin with a cloth or rub and peel off with the fingers.

4. Cut the leek into strips and then cut across into very small pieces. Peel the ginger and chop very finely.

5. Chop the squid bodies and tentacles very finely, transfer to a mortar and pound well with the pestle. To thicken the mixture add the cornflour and mix well.

6. For the batter blend together the egg white, cornflour and 1 tsp water. Shape the squid mixture into small balls about $\frac{3}{4}$ in (2 cm) in diameter. Heat the oil to 340°F (175°C). Coat the squid balls with the batter and deep-fry for about 3 minutes. Drain and keep hot.

7. Empty the oil from the wok and wipe clean; heat the peanut oil and stir-fry the ginger and leek until they start to release their aroma. Mix the sugar and soy sauce and pour into the wok.

8. Add the squid balls and cook just long enough for the sauce to be partially absorbed.

Stir-fried squid and seaweed

2 squid
1 oz (25 g) fresh seaweed or dried seaweed (kombu variety)
1 leek
1 clove garlic
3–4 mange-tout
salt
1 oz (25 g) lard
For the sauce:
2½ tbsp soy sauce
1 tbsp vinegar
2 tsp cornflour
Calories 206; protein 24.8 g; fat 10.5 g; sugar 5.2 g

1. Place the squid in a large bowl of water. Remove the central bone and the tentacles, together with the innards of the squid without breaking them up. Rub off the skin, slit the bodies and open them up and remove the cartilaginous tips on either side.

2. Cut the squid across into strips about 1¼ in (3 cm) wide; cut these strips into fairly small pieces and then make 2 slits in each piece, leaving the strips attached at one end. Blanch the squid in boiling water, refresh in cold water and drain.

3. Wash the seaweed and leave in cold water for a little while to become firm again (if dried seaweed is used, pre-soak); cut into strips. Slice the leek and garlic very thinly; boil the mange tout for a short time in salted water to intensify the colour, and cut diagonally in half.

4. Mix the sauce ingredients soy sauce, vinegar and cornflour with 2 tbsp water until the cornflour has thoroughly dissolved.

5. Heat the lard in the wok; stir-fry the garlic and leek and as soon as they start to give off their distinctive aroma, add the squid and the seaweed. Stir-fry briefly over a high heat; add the sauce and mix briskly. Add the mange-tout; when these have heated through the dish is ready to serve.

Stir-fried squid and asparagus

2 squid
1 tsp rice wine or dry sherry
1 tsp ginger juice
2 tsp cornflour
8 asparagus spears
$\frac{1}{3}$–$\frac{1}{2}$ Chinese white radish
1 boiled fresh or canned bamboo shoot
2 tbsp oil
8 fl oz (225 ml) stock (see recipe, p. 296)
$\frac{1}{2}$ tsp salt
1 tsp sugar
1 tbsp rice wine or dry sherry
2 tsp cornflour
1 tbsp rendered chicken fat
Calories 279; protein 26.6 g; fat 11.6 g; sugar 8.8 g

1. Place the squid in a large bowl of water. Remove the central bone and pull the tentacles carefully away from the bodies of the squid, removing the innards without breaking them; rub and peel off the thin skin and trim off the cartilaginous tips on either side of the opening of the body. Slit the squid open and cut the squid lengthways into three sections. Holding the knife at an oblique angle to the work surface, score the flesh lengthways and quite deeply and then cut the scored strips across into small pieces $\frac{1}{2}$–$\frac{3}{4}$ in (1–1$\frac{1}{2}$ cm) wide.

2. Flavour the squid with the rice wine and ginger juice, mixing well, and then coat with cornflour; blanch in boiling water and then refresh in cold water and drain.

3. Cut off any woody parts from the asparagus stems and simmer the spears in salted water until the tips are just tender, refresh in cold water and cut into 1$\frac{1}{2}$-in (4-cm) lengths.

4. Peel the Chinese white radish, cut into small rectangular pieces, boil until just tender and drain; cut the bamboo shoot into rectangular pieces.

5. Heat the oil in the wok and fry the radish and bamboo shoot pieces over a high heat. Add the stock and cook for about 5–7 minutes.

6. Add the salt, sugar and rice wine, stir and then add the pieces of asparagus. As soon as the liquid returns to the boil, add the squid and cook briskly for a few minutes until the squid has curled. Stir in the cornflour dissolved in 4 tsp water to thicken the sauce a little and finish by trickling in the rendered chicken fat, down the side of the wok. Stir once more and serve.

Squid with fresh ginger juice and green beans

A crisp, fresh-tasting dish to which the ginger juice gives a pleasantly strong, piquant flavour.

2 squid
salt
a few drops of sesame seed oil
7oz (200g) green beans
For the sauce:
2 tbsp fresh ginger juice
2 tbsp soy sauce
2 tbsp vinegar
1 tsp sugar
1 tbsp sesame seed oil
Calories 174; protein 24.7; fat 6.6g; sugar 2.8g

1. Clean the squid as instructed on page 175; slit them to open out flat with the inside facing upwards. Holding the knife at 45° to the work surface, score a lattice pattern.

2. Cut the squid bodies into bite-sized pieces, blanch in boiling water for 1–2 minutes, refresh in cold water. Drain and season with a pinch of salt and a few drops of sesame seed oil.

3. String the beans if necessary, wash and drain well. Sprinkle with 2 tbsp salt and mix well; boil rapidly for 2 minutes, refresh in cold water and then drain and cut into $1\frac{1}{4}$–$1\frac{1}{2}$ in (3–4cm) pieces.

4. Mix the sauce ingredients together in a bowl (ginger juice, soy sauce, vinegar, sugar and sesame seed oil).

5. Make sure that the squid and beans are well drained, then add them to the sauce and mix thoroughly so that they are well coated and flavoured.

Fried oysters

Oysters fried in a melting batter containing seaweed strips are equally good as a first course or snack with Chinese fortified wines.

14oz (400g) shelled oysters
⅓ leek
small piece root ginger
cornflour
1 leaf purple nori seaweed
1¾ pints (1 litre) oil for frying
For the batter:
2 small eggs
½ tsp salt
8 tbsp plain flour
For the garnish:
1 radish
Calories 277; protein 14.6g; fat 15g; sugar 20.4g

1. Choose oysters of roughly the same size for this recipe, place them in a large sieve and immerse in a bowl full of salted water, moving the sieve around in the water to remove grit and impurities. Drain the oysters and spread out in a sieve; pour plenty of boiling water over the oysters, allow to drain well and cool.

2. Chop the leek finely and grate the ginger. For the garnish, cut the radish into a flower shape and soak in cold water for 10 minutes, so that it opens out.

3. Mix the oysters with the chopped leek and the grated ginger in a dish and leave to absorb the flavours for 5 minutes. Take up the oysters and coat with cornflour.

4. Prepare the batter by beating the eggs in a bowl, stir in the salt and 2 tbsp water and then sift in the flour. Stir to blend.

5. Fold the leaf of nori seaweed in half, use kitchen tongs to hold very briefly over a flame (or place for a few seconds under a pre-heated grill). Wrap the seaweed in a cloth and rub gently to break the leaf into tiny pieces. Add to the batter and mix well.

6. Heat the oil in the wok to 350°F (180°C), dip the oysters in the batter and fry until crisp. Transfer to a serving dish and garnish with the radish. Season, according to taste, with lemon, mustard mixed with soy sauce or soy sauce and vinegar.

Stir-fried oysters and bean curd

A hot dish in which the bland bean curd absorbs the delectable if delicate flavour of the oysters and sesame seed oil.

10oz (300g) small shelled oysters
1 leek
small piece root ginger
1½ cakes bean curd
2 tbsp salted black beans, rinsed
4 tbsp peanut oil
few leaves of parsley
For the sauce:
1½ tbsp soy sauce
1 tbsp sugar
2 tbsp oil
2 tsp sesame seed oil
Calories 366; protein 17.9g; fat 27.1g; sugar 9.7g

1. Place the oysters in a large sieve and immerse in salted water, moving the sieve around in the water to remove any grit. Add a small piece of the leek and the ginger, finely sliced, to a large saucepan of boiling water, lower the oysters into the boiling water for a few seconds to blanch and then drain.

2. Cut the bean curd lengthways into three and then into smaller pieces about ½ in (1 cm) thick. Simmer in the flavoured water for 1 minute then drain carefully.

3. Chop the remaining leek and the salted black beans finely.

4. Mix the sauce ingredients.

5. Heat the wok, pour in the peanut oil and when it is very hot, fry the chopped leek and beans; add the oysters and the bean curd and stir-fry over a high heat, taking care not to break up the bean curd too much; pour in the sauce all at once and cook for 2 minutes to allow it to penetrate the oysters and bean curd. Turn onto a serving dish and garnish with parsley.

EGG DISHES

Eggs play a supporting role in Chinese cookery which is nonetheless vital since eggs can be used to complement or blend with an infinite variety of ingredients. A beaten egg added to soup not only makes it look attractive but also sets off the taste. Egg is unequalled as a binding agent (whites are used for making Chinese coconut cake) and the yolks are used for sealing such foods as spring rolls.

Hard-boiled eggs are peeled, simmered in stock flavoured with soy sauce, and eaten as a popular snack; or their shells are gently cracked and the hard-boiled eggs are then simmered in a mixture of tea and soy sauce; when they are peeled this gives them an attractive marbled effect.

"Thousand year old eggs" are the product of an extremely ancient and ingenious method of preserving duck eggs which keep less well than chickens' eggs. A mixture of lime, pine ash, salt, and rice husks is plastered all over the eggs, which are then buried in this rather slimy concoction for anything from 2 to 4 months. During this period the coating gradually dries and the lime produces a reaction in the eggs, transforming the whites into a firm, translucent amber-coloured jelly and making the yolks turn green. These duck eggs acquire a very distinctive taste and are usually served as a snack with slices of ginger which have been macerated in vinegar. Sometimes special seasonings are mixed with the preserving substance to add extra flavour. Pickled duck eggs are another favourite; these are eaten hot with a bowl of boiled rice (or, best of all, with Congee rice – the typical Shanghai breakfast). The yolks of duck eggs are also dried in the sun and used to fill moon cakes which are eaten as festival fare.

Although chicken and duck eggs are the most widely used, pigeons' eggs and quails' eggs also make frequent appearances on Chinese menus.

Pork and eggs

A full-flavoured and spicy dish which is best eaten with plain boiled rice.

14oz (400g) belly pork
4 dried Chinese mushrooms, pre-soaked
1 leek
2oz (50g) dried prawns
2–3 tbsp peanut oil
scant 3floz (75ml) soy sauce
1 tbsp rice wine or dry sherry
1 tsp sugar
pinch of five-spice powder
4 hard-boiled eggs
Calories 531; protein 18.6g; fat 49.1g; sugar 3.4g

1. Cut the pork into dice about ½in (1 cm) square; soak the Chinese mushrooms in water for 20 minutes and when they have softened and expanded, drain.

2. Remove the stalks from the mushrooms and cut the caps into pieces approx. ½in (1 cm) square. Chop the leek finely. Soak the dried prawns in water and when plump, drain and reserve the liquid.

1
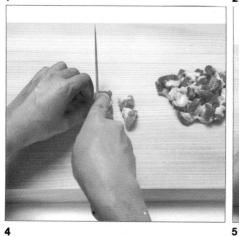

2

3

4

5

6

3. Heat the oil in the wok and stir-fry the leek; when it starts to release its aroma, add the prawns and stir-fry these for a few minutes.

4. Add the mushrooms and the pork and stir-fry over a high heat; when the meat has changed colour, add the soy sauce, rice wine, sugar and the five-spice powder. Transfer all the ingredients to a fairly deep saucepan.

5. Make approx. 1 pint (½–¾ litre) stock using the liquid in which the prawns were soaked, topped up with enough water to just cover all the ingredients in the saucepan.

6. Add the peeled hard-boiled eggs, placing them on top of the other ingredients so that they do not touch the bottom of the pan. Cover and simmer for about 1 hour.

Five-colour omelette

Simple and quick to prepare as well as attractive in presentation, this delicious dish can be enjoyed at any time of year.

2 slices cooked ham
½ bunch spring onions
4oz (125g) boiled fresh or canned bamboo shoots
3 fresh or canned Chinese mushrooms (egg mushrooms or straw mushrooms)
6 eggs
½ tsp salt
½ tsp sugar
pinch of monosodium glutamate
2–3 tbsp oil for frying
Calories 230; protein 11.2g; fat 19.1g; sugar 3.2g

1. Cut the ham into thin strips; chop the spring onion tops into pieces about 1½–2 in (4–5 cm) long, discarding the bulbs. If spring onions are not in season, use finely shredded leek.

2. Wash the bamboo shoots well if fresh shoots are used and boil until tender; shred the fresh or canned shoots into small strips the same size as the ham, and do likewise with the mushrooms having first removed their stalks.

3. Beat the eggs in a bowl, using chopsticks.

4. Mix in the salt, sugar and monosodium glutamate and beat the eggs briefly but energetically, lifting the mixture to incorporate as much air as possible.

5. Add the ham, spring onions, bamboo shoots and mushrooms and stir well.

6. Heat the oil in the wok; pour the omelette mixture into the wok all at once and cook until just set, using a palette knife or a Chinese scoop or turner to make sure the ingredients are evenly spread throughout the omelette.

7. When the omelette has set on one side, divide into three portions and turn over, then scoop the three portions together again.

8. When the omelette has set into a nicely rounded shape, cover and cook for a very short time and then serve.

Fried eggs, tomatoes and mushrooms

A simple dish, easy to prepare, with a lively flavour. It goes well with boiled rice.

¼oz (5g) dried Chinese wood ear mushrooms
2 eggs
salt
2 ripe tomatoes
oil for frying
1 tsp sugar
1 tbsp soy sauce
pinch of monosodium glutamate
Calories 128; protein 4.1 g; fat 10.5 g; sugar 5.7 g

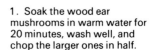

1. Soak the wood ear mushrooms in warm water for 20 minutes, wash well, and chop the larger ones in half.

2. Beat the eggs in a bowl together with a pinch of salt.

3. Make a shallow cross cut in the skin on the top of each tomato and place in a bowl; cover with boiling water and remove after 5–10 seconds; rinse in cold water remove the stalks and peel off the skin. Chop roughly.

4. Heat the wok and pour in 3–4 tablespoons oil; when the oil is hot, pour in the beaten eggs.

5. Scoop and turn the omelette mixture, until it is half-cooked – just set.

6. Remove the omelette mixture from the wok; pour in 2 tbsp more oil and heat. Add the chopped tomato and stir-fry lightly. When the tomato has just heated through, return the eggs to the pan, add the mushrooms and cook briefly, scooping and turning.

7. Sprinkle with the sugar, soy sauce and monosodium glutamate, mixing quickly before serving.

Tea eggs

Once the eggs have been boiled in a mixture of tea and soy sauce they are peeled to reveal an attractive marbled pattern; their taste is also enhanced.

6 eggs
2 tsp tea leaves
1 star anise
1 tsp sugar
salt
1 tbsp soy sauce
2 small cucumbers
1 tsp black bean paste
a few drops of sesame seed oil
Calories 152; protein 9.9g; fat 11.1g; sugar 2.5g
Serves 6

1. Hard-boil the 6 eggs for 10 minutes. Drain and rinse immediately in plenty of cold water.

2. Roll the eggs very carefully against the work surface, pressing gently so as to form tiny cracks in the shell without rupturing the thin inner skin.

3. Place the eggs in a saucepan with $1\frac{1}{2}$ pints ($\frac{3}{4}$ litre) water, the tea, star anise, sugar, $\frac{1}{4}$ tsp salt and the soy sauce. Boil gently for up to 1 hour, turning the eggs now and then so that they colour evenly. Allow the eggs to cool in the liquid.

4. Remove the eggs from the pan and peel off their shells very carefully taking care not to tear the delicate skin immediately under the shell.

5. Prepare the cucumbers by first slicing them lengthways in half, score the skins obliquely making a lattice pattern and then cut into pieces $1\frac{1}{4}$ in (3cm) long; place in a bowl and sprinkle with 1 tsp salt; when the cucumbers have softened rinse with cold water and drain. In a separate bowl mix the black bean paste, the soy sauce and the sesame seed oil, add the cucumbers and mix rapidly.

6. Arrange the cucumbers in the bottom of a bowl or serving plate and top with the tea eggs.

Scrambled eggs with prawns

The complementary flavours of the prawns and eggs make a clever combination for this quick and easy dish.

5oz (150g) prawns
½ egg white
1 tsp cornflour
oil for frying
6 eggs
½ tsp salt
½ tsp sugar
pinch of monosodium glutamate
3–4 tbsp peanut oil
1 tbsp rice wine or dry sherry
Calories 310; protein 15g; fat 26.2g; sugar 1.9g

1. Shell the prawns and if large remove the black vein running down their backs with a cocktail stick, rinse and drain.

2. Place the prawns in a bowl, add the white of egg and the cornflour and mix well with the fingers.

3. Heat enough oil for deep-frying to 250°F (120°C), add the prawns and fry lightly. As soon as they change colour, remove from the oil and drain. (If cooked prawns are used, merely heat them through in the oil.)

4. Beat the eggs with the salt in a bowl; add the sugar and monosodium glutamate and stir well.

5. Heat the peanut oil in the wok; pour in the beaten eggs and stir and turn them with a scoop or palette knife until half cooked.

6. Add the prawns and mix quickly; sprinkle with the rice wine and stir briefly before transferring to a warmed serving platter. Eat while still piping hot.

VEGETABLES

It has already been pointed out that a good Chinese cook aims to achieve balance and harmony between the various ingredients he prepares. This means that vegetables play a far more important part in Chinese cuisine than is the case with western food, where they are usually relegated to a supporting rôle. The word ts'ai *which denotes the dishes forming the component parts of a meal actually means "vegetables". There has always been a great choice and abundance of vegetables in China – mainly due to the favourable climate but also stemming from the Chinese habit of raising fast-growing vegetables sown between the main crops of rice and cereals, thus making the most of the limited area of arable land available. Plants which do not spread out and take up too much ground space are therefore favoured and squashes or pumpkins are ripened on the roofs of houses; vegetables such as bean sprouts can even be grown indoors.*

In addition to this, the age-old Chinese flair for making the most of every food source offered by nature means that such plants as bamboo shoots, seaweed, and water chestnuts are gathered and consumed; such beauties of nature as the lotus are fully exploited, hence the widespread inclusion of lotus leaves, seeds and roots in so many recipes.

The teachings of Buddhism, which advocate vegetarianism have had a considerable influence on Chinese eating habits, and in fact the influence of the philosophy itself is far less prominent in China than its influence on the cuisine. Preserved vegetables are an important addition to the Chinese diet; when vegetables are plentiful, the surplus can be dried or pickled for use when the fresh article is out of season or scarce.

Stir-fried green beans with mushrooms

A simple recipe requiring ingredients which are available all year round. It goes well with a meat dish.

½lb (250g) green beans
4oz (125g) button mushrooms
oil for frying
1 tsp salt
2 tbsp soy sauce
1 tsp sugar
1 tsp rice wine or dry sherry
pinch of monosodium glutamate
a few drops of sesame seed oil
1 tsp cornflour (optional)
Calories 96; protein 2.3g; fat 7.7g; sugar 6.1g

1. Trim, wash and dry the beans and slice them obliquely into 1½–2-in (4–5-cm) lengths.

2. Trim and wash the mushrooms, cutting the larger ones in half.

3. Heat the wok over a high heat and pour in 2 tbsp oil, swirling it round the inside of the wok to coat it thoroughly.

4. When the oil is very hot add the beans and stir-fry.

5. Once the beans have absorbed most of the oil, season with salt and pour in 8 fl oz (225 ml) water; cover and cook until tender and then transfer to a plate and discard the liquid from the wok.

6. Heat the wok again over a high heat; pour in 2 tbsp oil and when it is very hot return the beans to the pan. Add the mushrooms and stir-fry.

7. Mix together the soy sauce, sugar, rice wine and monosodium glutamate and stir into the green beans and mushrooms. Add a few drops of sesame seed oil for extra flavour.

8. If the sauce needs thickening, stir in the cornflour mixed well with 2 tsp water.

Stir-fried mange-tout with black bean paste

A vegetable dish with a well defined, mildly spicy flavour.

¾lb (350g) mange-tout
oil for frying
1 tsp salt
1 tsp finely chopped garlic
1 tsp black bean paste
1 tbsp soy sauce
1 tsp sugar
pinch of monosodium glutamate
a few drops of sesame seed oil
Calories 119; protein 3.8g; fat 7.9g; sugar 9.7g

1. Trim the mange-tout and remove the strings; wash and dry.

2. Heat 2 tbsp oil in the wok, add the mange-tout and stir-fry lightly; season with salt and pour in 8floz (225ml) water.

3. Cover and cook until the mange-tout are tender but still crisp, and drain.

4. Remove any liquid left in the wok; pour in 2 tbsp oil and when the oil is quite hot, add the chopped garlic.

5. As soon as the garlic starts to release its aroma, return the mange-tout to the wok and mix in the black bean paste, the soy sauce, sugar and monosodium glutamate. Stir-fry just long enough for the mange-tout to absorb the flavour of the dressing.

6. Sprinkle with a few drops of sesame seed oil for extra flavour and sheen.

Stir-fried cucumbers with dried prawns

An original combination of cucumbers and prawns provides a delicious, quick and easy dish.

2 tbsp dried prawns
2 small cucumbers
oil for frying
1 slice root ginger
1 tsp sugar
$\frac{1}{2}$ tsp salt
1 tbsp soy sauce
pinch of monosodium glutamate
1 tsp cornflour
Calories 58; protein 0.9g; fat 5.1g; sugar 2.2g

1. Wash the prawns and soak in water to soften and plump up; drain and reserve the liquid and chop the prawns into small pieces.

2. Slice the cucumbers lengthways in half and then cut diagonally into 2-in (5-cm) lengths.

3. Pour 2 tbsp oil into the wok and heat; when the oil is very hot, stir-fry the ginger until it releases its aroma.

4. Add the chopped prawns and stir-fry; add the cucumbers and stir-fry, keeping the heat high.

5. Season with the sugar, salt, soy sauce and monosodium glutamate and moisten with some of the liquid reserved from soaking the prawns. Cover and cook over a low heat until the liquid has been partially absorbed.

6. Thicken the remaining juices a little by stirring in the cornflour mixed with 2 tsp water.

Cucumbers and scallops with mushrooms

A delicate combination of flavours which makes a delicious and exotic dish, useful when unexpected guests arrive, since it mainly comprises canned ingredients.

4 small cucumbers
1 can Chinese egg mushrooms
1 can scallops
¾ pint (½ litre) stock (including liquor from canned scallops)
3 tbsp peanut oil
1–2 tbsp rice wine or dry sherry
1 tsp salt
2 tsp cornflour
a few drops of sesame seed oil
Calories 185; protein 18.4g; fat 10.5g; sugar 11.4g

1. Peel the cucumbers and cut diagonally into slices about ¼ in (5mm) thick.

2. Drain the mushrooms and cut into thin slices.

3. Drain the scallops, reserving the liquor; chop them finely and add the reserved juice to the stock, making up ¾ pint (½ litre).

4. Heat the wok; pour in the peanut oil and when the oil is hot, stir-fry the scallops.

5. Add the cucumbers and the egg mushrooms, stir-fry briefly and then trickle in the rice wine down the side of the wok. Pour in the stock.

6. When the liquid comes to the boil, season with salt and continue cooking on a slightly lower heat.

7. When the cucumbers are tender but still crisp, stir in the cornflour mixed with 4 tsp water, to thicken the sauce.

8. To give extra flavour stir in a few drops of sesame seed oil just before serving.

Aubergines Szechuan style

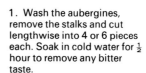

The flavour of the fried aubergine is improved by the addition of minced pork.

6 small aubergines
oil for frying
1 tsp finely chopped garlic
1 tbsp finely chopped leek
1 tsp finely chopped ginger
4oz (125g) minced pork
1 tsp rice wine or dry sherry
For the sauce:
1 tbsp sugar
2 tbsp soy sauce
1 tsp vinegar
pinch of monosodium glutamate
Calories 241; protein 5.4g; fat 21g; sugar 7.5g

1. Wash the aubergines, remove the stalks and cut lengthwise into 4 or 6 pieces each. Soak in cold water for ½ hour to remove any bitter taste.

2. Dry the aubergine slices thoroughly with a cloth and fry them in very hot oil.

3. Mix all the sauce ingredients together.

4. Heat 2 tbsp oil in the wok and stir-fry the garlic, leek and the ginger; once these have started to release their aroma, add the minced pork.

5. Fry the pork making sure that it does not form lumps; sprinkle with rice wine, add the fried aubergines and pour in the sauce. Stir and turn quickly to distribute the flavour evenly.

Chinese white radish with pork and prawns

The finely chopped pork and prawns enhance the subtle flavour of the white radish. An extremely economical dish.

2 tbsp dried prawns
1 lb (500 g) Chinese white radish
oil for frying
1 tbsp finely chopped leek
1 tsp finely chopped root ginger
2 oz (50 g) finely chopped or minced pork
1 tbsp rice wine or dry sherry
8 fl oz (225 ml) stock
2 tsp sugar
3 tbsp soy sauce
pinch of monosodium glutamate
Calories 126; protein 4.2 g; fat 8.1 g; sugar 8 g
Serves 4–5

1. Wash the dried prawns and soak in lukewarm or cold water until they have softened and swelled; chop into small pieces.

2. Peel the Chinese white radish, cut lengthways into four or, if very large, into six and then slice diagonally into small pieces.

3. Heat the wok over a fairly high heat and pour in 2–3 tbsp oil. When the oil is very hot, stir-fry the chopped leek and ginger.

4. Once these start to release their aroma, add the prawns.

5. When the prawns have heated through, add the minced pork and mix well, frying and turning with a wooden spoon or scoop to prevent the meat forming into lumps.

6. When the meat is cooked and well coloured, add the white radish, mix and turn briefly and then sprinkle with rice wine.

7. Stir-fry over a high heat, then pour in the stock and flavour with the sugar, soy sauce and monosodium glutamate.

8. Cover and cook over a low heat until the liquid has almost completely evaporated and the white radish is tender; any remaining juices should be absorbed by the white radish.

Stir-fried potatoes with pork

A dish which commends itself to any cook since it is extremely economical and digestible.

5oz (150g) pork, very thinly sliced
1 tsp sugar
1 tbsp soy sauce
1 tsp cornflour
peanut oil
1 lb (500g) waxy potatoes
8 floz (225ml) stock
1 tsp sugar
¼ tsp salt
pinch of monosodium glutamate
Calories 276; protein 8.7g; fat 16.2g; sugar 23.8g

1. Cut the thin slices of pork into small pieces, place in a bowl or deep dish and sprinkle with the sugar, soy sauce, cornflour and 1 tbsp peanut oil and mix well by hand to ensure even coating.

2. Peel the potatoes and boil them whole until only just tender.

3. Cut the potatoes into thin slices.

4. Heat 2 tbsp peanut oil in the wok, add the marinated pork and stir-fry lightly over a high heat.

5. After 2–3 minutes, add the potatoes and stir-fry. Pour in the stock and season with sugar, salt and monosodium glutamate.

6. Cover and turn down the heat; continue cooking for a short while until the meat and potatoes are tender and have absorbed the seasoning.

Bamboo shoots with spinach and mushrooms

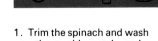 25'

The attractive colour contrasts of the ingredients make this light vegetable dish very appetising.

approx. 1 lb (500g) fresh spinach
3½ oz (100g) bamboo shoots
4–5 Chinese winter mushrooms or straw mushrooms
oil for frying
1 tsp salt
2 fl oz (50ml) stock
1 tbsp oyster sauce
pinch of monosodium glutamate
a few drops of sesame seed oil
1 tsp cornflour
Calories 93; protein 3.1 g; fat 7.9g; sugar 5.2g

1. Trim the spinach and wash very thoroughly, pat dry and cut into 2–2½-in (5–6-cm) pieces.

2. Boil the bamboo shoots until tender and slice thinly into small pieces. (If canned, drain and slice.)

3. Soak the mushrooms in water for 20 minutes if dried, remove the stalks and cut the larger caps in half.

4. Heat 2 tbsp oil in the wok, stir-fry the spinach briefly and then add salt and 8 fl oz (225ml) water. Cover and cook over a low heat until the spinach is tender, remove the spinach and drain.

5. Clean the wok and heat 2 tbsp fresh oil; when this is very hot, add the bamboo shoots and the mushrooms and stir-fry.

6. When the bamboo shoots and mushrooms are nearly done, add the spinach, the stock, oyster sauce and the monosodium glutamate, finishing with a few drops sesame seed oil.

7. Cover and cook for 2–3 minutes to allow the vegetables time to absorb flavour and moisture; before serving thicken the sauce by stirring in the cornflour mixed with 2 tsp water.

Chinese white radish with crab meat

The delicate flavours of Chinese white radish and chicken are enhanced by the sprinkling of crab meat.

1 chicken wing
small piece leek, thinly sliced
small piece root ginger, thinly sliced
a few drops of rice wine or dry sherry
salt
1 small can crab meat
1¼–1½lb (600–700g) Chinese white radish
3 tbsp peanut oil
1 tsp salt
1–2 tbsp rice wine or dry sherry
stock, (see recipe, p. 296)
4 tsp cornflour
a few drops of ginger juice
4–5 spring onion stems
Calories 313; protein 15.7g; fat 21.7g; sugar 11.7g

1. Place the chicken wing in a shallow dish, top with the thinly sliced leek and ginger and sprinkle with a few drops of rice wine and a pinch of salt. Place the dish in a bamboo steamer and cook for 15 minutes over a moderate heat. Allow to cool.

2. When the chicken has cooled down enough to handle but is still quite hot, tear off the flesh into small shreds. Reserve the cooking liquid. Drain the can of crab meat, reserving the liquor, and chop.

3. Cut the Chinese white radish into $1\frac{1}{2}$-in (4-cm) sections, then into thin slices and finally shred these slices to the same size as the chicken. Combine the crab liquor and the juices from the steamed chicken with the stock to make a scant 1 pint (generous $\frac{1}{2}$ litre).

4. Heat the wok and pour in the peanut oil; when this is hot add the white radish and stir-fry until fairly tender.

5. Season with $\frac{1}{2}$ tsp salt and flavour with the rice wine, trickling this in down the side of the wok. Pour in the stock and cook over a moderate heat; remove any scum which forms during cooking.

6. When the Chinese white radish is tender, add more salt to taste, a little at a time. If there is too much liquid, reduce by continuing to cook a little longer.

7. Add the shredded chicken and the crab meat, reserving a little crab for decoration. Stir and turn quickly with a palette knife or scoop.

8. Stir in the cornflour dissolved in 2 tbsp water to thicken the sauce; turn off the heat, add the ginger juice and stir. Garnish with chopped spring onion and the remaining pieces of crab.

Stir-fried Chinese greens

A fresh, light and very simple dish.

approx. 2lb (1kg) Chinese mustard greens
2–3 tbsp peanut oil
1 tsp salt
pinch of monosodium glutamate
8 fl oz (225ml) stock
Calories 52; protein 0.8g; fat 5.1g; sugar 1.3g

1. Wash the greens thoroughly, drain in a colander or salad shaker and cut into pieces 2–2½ in (4–5cm) long.

2. Heat the wok and pour in the peanut oil; as soon as the oil is quite hot, add the mustard greens and stir-fry over a high heat.

3. Season with salt and monosodium glutamate and pour in the stock. Cover and cook until just tender.

4. Drain and serve.

Fried aubergines with sweet and sour sauce

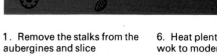

The aubergines are fan-cut, fried and served with a spicy sweet and sour sauce. The dish is finished with sesame seeds for extra flavour.

6 small aubergines
1 tbsp white sesame seeds
1 chili pepper
1 clove garlic
1 tbsp vinegar
1 tbsp sesame seed oil
2 tbsp soy sauce
1 tbsp sugar
oil for frying
Calories 160; protein 1.7g; fat 14g; sugar 7.8g

1. Remove the stalks from the aubergines and slice lengthways in half. Score the outside of each half deeply and diagonally, without cutting right through, so that each half aubergine will fry quickly but remain in one piece.

2. Toast the sesame seeds under a hot grill.

3. Remove the seeds from the chili pepper and cut the flesh into rings, about $\frac{1}{8}$ in (3mm) thick.

4. Crush the garlic clove.

5. Place the vinegar, sesame seed oil, soy sauce, sugar, sesame seeds, chili pepper and garlic in a bowl and mix well.

6. Heat plenty of oil in the wok to moderately hot and deep-fry the aubergines, turning them carefully every so often. Remove and drain well.

7. Arrange the aubergines, skin side upwards, on a heated serving platter, pour the sauce evenly all over them and leave to stand for a couple of minutes before serving so that the aubergines can absorb the sauce.

Ch'ao tou ya (stir-fried bean sprouts)

Not only is this vegetable very quick to prepare but it is also available all the year round.

1 lb (450 g) fresh bean sprouts
3 tbsp peanut oil
2 or 3 cloves garlic, crushed
2 slices root ginger, finely chopped
½ tsp salt
pinch of freshly ground pepper
1 tbsp lard or cooking fat
1½ tbsp light soy sauce
3 small leeks, white part only, finely shredded into strips about
    ¾ in (2 cm) long
1 tsp sesame seed oil
Calories 116; protein 3.4 g; fat 4.3 g; sugar 3.2 g
Serves 6

1. Rinse the bean sprouts and remove the little black seeds from one end and the thread-like root from the other. Drain well.

2. Heat the peanut oil in the wok and stir-fry the garlic with the ginger very briefly.

3. Add the bean sprouts, salt and pepper and stir-fry quickly for a few seconds only.

4. Add the lard, soy sauce and the leeks.

5. Stir-fry for 2 minutes over a high heat. When the bean sprouts are ready (they should still be crisp) sprinkle with the sesame seed oil.

BEAN CURD DISHES

The two most important products obtained from soya beans are soy sauce and the very nutritious and versatile white bean curd, which is known as tofu. These curd cakes look similar in texture to cheese, through their taste is quite different and rather bland. To make bean curd, yellow soya beans are soaked and softened in water and then crushed to a powder; this is then ground again with added water to form a purée or paste which is strained through cheesecloth. The filtered liquid is heated, combined with a little thickening agent, and then left to set in moulds. The purer and fresher the water used when making bean curd, the better it will be.

Buddhist monks introduced tofu and pioneered its skilful use to replace meat which was, of course, forbidden by their religion; bean curd and its derivatives were moulded and shaped to look like fish, seafood, and other ingredients for which they were substitutes. Bean curd can be dried, fermented, or frozen and can also be spiced to give it a stronger flavour.

Bean curd with black beans Szechuan style

2 cakes bean curd
1 chili pepper
1 tbsp salted black beans, rinsed
oil for frying
1 tbsp finely chopped leek
1 tsp finely chopped garlic
1 tsp finely chopped root ginger
5 oz (150 g) finely chopped or minced pork
1 tsp cornflour
For the sauce:
3 fl oz (75 ml) stock
2 tbsp soy sauce
2 tbsp sugar
1 tbsp black bean paste
1 tsp hot black bean paste
$\frac{1}{4}$ tsp salt
1 tbsp rice wine or dry sherry
pinch of monosodium glutamate
Calories 279; protein 17.3 g; fat 20 g; sugar 9 g

1. Cut the bean curd cakes into small cubes about $\frac{1}{2}$–$\frac{1}{4}$ in ($1\frac{1}{2}$–2cm) square. Place in one layer in a flat tin propped up at one end so that the liquid from the bean curd will drain to the bottom.

2. Remove the seeds from the chili pepper and cut the flesh into rings $\frac{1}{4}$ in (5mm) thick; chop the black beans finely, holding the knife at both ends and pivoting on the sharper end from left to right while chopping.

3. Prepare the sauce by mixing thoroughly the stock, soy sauce, sugar, black bean paste and hot black bean paste, salt, rice wine and monosodium glutamate.

4. Heat 2–3 tbsp oil in the wok and stir-fry the finely chopped leek, garlic and ginger briskly without allowing them to colour too much.

5. When these ingredients start to release their aroma, add the minced pork, the salted black beans and the chili pepper. Stir-fry, taking care that the meat does not stick together.

6. When the pork is cooked, add the bean curd, being careful not to break it.

7. Pour in the sauce; gently stir and turn all the ingredients once without breaking the bean curd, if possible. Cover and cook for about 15 minutes over a low heat, shaking the wok gently from time to time.

8. When the bean curd has absorbed most of the sauce, thicken the remainder by adding the cornflour mixed with 2 tsp water.

Steamed bean curd and white of egg

1 cake bean curd
2 slices cooked ham
2 tbsp frozen peas
5 egg whites
4 floz (125ml) milk
scant 3 floz (75ml) stock
$\frac{1}{2}$ tsp salt
1 tsp sugar
pinch of monosodium glutamate
1 tsp cornflour
For the sauce:
6 floz (175ml) stock
1 tbsp rice wine or dry sherry
$\frac{1}{4}$ tsp salt
$\frac{1}{4}$ tsp sugar
pinch of pepper
pinch of monosodium glutamate
Calories 127; protein 12.5g; fat 6.5g; sugar 5.4g
Serves 4–5

1. Cut the bean curd into 4 pieces and push through a sieve. Allow to stand for a little while and then transfer to a piece of cheesecloth to drain away excess moisture.

2. Cut the ham into small strips about $\frac{1}{4}$ in (5mm) wide; place the frozen peas in a bowl and cover with boiling water; leave to stand for a couple of minutes and then drain.

3. Place the egg whites in a bowl, mix gently with chopsticks or a fork, making sure that no bubbles form. Add the bean curd and mix with a wooden spoon.

4. Add the milk, stock, salt, sugar and a pinch of monosodium glutamate.

5. To achieve a particularly smooth, velvety consistency, push the mixture through a sieve with a slightly wider mesh than previously used; transfer the mixture to a heatproof serving bowl.

6. Place the bowl in the steamer, which should be placed over boiling water 10 minutes in advance. Steam the bean curd mixture for 20–25 minutes over a gentle heat until it has set. (The top should feel firm when pressed very lightly with the fingers.)

7. Prepare the sauce meanwhile by placing the strips of ham and peas together with all the sauce ingredients in a small saucepan. Bring to the boil; add the cornflour dissolved in 2 tsp water at once; set the thickened sauce aside.

8. When the bean curd is set cut into it with a spoon, scooping out an egg-shaped piece and let it fall back gently into the bowl upside down, repeat all the way round the bowl so that the curd looks rather like the petals of a flower. Pour in the sauce and serve.

209

Fried bean curd in soy sauce

 40'

2 cakes fried bean curd
1 large piece root ginger
3–4 dried Chinese mushrooms, pre-soaked
1 tbsp dried Chinese wood ear mushrooms, pre-soaked
approx. 30 dried lily bud stems, pre-soaked
5oz (150g) leg of pork
1 tsp rice wine or dry sherry
½ tsp soy sauce
2 tsp cornflour
oil for frying
3½oz (100g) green beans
peanut oil
cornflour
salt
For the sauce:
3 tbsp soy sauce
½ tsp sugar
1 tbsp rice wine or dry sherry
1 tbsp sesame seed oil
Calories 448; protein 24g; fat 30.7g; sugar 26.3g

1. Cut the fried bean curds into slices about ¼ in (6mm) thick; shred the ginger.

2. Drain the soaked Chinese mushrooms, dry and cut into thin slices. Drain the soaked wood ear mushrooms.

3. Drain the lily bud stems, remove any woody parts and tie each stem into a knot.

4. Cut the pork into narrow strips, sprinkle with rice wine and soy sauce and leave to marinate for 10 minutes.

5. Mix the cornflour with the pork and then stir-fry lightly in fairly hot oil.

6. Heat 2–3 tbsp peanut oil in the wok. Stir-fry the ginger briefly then add the Chinese mushrooms, the fried bean curds, lily bud stems, the wood ears and the fried pork; stir-fry over a fairly high heat.

7. Pour in the sauce ingredients and cook briskly over a high heat for 3–4 minutes, stirring and turning. Thicken the sauce by stirring in 2 tsp cornflour mixed with 4 tsp water.

8. Blanch the green beans quickly in boiling salted water, drain and cut each bean diagonally into two or three pieces; stir-fry briskly in a little peanut oil and season with a little salt.

9. Transfer the bean curd and other ingredients to a heated serving plate and surround with the beans.

SOUPS

"When Tung-po was living as a hermit he used to cook a vegetable soup which although it contained no fish, meat, or five-spice powder, was full of the savour and goodness of simple things".

Su Shih, *In praise of Tung-po's Soup*

Soup is usually served as the last course of a Chinese meal, but, as is so often the case in Chinese cooking, this is not a hard and fast rule. Such highly prized delicacies as Shark's Fin Soup and Bird's Nest Soup are substantial and nutritious, made with fish or meat, eggs, mushrooms, and various other vegetables. These special thick soups are served in small bowls immediately after the first course.

The soup which is most often served is, in contrast, a very light, clear vegetable broth, containing a few small pieces of meat. It is brought to the table in a large tureen and each person helps himself, ladling the soup into his own bowl and sipping it throughout the meal in place of other thirst-quenching drinks; at the end of the meal, a further, more generous helping is consumed as an effective aid to digestion.

Yu Ch'i (shark's fin soup)

An extremely expensive delicacy, only served at banquets and on special occasions. Originally a Peking speciality.

About 3½ oz (100g) dried shark's fin
3¼ pints (1¾ litres) light stock
2 spring onions or thin, young leeks
3 slices root ginger
2 tbsp peanut oil
8oz (250g) chicken meat, shredded
2oz (50g) fresh boiled or canned bamboo shoots, shredded
1oz (25g) dried Chinese winter mushrooms, pre-soaked
1 tbsp rice wine or dry sherry
2 tbsp light soy sauce
1 tbsp red wine vinegar
½ tsp sugar
½ tsp salt
3 tbsp cornflour
Calories 120; protein 6.6g; fat 4.5g; sugar 7g
Serves 8–10

1. Soak the shark's fin for 4 hours in cold water; rinse several times. Boil the fin for up to 2 hours, changing the water several times and picking out any remaining foreign particles.

2. Rinse the shark's fin under cold running water for 10 minutes and then pat dry.

3. Place the shark's fin in a flameproof casserole, pour in 1¼ pints (¾ litre) stock and add the spring onions and the ginger. Bring to the boil, cover and boil for 15 minutes. Drain the shark's fin, discarding the broth.

4. Heat the peanut oil in a flameproof casserole, add the shredded chicken meat and stir-fry until the flesh is lightly coloured.

5. Add the remaining stock and bring to the boil. Add the shark's fin, bamboo shoots, sliced mushrooms, rice wine, soy sauce, vinegar, sugar and salt and simmer over a low heat for 15–20 minutes.

6. Stir in the cornflour mixed with 5 tbsp water and simmer until the soup has thickened, stirring from time to time. Serve very hot in small bowls; a little vinegar may be added if desired.

Won ton soup

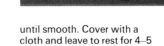 45'

¾ lb (350 g) prawns, peeled, de-veined and chopped
2½ oz (65 g) leek, shallot or spring onion cut into thin rings
1 beaten egg
For the marinade:
1 tsp sugar
½ tsp salt
½ tsp monosodium glutamate
2–3 drops of sesame seed oil
For the soup:
2½ pints (1½ litres) chicken stock (see recipe, p. 296)
1 tsp salt
½ tsp monosodium glutamate
2 tbsp light soy sauce
4–5 drops of sesame seed oil
For the won ton:
4 oz (125 g) strong flour
6 tbsp mixture of beaten egg and water
cornflour
Calories 430; protein 16.5 g; fat 25.6 g; sugar 23 g
Serves 6–8

1. Prepare the won ton: Sift the flour on to a pastry board, make a well in the centre and pour in all but 1 tbsp of the beaten egg and water mixture; add the last tbsp if required. Mix in the flour and then work the dough for about 5 minutes until smooth. Cover with a cloth and leave to rest for 4–5 hours at room temperature.

2. Knead the dough briefly once more and lightly dust the pastry board and rolling pin with cornflour. Roll out into a very thin, almost transparent sheet and cut out about 48 circles 3 in (7 cm) in diameter. Dust them with cornflour, pile them on top of each other and keep in the refrigerator, covered with a clean cloth until needed.

3. Mix the chopped prawns thoroughly with the marinade and place in the refrigerator for 30 minutes.

4. Spread the pastry circles on a board, shaking off the excess cornflour. Place a generous 1 tsp of prawn mixture in the centre of each circle and brush the surrounding pastry with beaten egg.

5. Gather the pastry over the filling, twist very slightly and seal, pressing gently.

6. Bring a large saucepan of boiling salted water to the boil and lower the won ton dumplings into it; boil for 2 minutes or until the dumplings rise to the top. Drain.

7. Distribute half the chopped leek evenly in the soup bowls and place the won ton on top.

8. Bring the chicken stock and other ingredients to the boil, add the remainder of the chopped leek and boil for 1 minute more. Pour into the bowls and serve.

213

Pork and prawn balls in broth

For the prawn balls:
7oz (200g) shelled prawns, de-veined
2½oz (60g) fresh pork fat
1 tsp rice wine or dry sherry
½ tsp ginger juice
½ egg white
½ tsp salt
1 tbsp cornflour

For the pork balls:
3 dried Chinese winter mushrooms, pre-soaked
⅓ leek
7oz (200g) minced pork
½ tbsp rice wine or dry sherry
pinch of pepper
½ tsp salt
scant 1 tsp mixed peanut and sesame seed oil
1 small or ½ large beaten egg
½ tbsp cornflour
For the broth:
3–3½ pints (1¾–2 litres) stock (see recipe, p. 296)
2 generous tsp salt
2 tbsp rice wine or dry sherry
½–1 small cucumber
pinch of pepper
a few drops of sesame seed oil
Calories 397; protein 22g; fat 30.9g; sugar 5.9g
Serves 4–6

1

2

3

4

1. Prepare the prawn balls. Chop the prawns very finely and pound with the blunt edge of a cleaver to form a thick paste.

2. Chop the pork fat into small dice about ¼ in (5mm) square – if chopped any finer it may melt during cooking.

3. Place the prawns in a bowl, add the rice wine and ginger juice and mix well; stir in the pork fat, egg white, salt and the cornflour.

4. Shape the mixture into balls about ½–¾ in (1½–2cm) across; a quick and easy method is to take a small portion of mixture, form a fist enclosing it and then squeeze out a ball of mixture through the aperture formed by the thumb and forefinger.

5. Prepare the pork balls next: drain the mushrooms, remove the stalks and chop the caps; chop the leek finely.

6. Place the minced pork in a bowl with the rice wine and pepper, mix and then add the leek, mushrooms, salt, mixed peanut and sesame seed oil beaten egg and cornflour and work together to form a smooth, well blended mixture. Shape into balls.

7. Pour the stock into a deep saucepan or flameproof casserole and bring to the boil; add the pork balls followed by the prawn balls. Cut the cucumber into paper-thin slices.

8. As soon as the stock returns to the boil, skim off any scum; flavour with salt and rice wine and add the sliced cucumber. Season with pepper and a few drops of sesame seed oil.

5

6

7

8

Mushroom soup

This soup is something of a luxury, since it contains several varieties of delicious and sought-after mushrooms.

4–5 dried winter Chinese mushrooms, pre-soaked
½–1 can straw mushrooms
1 oz (25g) dried wood ears, pre-soaked
2–4 leaves Chinese cabbage
small piece carrot
3 tbsp peanut oil
1 tsp salt
2–2½ pints (1¼–1½ litres) stock
½ tbsp soy sauce
1 tbsp rice wine or dry sherry
½ tsp vinegar
½ tbsp cornflour
pinch of pepper
a few drops of sesame seed oil
Calories 105; protein 4g; fat 10.4g; sugar 9.1g
Serves 4–6

1. Drain the winter mushrooms, remove the stalks and slice the caps thinly. Drain the straw mushrooms and slice.

2. Cut off the stalks of the wood ears and separate the mushrooms. Cut the Chinese cabbage and the peeled carrot into very small, thin strips.

3. Heat the peanut oil in the wok; add the winter mushrooms, the straw mushrooms, the Chinese cabbage and the carrot; stir-fry over a fairly high heat. When the vegetables are quite tender, season with salt.

4. Pour in the stock, soy sauce, rice wine and vinegar and as soon as the liquid comes to the boil, lower the heat and continue cooking for about 5–6 minutes, to give the vegetables time to absorb some of the liquid and flavours. Add the wood ears.

5. When the vegetables are cooked, stir in the cornflour mixed with 1 tablespoon water to thicken.

6. Just before serving add a pinch of pepper and a few drops of sesame seed oil.

Steamed egg soup with crab meat

An exquisitely delicate soup in which crab meat adds flavour to the steamed egg mixture.

5 eggs
salt
pinch of monosodium glutamate
1½ pints (850ml) stock
small can crab meat, drained
3–4 strands chives
¼ tsp sugar
1 tbsp rice wine or dry sherry
1 tsp cornflour
Calories 158; protein 16.6g; fat 7.3g; sugar 2.4g

1. Set the bamboo steamer over boiling water. Break the eggs into a bowl and stir gently, add a pinch of salt, a pinch of monosodium glutamate and 1¼ pints (¾ litre) stock. Mix slowly so that the mixture does not become at all frothy.

2. Select a deep, heatproof bowl which will fit in the steamer and which is also decorative, since the soup will be served in this bowl. Pour the egg mixture through a fine sieve into the bowl.

3. Place the bowl in the bamboo steamer, which should be full of steam; steam for 20–25 minutes until the surface is firm to the touch.

4. While the egg mixture is being steamed, chop the crab meat into small pieces and snip the chives into 1–1½-in (3–4-cm) lengths.

5. Place the crab meat, chives, the remaining stock, the sugar, rice wine, ¼ tsp salt and a pinch of monosodium glutamate in a small saucepan; cook for a few minutes over a moderate heat and then thicken by stirring in the cornflour mixed with 2 tsp water.

6. Pour onto the steamed egg mixture and serve.

Crab soup

1 can crab meat
1 egg
3 dried Chinese winter mushrooms, pre-soaked
3½oz (100g) boiled fresh or canned bamboo shoots
1 leek
a little parsley
small piece root ginger
1 tbsp oil (or lard, or cooking fat)
1 tsp soy sauce
1 tbsp rice wine or dry sherry
scant 2½ pints (1½ litres) hot stock or water
generous 2 tsp salt
pinch of pepper
pinch of monosodium glutamate
1½ tbsp cornflour
Calories 107; protein 7.7g; fat 5.5g; sugar 6.9g

1. Drain the crab meat and chop.

2. Drain the soaked mushrooms, remove the stalks and slice the caps into thin strips. Cut the bamboo shoots into strips of the same size. Cut the leek diagonally into thin slices; chop the parsley finely and grate the ginger.

1

2

3

4

5

6

3. Heat the oil in the wok; stir-fry the mushrooms, add the leek and when this starts to release its aroma, add the bamboo shoots, the crab meat and the grated ginger. Stir-fry over a high heat.

4. Sprinkle with soy sauce and the rice wine; pour in the heated stock or water and as soon as the liquid comes to the boil, skim off any scum.

5. Season with salt, pepper and monosodium glutamate. Stir in the cornflour mixed with 3 tbsp water to thicken the soup.

6. Pour the beaten egg into the soup and mix with chopsticks so that the egg sets and is evenly distributed throughout the soup. Sprinkle with finely chopped parsley and serve.

Chicken wings and cucumbers in broth

This soup requires painstaking preparation and is usually served when entertaining special guests.

14oz (400g) chicken wings
1 dried Chinese winter mushroom
3 small (1 large) cucumbers
salt
pinch of monosodium glutamate
1 tbsp rice wine or dry sherry
pinch of pepper
Calories 267; protein 19.5g; fat 18.8g; sugar 3.9g

1. Cut the chicken wings in half.

2. Place the wings in a bowl; cover with boiling water, stir, drain and remove any quills. Wash in cold water and drain.

3. Place the chicken wings in a large saucepan; add $3\frac{1}{4}$ pints (1.8 litres) water and bring to the boil quickly over a high heat; reduce the heat and cook for 30 minutes until the chicken flesh is tender; remove any scum from the surface. Meanwhile soak the Chinese mushroom in warm water for 20 minutes, remove the stalk and add the mushroom to the chicken and stock.

4. Peel the cucumbers carefully, cut them lengthways in half and then cut each strip diagonally into 4 pieces (if larger cucumbers are used, cut into quarters and then into pieces).

5. Set the bamboo steamer over boiling water. Bring a saucepan of water to the boil, add a pinch of salt and the cucumbers and simmer for 3 minutes; drain the cucumbers and refresh in cold water.

6. When the chicken wings are done, remove from the stock. Place the mushroom rounded side down in the centre of a small, heatproof dish and arrange the chicken wings around it. Insert the pieces of cucumber between the chicken wings.

7. Strain the chicken stock, add the rice wine and a pinch each of pepper, salt and monosodium glutamate. Pour enough of the stock into the dish containing the chicken wings, mushroom and cucumbers to come four-fifths of the way up the dish. Place the dish in the bamboo steamer, reserve the remainder of the stock, keeping it hot, and steam the wings and cucumbers for about 15 minutes.

8. Pour the juices from the dish into the reserved stock. Place the serving bowl over the small dish from the steamer and turn the chicken wings, cucumbers and mushroom upside down into the serving bowl. Pour the hot broth gently into the serving bowl.

221

Lettuce and fillets of fish in broth

3½oz (100g) fillets of white fish such as halibut, cod, carp, etc.
1 tsp ginger juice
rice wine or dry sherry
salt
monosodium glutamate
1 tsp cornflour
1 lettuce
small piece root ginger
1 tsp peanut oil
1 tsp soy sauce
scant 2½ pints (1½ litres) hot light stock or water
pinch of pepper
a few drops of sesame seed oil
Calories 55; protein 5.8g; fat 2.4g; sugar 2.6g

1. Slice the fish fillets diagonally into thin pieces and sprinkle with ginger juice, 1 tsp rice wine, a pinch of salt, a pinch of monosodium glutamate and the cornflour. Mix by hand to flavour and coat evenly.

2. Detach all the leaves from the lettuce and wash well. Cut the ginger into thin slices.

3. Heat the peanut oil in the wok, stir-fry the ginger, moisten with the soy sauce and continue to cook until the full aroma is released. Pour in the hot stock or water and season to taste with salt.

4. Turn down the heat, add the pieces of fish a few at a time and when the liquid has come to the boil, season with monosodium glutamate, salt, pepper, a few drops of rice wine and sesame seed oil; add the lettuce leaves and turn off the heat.

West Lake beef soup

A classic soup from Shanghai.

3½ oz (100g) thinly sliced beef
3 egg whites
½ leek
a few honey fungus mushrooms
1 tbsp peanut oil
1 tbsp rice wine or dry sherry
scant 2½ pints (1½ litres) hot light stock or water
4 tsp salt
pinch of monosodium glutamate
2 tbsp cornflour
pinch of pepper
To flavour:
1 tsp soy sauce
1 tsp rice wine or dry sherry
½ tsp sugar
½ tsp cornflour
Calories 75; protein 6.1g; fat 1.3g; sugar 6.3g

1. Cut the sliced beef diagonally into strips about ¼ in (5mm) wide. Mix all the flavouring ingredients together in a bowl.

2. Beat the egg whites with chopsticks or a fork; shred the leek. Trim off the stalks of the mushrooms and set aside.

3. Heat the peanut oil in the wok, add the rice wine and then pour in the hot stock and bring to the boil.

4. Mix the flavouring mixture with the beef and leave to stand.

5. Once the stock has come to the boil, add the beef a little at a time; season with salt and monosodium glutamate. Stir in the cornflour mixed with an equal quantity of water to thicken.

6. Pour the egg whites into the broth all at once, mixing quickly to blend evenly; add the mushrooms, shredded leek and a pinch of pepper. Allow to boil for a few seconds and then turn off the heat.

Meat balls in broth

½ lb (250 g) minced pork
½ onion, finely chopped
2 tsp rice wine or dry sherry
pinch of pepper
sesame seed oil
3 dried Chinese winter mushrooms, pre-soaked
1 small beaten egg
¼ tsp salt
1 tbsp cornflour
1 tomato
2 cabbage leaves
1–1½ oz (25–40 g) transparent noodles
2–2½ pints (1¼–1½ litres) stock or water
For the final seasoning:
1 tsp salt
1 tsp rice wine or dry sherry
pinch of pepper
Calories 273; protein 13.2 g; fat 18.4 g; sugar 13.4 g

1. Place the minced pork in a bowl, add the finely chopped onion, the rice wine, pepper and 1 tsp sesame seed oil; work the mixture well by hand.

2. Drain the Chinese mushrooms, remove the stalks, chop the caps finely and add to the meat mixture. Mix in the beaten egg, the salt and cornflour in this order. Blend each ingredient in thoroughly before adding the next one.

3. Take a ripe tomato, blanch in boiling water, refresh in cold water and skin. Slice crossways in half, remove the seeds and cut each half into slices just over $\frac{1}{2}$ in (1 cm) thick.

4. Cut out the ribs of the cabbage leaves and cut the leaves into small pieces. Place the transparent noodles in a bowl, cover with boiling water and leave to soften. Drain and snip into fairly short lengths.

5. Bring the stock to the boil in a large saucepan; lightly oil the palms of the hands with sesame seed oil and shape the pork mixture into small balls, taking a small quantity of meat in one hand, forming a fist enclosing the meat and squeezing a well-rounded ball out through the opening formed by thumb and forefinger.

6. The meat balls should be about 1 in (2$\frac{1}{2}$ cm) in diameter; lower into the boiling stock one by one.

7. Remove any scum from the stock, add the cabbage and the tomato and boil for a few minutes longer, skimming off any scum as it forms.

8. Add the final seasoning of salt, rice wine and pepper and shortly before serving add the transparent noodles, boil fast for 1 minute and turn off the heat. Serve very hot.

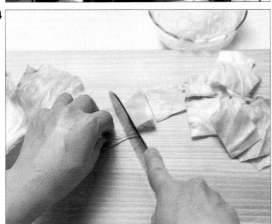

225

Cucumber and chicken soup

1 chicken wing
salt
rice wine or dry sherry
$\frac{1}{4}$ leek, sliced diagonally
small piece root ginger, shredded
1–1$\frac{1}{2}$ oz (25–40 g) transparent noodles
1 small cucumber ($\frac{1}{2}$ if large)
1$\frac{3}{4}$–2 pints (1–1$\frac{1}{4}$ litres) stock
a few drops of sesame seed oil
pinch of pepper
Calories 113; protein 4.1 g; fat 6.3 g; sugar 9.4 g

1. Set the bamboo steamer over boiling water. Place the chicken wing in a heatproof dish, sprinkle with 1 generous tsp salt and $\frac{1}{2}$ tbsp rice wine and top with the sliced leek and shreds of ginger. Place the dish in the bamboo steamer and steam for 15–20 minutes.

2. When the chicken is cooked, remove the skin and bones; tear the chicken flesh

1

2

3

4

5

6

into long, thin strips by hand; remove and discard the leek and ginger and pour the cooking juices which have collected into the stock.

3. Rinse the transparent noodles; place in a bowl and cover with boiling water.

Leave to soften for 5 minutes. Drain and cut into fairly short lengths.

4. Slice the cucumber diagonally into thin rounds, then cut each slice into thin strips.

5. Pour the stock into a deep saucepan, bring to the boil and add salt and rice wine to taste (the best stock should be used for this soup, made with chicken bones and wing-tips).

6. Add the noodles to the stock followed by the strips of chicken and the cucumber. Adjust the seasoning adding a few drops sesame seed oil and a pinch of pepper. Turn off the heat and serve.

Peking bean curd soup

1–2 cakes bean curd
3 slices belly of pork
3 dried Chinese winter mushrooms, pre-soaked
5 leaves Chinese cabbage
3½oz (100g) minced pork
2 tsp finely chopped leek
1 tsp grated root ginger
soy sauce
salt
pinch of pepper
pinch of monosodium glutamate
1 tsp sugar
a few canned gingko nuts
1 tbsp rice wine
1 scant tbsp cornflour
Calories 187; protein 12.5g; fat 11.5g; sugar 9.9g

1. Cut each cake of bean curd into 8 pieces; cut the belly pork into pieces 2in (5cm) long; drain the Chinese mushrooms, remove the stalks, quarter the caps and then cut obliquely into thin slices.

2. Cut the Chinese cabbage leaves lengthways in half, then into 2-in (5-cm) pieces and finally shred diagonally.

3. Place the minced pork in a bowl and add the chopped leek, grated ginger, ¼ tsp soy sauce, ¼ tsp salt, a pinch of monosodium glutamate and a pinch of pepper. Blend well to form a firm, smooth mixture. Shape into small balls.

4. Bring 2½ pints (1½ litres) water to the boil in a large flameproof casserole. Lower the pork balls into the boiling water, followed by the mushrooms and the pork. Cook for a while before adding 1 tbsp soy sauce, 1½ tsp salt, a pinch of monosodium glutamate, a pinch of pepper and the sugar. Then stir in the cabbage.

5. When the Chinese cabbage is just tender, adjust the seasoning if necessary; add the bean curd, gingko nuts, rice wine and cornflour mixed with 2 tbsp water and boil for a few moments longer.

6. Serve the soup straight away, while piping hot.

Bamboo shoot soup

A fairly thick soup which is served as a foil to rich, spicy dishes.

5 oz (150 g) boiled fresh or canned bamboo shoots
¾ pint (½ litre) stock
½ tsp salt
pinch of pepper
generous 1 tbsp rice wine or dry sherry
1 scant tsp cornflour
small bunch parsley, coarsely chopped
2–3 drops of peanut oil
2–3 drops of sesame seed oil
Calories 44; protein 1.4g; fat 2.6g; sugar 3.9g

1. Cut the bamboo shoots lengthways in half and then into thin slices, cutting out a comb pattern down the straight side for decorative effect (see picture).

2. Bring the stock to the boil in a large saucepan, add the bamboo shoots and when the stock returns to the boil, season with salt, pepper and rice wine; stir in the cornflour mixed with 1 tbsp water, to thicken.

3. Sprinkle with coarsely chopped parsley, quickly add the peanut oil and the sesame seed oil and turn off the heat.

Chicken soup

14oz (400g) Chinese white radish
10oz (300g) carrot
4in (10cm) length of leek
small piece root ginger
1¼lb (600g) chicken wings and legs
1¼ tsp salt
pinch of monosodium glutamate
pinch of pepper
1 tbsp rice wine or dry sherry
Calories 249; protein 23.7g; fat 12.1g; sugar 8.6g

1. Wash the white radish thoroughly and peel; cut lengthways in half and then into 2-in (5-cm) lengths. Round off all the edges to make evenly shaped pieces.

2. Wash the carrot well and cut in the same way as the white radish, but in smaller

1

2

3

4

5

6

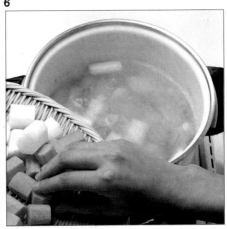

pieces. Cut the leek in half. Pound the ginger lightly with the flat of the cleaver.

3. Chop the chicken into portions about 1¼–1½ in (3–4cm) square; place in a bowl and cover with boiling water. Drain.

4. Use kitchen tweezers to pluck any remaining small feathers, quill roots etc. Rinse in cold water.

5. Place the chicken pieces in a large saucepan with the leek and ginger; pour in sufficient water to cover. As soon as the water has come to the boil, lower the heat and simmer for 20 minutes. Skim off any scum which forms.

6. When the chicken is nearly done, remove and discard the leek and ginger. Season with salt and monosodium glutamate, add the white radish and carrot, cook until these are tender and then season with pepper, the rice wine and a little more salt if necessary.

Bean curd and tomato soup

The contrast in colour and taste between the bean curd and tomatoes is brought out by the use of chili oil.

7oz (200g) belly of pork, thinly sliced
soy sauce
2 tsp rice wine or dry sherry
2 cakes bean curd
2 tomatoes
a little parsley
2 tbsp oil
1 tsp chili oil
pinch of monosodium glutamate
pinch of pepper
Calories 308; protein 11.4g; fat 24.4g; sugar 2.5g

1. Cut the slices of belly pork into 2-in (5-cm) lengths. Put into a bowl and sprinkle with 2 tsp soy sauce and the rice wine. Leave to marinate.

2. Cut each bean curd cake into 8 pieces; remove the stalks from the tomatoes and quarter or cut into 8 segments if large. Chop the parsley.

3. Heat the oil in the wok, add the marinated pork and stir-fry until lightly browned. Add the pieces of bean curd (handling them gently so that they do not break up), and the tomatoes and stir-fry briefly.

Add 2 tbsp soy sauce, the chili oil, monosodium glutamate and pepper and 4 fl oz (125 ml) hot water. As soon as the water comes to the boil, transfer carefully into a serving dish, sprinkle with parsley and serve.

Chinese cabbage and chicken soup

A whole chicken is simmered in this wholesome soup.

a boiling fowl weighing about 3lb (1.3kg)
1 small Chinese cabbage
2 tsp salt
pinch of monosodium glutamate
1 tbsp rice wine or dry sherry
pinch of pepper
Calories 378; protein 31.9g; fat 25.8g; sugar 2.2g
Serves 5–6

1. Clean the chicken, wash well in cold water and pour boiling water over the skin and inside the cavity to dislodge any remaining particles and loosen the quills. Pick off any stray quills with tweezers.

2. Place the chicken in a large, heavy flameproof casserole or saucepan, cover with water and bring to the boil over a high heat. As soon as the water has boiled, skim and turn down the heat. Simmer for about 40 minutes.

3. Remove and discard the outer leaves of the Chinese cabbage, until the cabbage is about 5in (12cm) wide. Cut in half and then slice each half into 4–6 pieces.

4. When the chicken is nearly done, season with salt, monosodium glutamate and rice wine, add the Chinese cabbage and cook until the chicken and cabbage are tender.

5. Transfer the chicken carefully into a flameproof serving dish, arrange the cabbage leaves around it and pour in the broth. Bring back to the boil, add a little pepper and serve very hot.

Five-colour soup

5 chicken wings
10 quails' eggs
1 tbsp soy sauce
oil for frying
10 scallops
2 oz (50 g) belly of pork, cut in 3 slices
3 dried Chinese winter mushrooms, pre-soaked
3½ oz (100 g) boiled fresh or canned bamboo shoots
4 leaves Chinese cabbage
½ leek
1½–2 oz (40–50 g) transparent noodles
1 tbsp peanut oil
1 tbsp rice wine or dry sherry
1¼ tsp salt
pinch of monosodium glutamate
pinch of pepper
Calories 434; protein 22.3 g; fat 35.4 g; sugar 6.7 g

1. Set the bamboo steamer over boiling water. Wash the chicken wings and chop in half, placing them in a heatproof dish together with the quails' eggs. Cook in the bamboo steamer for 5 minutes, then remove and shell the eggs. Drain the chicken well.

2. Sprinkle the chicken wings and eggs with 2 tsp soy sauce and mix well. Heat enough oil for deep-frying and fry the wings and eggs until they are golden brown.

3. Shell and trim the scallops and wash them thoroughly; chop the pork into strips 2–2½ in (5–6 cm) long.

4. Drain the Chinese mushrooms, remove the stalks and cut the caps obliquely into thin slices. Slice the bamboo shoots thinly.

5. Cut the Chinese cabbage leaves lengthways in half, then into 2-in (5-cm) pieces and finally slice diagonally into thin strips. Cut the leek into 1¼-in (3-cm) lengths.

6. Place the transparent noodles in a bowl, cover with boiling water and when soft, drain and snip into 5-in (12-cm) lengths.

7. Heat the peanut oil in the wok and stir-fry the leek until it releases its aroma; sprinkle with 1 tsp soy sauce and with the rice wine; once these are warmed through, add 2 pints (1.1 litres) boiling water.

8. Line the bottom of flameproof casserole with the cabbage leaves; place all the ingredients except for the scallops on the cabbage leaves, pour the stock slowly into the casserole and season with salt and monosodium glutamate.

9. As soon as the soup has come to the boil, lower the heat and simmer until all the ingredients are nearly done, add the scallops and cook for a few minutes only, season with pepper and serve.

Eight-treasure soup

14oz (400g) chicken wings
12 dried Chinese winter mushrooms, pre-soaked
2 sheets dried bean curd
10oz (300g) taro root
3½oz (100g) carrot
small quantity spinach
a few gingko nuts
a few dried lily bud stems, pre-soaked
4 tbsp cornflour
a little mustard
For the marinade:
1 tsp soy sauce
1 tsp rice wine or dry sherry
1 tsp sesame seed oil
¼ tsp salt
pinch of monosodium glutamate
pinch of pepper
Flavourings for the stock:
4 tbsp soy sauce
scant 2 tbsp sugar
2 tbsp rice wine or dry sherry
2 generous tsp salt
pinch monosodium glutamate
Calories 385; protein 23.8g; fat 20.4g; sugar 30.3g

1. Chop the chicken into fairly generous pieces and sprinkle with the marinade. Mix and leave to stand.

2. Drain the mushrooms, remove the stalks and cut the caps into thin slices.

3. Soak the dried bean curd in several changes of hot water and cut each sheet into 6 pieces.

4. Peel the taro root and cut into ½-in (1-cm) slices.

5. Cut evenly spaced grooves lengthwise into the outside of the carrot and slice into ¼-in (5-mm) rounds to form flower-shapes. Blanch the spinach for a few seconds in boiling water, drain and cut into 1½-in (4-cm) lengths.

6. Shell the gingko nuts, boil in slightly salted water and peel off the thin inner skin (or use the shelled canned variety). Drain the lily bud stems and trim; tie each stem in a knot.

7. Bring 3¼ pints (1¾ litres) water to the boil in a flameproof casserole. Add the flavourings for the stock, the Chinese mushrooms, taro root, carrots and the dried bean curd. Simmer for about 10 minutes. Coat the chicken wings with cornflour and add to the stock with the gingko nuts and the lily bud stems.

8. Simmer for 1–2 minutes, adjust the seasoning and add the spinach. Serve, using a little mustard for extra flavour.

Beef and white radish soup

A substantial, thick soup which needs lengthy cooking and can be served as a main course; its robust flavour goes well with boiled rice.

14oz (400g) flank of beef
1¼lb (600g) Chinese white radish
7oz (200g) carrots
½–1 leek
small piece root ginger
1 clove garlic
1–2 chili peppers
2 tbsp oil
1 tsp salt
pinch of pepper
pinch of monosodium glutamate
For the sauce:
1–2 tsp hot black bean paste
2 tbsp hoisin sauce
2 tsp sugar
3 tbsp soy sauce
Calories 379; protein 22.2g; fat 23.2g; sugar 18.9g

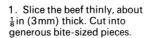

1. Slice the beef thinly, about ⅛in (3mm) thick. Cut into generous bite-sized pieces.

2. Peel the Chinese white radish and slice diagonally using the rolling cut technique (see p. 306); cut the carrot in the same way.

1

2

3

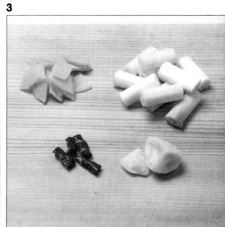

4

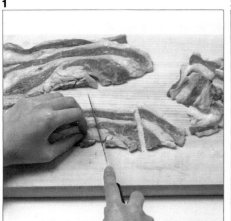

5

6

3. Cut the leek into 1¼–1½-in (3–4-cm) lengths; slice the ginger finely and pound the garlic with the flat of the cleaver. Cut the chili peppers in half and remove the seeds.

4. Heat the oil in the wok and stir-fry the garlic over a moderate heat until it releases its aroma; add the leek and the ginger and stir-fry well. Add the chili peppers and the beef.

5. Turn up the heat and stir-fry until the beef has changed colour. Blend the sauce ingredients in a bowl, pour over the beef and stir-fry until the ingredients are golden brown.

6. Place the carrot and Chinese white radish in a flameproof casserole, spoon the beef mixture on top and fill with hot water almost to the rim of the dish. Season with salt, pepper and monosodium glutamate and cook for 1 hour or more over a low heat, until the beef is very tender.

Pork and vegetable soup

A straightforward recipe; the soy sauce and vinegar counteract the rich, rather fat pork.

7oz (200g) belly of pork
10oz (300g) Chinese white radish
14oz (400g) Chinese cabbage
1 tsp salt
pinch of monosodium glutamate
1 tbsp rice wine or dry sherry
pinch of pepper
wine or cider vinegar
soy sauce
Calories 201; protein 9.2g; fat 15.6g; sugar 4.8g

1. Place the piece of pork in a deep saucepan, cover with water and bring to the boil.

2. Lower the heat as soon as the water has boiled and simmer for about 15 minutes. Drain and cool; cut into thin slices. Strain the cooking liquid and reserve.

3. Peel the white radish and slice into 2½-in (6-cm) lengths; cut these pieces into rectangles 1 in (2½ cm) long and ⅛ in (3 mm) thick.

4. Cut the Chinese cabbage lengthways in half and then into 2½-in (6-cm) lengths.

5. Pour the reserved stock into a large saucepan and bring to the boil, season with the salt and monosodium glutamate, add the Chinese white radish and cook for about 5 minutes; add the Chinese cabbage and simmer for 5 minutes more.

6. When the vegetables are tender, sprinkle the pieces of pork into the soup; season with rice wine and pepper and serve at once. Serve with a mixture of vinegar and soy sauce for each person to add as desired.

Pork and mushroom soup with quails' eggs

1¼ lb (600 g) belly of pork
5 dried Chinese winter mushrooms. pre-soaked
2 leaves dried seaweed (kombu variety) each about 12 in (30 cm) long
7 oz (200 g) boiled fresh or canned bamboo shoots
15–20 quails' eggs
6 fl oz (175 ml) soy sauce
1 tbsp rice wine or dry sherry
pinch of monosodium glutamate
Calories 719; protein 33.1 g; fat 16.4 g; sugar 10.2 g

1. Dice the pork into pieces about ¾ in (2 cm) square; place in a large saucepan or flameproof casserole.

2. Drain the Chinese mushrooms, remove the stalks and cut the caps in half or quarters; slice diagonally into slivers. Reserve the water in which the mushrooms were soaked.

3. Wipe the seaweed leaves with a damp cloth and add to the pork. Pour in 2 pints (1.1 litres) water and the reserved mushroom liquid; bring to the boil.

4. Once the water has boiled, turn down the heat and cook slowly until the pork is so tender that it can be pierced easily with chopsticks. Remove the seaweed when soft.

5. Set the bamboo steamer over boiling water. Cut the bamboo shoots lengthways into quarters then slice diagonally into irregular pieces. Place the quails' eggs on a plate in the bamboo steamer and steam for 5 minutes; shell. Cut the seaweed into strips and knot each strip.

6. Add the soy sauce, rice wine and monosodium glutamate to the soup, followed by the mushrooms, bamboo shoots, seaweed and quails' eggs, boil for a few seconds and then reduce the heat; simmer until all the ingredients are well-coloured and have absorbed the soy sauce and other flavourings. Add a little water if the mixture becomes too dry.

7. Transfer the pork and vegetables with a slotted spoon to a serving dish and pour in the liquid.

239

Chinese cabbage and pork soup

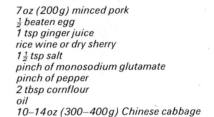

7oz (200g) minced pork
½ beaten egg
1 tsp ginger juice
rice wine or dry sherry
1½ tsp salt
pinch of monosodium glutamate
pinch of pepper
2 tbsp cornflour
oil
10–14oz (300–400g) Chinese cabbage
½ leek
small piece root ginger
½ tbsp soy sauce
Calories 208; protein 11.1 g; fat 14.5g; sugar 6.7g

1. Place the pork in a bowl, and add the beaten egg, ginger juice, 1 tsp rice wine, ½ tsp salt, pinch of monosodium glutamate, pinch of pepper, 2 tbsp water, and the cornflour. Mix until smooth and well blended. In order to achieve a very dense mixture, gather the meat in one hand and slap against the inside of the bowl several times; mix and knead well once more.

1

2

3

4

5

6

2. Oil a plate very lightly, place the meat on it and press out into a large patty about ½ in (1 cm) thick using a wooden or plastic spatula rinsed in cold water.

3. Cut across the Chinese cabbage, slicing it into pieces ½ in (1 cm) wide; cut the leek into rings ¼ in (5mm) thick, peel the ginger and cut into thin slivers.

4. Heat 1 tbsp oil in the wok; stir-fry the leek and ginger and when they start to release their aromas, add the soy sauce and 1 tbsp rice wine, followed by 1¾ pints (1 litre) water.

5. Season with 1 tsp salt and a pinch of monosodium glutamate, add the Chinese cabbage and slide the pork patty carefully on top.

6. Cover and cook over a gentle heat for about 10 minutes; adjust the seasoning and sprinkle with freshly ground pepper. Transfer all the ingredients carefully to a flameproof casserole; bring to boiling point and serve.

Fish balls in broth

A mixture of fish balls and slices of fish in a clear soup; a light and digestible dish.

7oz (200g) swordfish (if not available, use any firm white fish such as halibut)
salt
pepper
7oz (200g) raw, flaked white fish
rice wine or dry sherry
*1 bunch Chinese spring chrysanthemum flowers (*not *the normal garden variety), (optional)*
1 stick celery
scant 2½ pints (1½ litres) stock
pinch of monosodium glutamate
Calories 161; protein 24.5g; fat 2.9g; sugar 7.8g

1. Pound the swordfish lightly with the flat of the cleaver blade; cut into rectangular pieces ½in (1 cm) by ¾in (2cm) and ½in (1 cm) thick. Season lightly with salt and pepper.

2. If the flaked fish is dry, soften with a little rice wine and water. Put in a dish with the swordfish cover and leave in the refrigerator for about 6 hours.

3. Tear the chrysanthemum flowers into small pieces by hand; remove the strings from the celery and slice thinly.

4. Shape the minced fish into small balls. Pour the stock into a large saucepan or flameproof casserole, season with 2 tsp salt and a pinch of monosodium glutamate and once it has come to the boil, add the fish balls and sliced swordfish.

5. When the fish rises to the surface add the celery and chrysanthemum flowers; season with pepper and 1 tbsp rice wine.

MONGOLIAN HOT POT COOKING

The Mongolian hot pot is a legacy of the ancient northern Chinese custom of using a stove for the dual purpose of cooking food and providing warmth for their dwellings, lashed by the icy northern winds during the freezing winter evenings.

A table ready-prepared for a Huo Kuo or "Fire Pot" meal is one of the most enchanting and welcoming sights imaginable. In the centre of the table is a great pot of shining brass. It has a chimney full of red-hot, glowing coals, and hot, flavoursome broth steaming in the surrounding moat. All around, numerous dishes are placed, on which various raw meats, fish and vegetables are elegantly set out, all cut into small slivers which will cook quickly in the simmering broth. Several different kinds of sauces are placed around the table.

Each person cooks his or her own food by holding the delicious morsels in the broth with chopsticks, "rinsing" the food as the Chinese call it, and sipping some of the strong wines or spirits of the north as they do so. The recipes overleaf are adaptations of the hot pot method in that the food is pre-cooked and merely kept hot in the broth as it simmers gently in the bowl of the hot pot.

Huo Kuo

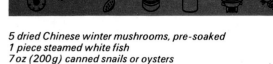

14oz (400g) minced pork
3 eggs
2 tbsp finely chopped leek
salt
pinch of monosodium glutamate
pinch of pepper
oil for frying
cornflour

5 dried Chinese winter mushrooms, pre-soaked
1 piece steamed white fish
7oz (200g) canned snails or oysters
2 cakes fried bean curd
½ a large Chinese cabbage
transparent noodles
gingko nuts
scant 2½ pints (1½ litres) stock
1 tbsp rice wine or dry sherry
Calories 479; protein 29.1; fat 33.9g; sugar 14.1g

1. Mix the minced pork in a bowl with 1 egg, the chopped leek, ½ tsp salt, a pinch of monosodium glutamate and a pinch of pepper. Mix by hand until smooth and well blended.

2. Use three-quarters of this mixture to shape small balls 1 in (2½ cm) in diameter. Heat enough oil for deep-frying until very hot; carefully lower in the meat balls then turn off the heat immediately. Wait 3 minutes and then turn on the heat again. Fry briskly.

3. Set the bamboo steamer over boiling water. Beat 2 eggs well with a pinch of salt and 1 tbsp cornflour dissolved in 1 tbsp water. Heat a little oil in a frying pan and fry the egg mixture to make a very thin rectangular omelette, rather like a pancake, measuring 6 × 8 in (15 × 20 cm). Place

1

2

3

4

5

6

the omelette on a board and spread the remaining minced meat mixture carefully over it; sprinkle with a little more salt and monosodium glutamate and then with 4 tbsp cornflour. Roll up and steam for 8 minutes; cut into slices.

4. Drain the mushrooms. Remove the stalks and slice the caps thinly. Cut the fish into several pieces. Drain the canned snails or, if oysters are to be used, clean well. Blanch the fried bean curd in boiling water for 1 minute. Drain and cut into slices.

5. Boil the Chinese cabbage in salted water; chop into pieces 1½ in (4cm) wide; soften the noodles in boiling water, drain and cut into 4½-in (12-cm) lengths. Boil the gingko nuts and peel off the thin inner skin or use canned nuts.

6. Line the bottom of the hot pot with the cabbage. Arrange the other ingredients as shown on facing page, pour over the cooking stock and add 2 tsp salt, a pinch of pepper and the rice wine. Simmer until all ingredients are tender.

Seafood hot pot

1 whole white fish (such as bream, porgy or carp) or 10 oz
(300 g) sliced fish
5 large prawns
1 squid
10 clams
3½ oz (100 g) belly of pork
10 oz (300 g) Chinese white radish
1 leek
small piece root ginger
petals of Chinese spring chrysanthemum flowers (not the
    normal garden variety)
1 tbsp peanut oil
1 tbsp rice wine or dry sherry
2 tsp salt
pinch of monosodium glutamate
pinch of pepper
wine vinegar
soy sauce
Calories 325; protein 42.8 g; fat 13.8 g; sugar 4.8 g

1. De-scale and gut the fish; cut away the gills. Cut in half by running a knife down the backbone and work both sides away from the bones. Cut into bite-sized pieces. Reserve the head.

2. Slit the prawns down their backs to de-vein but do not remove the shells. Clean the squid; remove head, ink sac and central bone, rub off the skin, slit and open out; score the inside in a lattice pattern and then cut into small pieces. Rinse the clams completely free of sand in several changes of water.

3. Cut the pork into 2-in (5-cm) pieces.

4. Peel the Chinese white radish, cut into pieces 1 in (2.5 cm) wide, 2 in (5 cm) long and ¼ in (5 mm) thick.

5. Slice the leek diagonally into 1-in (2½-cm) sections; slice the ginger thinly (chop 1 slice and reserve for the dipping sauce); wash the chrysanthemum flowers and pluck off the petals.

6. Heat the peanut oil in the wok and stir-fry the leek and the ginger. Sprinkle with rice wine and pour in scant 2½ pints (1½ litres) hot water. Add the pork and Chinese white radish and season with salt and monosodium glutamate; cook until the vegetables are quite tender.

7. Transfer to the hot pot or flameproof casserole, bring back to the boil and add the fish (including the head) and clams followed by the prawns and squid. Add the chrysanthemum petals; sprinkle with a pinch of pepper and serve. Pass round soy sauce mixed with wine vinegar and finely chopped ginger as a dipping sauce.

RICE DISHES

When one Chinese person meets another the customary greeting is: "Chueh fan mei-yu?" – literally, "Eat rice? Yes? No?", rather like the automatic rhetorical question in English "How do you do?" or the more commonly used "How are you?" The Chinese phrase reveals the fundamental importance of rice in the everyday life of millions of Chinese.

Rice has been a staple food in China for over 4,000 years. There is a vast number of different varieties of rice grown in China – some say as many as 7,000, but this is certainly an exaggeration. The polishing of rice is an ancient custom: 2,500 years ago Confucius wrote that rice should be clean and white. When cooked, the rice grains should be fluffy and separate, and the knowledgeable Chinese cook will take great care to wash the rice very thoroughly beforehand (thus, incidentally, removing some of its nutritional value). Only certain varieties, such as glutinous rice, with its short, round grains, should be sticky; it is used for special dishes, puddings and desserts.

In the recipes in this section, it should be noted that unless otherwise stated or where the recipe obviously calls for uncooked rice, the weights given are for cooked rice. As a very approximate guide, uncooked rice yields roughly two-and-a-half times its uncooked weight, absorbing a great deal of water as it cooks.

Yangchow fried rice

3–4 dried Chinese winter mushrooms, pre-soaked
sugar
soy sauce
sesame seed oil
3½oz (100g) prawns
1 egg white
2 tsp cornflour
oil for frying
5oz (150g) boneless chicken breast
1½lb (700g) cooked rice
5oz (150g) cold roast pork
3oz (75g) shelled peas
2 eggs
2 tsp salt
pinch of pepper
1–2 tbsp rice wine or dry sherry
Calories 784; protein 44.6g; fat 20.2g; sugar 100.5g

1. Drain the mushrooms, remove the stalks and chop into pieces $\frac{1}{2}$ in (1 cm) square. Sprinkle with a mixture of a little sugar, soy sauce and sesame seed oil.

2. Wash the prawns (if raw) and shell; de-vein with a cocktail stick, mix with $\frac{1}{2}$ egg white and 1 tsp cornflour by hand. Heat enough oil for deep-frying to 250°F (120°C), add the prawns and fry lightly. Drain.

3. Cut the chicken into $\frac{1}{2}$-in (1-cm) dice, mix with the other $\frac{1}{2}$ egg white and 1 tsp cornflour by hand and fry in the hot oil taking care that the pieces do not stick to one another. Drain and clean out the wok.

4. Cut the pork into $\frac{1}{2}$-in (1-cm) dice. If frozen peas are used, cover with boiling water and then drain well. If fresh peas are used, boil in lightly salted water.

5. Heat 1–2 tbsp oil in the wok; pour in the beaten eggs, stir and when cooked, cut into pieces about $\frac{1}{2}$ in (1 cm) square. Drain.

6. Clean the wok again and heat 3–4 tbsp fresh oil. Add the mushrooms, pork, prawns and the chicken. Stir-fry over a moderate heat and season with 1 tsp salt.

7. When these ingredients have absorbed the oil and salt, add the cooked rice (which should be tender but firm); mix and turn thoroughly to prevent it sticking.

8. Add the peas and the cooked egg and season with the remaining salt and a pinch of pepper; sprinkle with rice wine and stir-fry over a high heat, taking care that the rice does not stick and that the grains remain separate.

Five-colour fried rice

A delicious dish which can be prepared quickly and served to special guests.

3 dried Chinese winter mushrooms, pre-soaked
2oz (50g) cooked ham
3½oz (100g) pork
1 leek
1–2 tbsp cooked peas
2 eggs
salt
monosodium glutamate
oil
2 tsp soy sauce
pinch of pepper
1¾lb (800g) cooked rice
Calories 617; protein 19.3g; fat 30.3g; sugar 84.2g

1. Drain the mushrooms, remove the stalks and cut the caps into $\frac{1}{4}$-in (5-mm) squares; dice the ham and pork to the same size, chop the leek finely. Shell the prawns and chop into $\frac{1}{4}$-in (5-mm) pieces.

2. Beat the eggs and season with a pinch each of salt and monosodium glutamate; heat 1 tbsp oil in the wok; pour in the eggs and cook, stirring to scramble; set aside on a plate.

3. Wipe the wok and heat 2 tbsp fresh oil; stir-fry the mushrooms gently over a moderate heat until their full aroma is released.

4. Add the pork and stir-fry, stirring to keep the pieces from sticking to one another; when the pork has changed colour, add the prawns and the ham. Fry lightly.

5. Once the prawns have changed colour (if raw) or have heated through if pre-cooked, pour in the soy sauce, trickling it in down the side of the wok. Give the soy sauce time to flavour the other ingredients, stirring and turning, and then season with a pinch each monosodium glutamate and pepper. Remove the mixture from the wok and set aside.

6. Clean the wok, pour in 4 tbsp fresh oil and heat; stir-fry the leek to flavour the oil but do not allow to brown.

7. Add the rice and stir-fry over a moderate heat, stirring and turning continuously, taking care not to crush the rice grains. Season with $\frac{1}{2}$ tsp salt and a pinch of monosodium glutamate.

8. When the rice is well mixed and coated with oil, add the reserved meat and prawn mixture and stir-fry; add the scrambled egg and peas and mix once more before serving.

251

Fried rice with smoked salmon and chicken

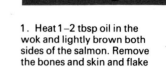

The smoked salmon imparts an original and enjoyable flavour to this rice dish.

4 fl oz (125 ml) oil
3½–5 oz (100–150 g) smoked salmon
3½ oz (100 g) boneless chicken breast
Marinade for chicken:
¼ tsp salt
pinch of monosodium glutamate
pinch of pepper
1 tsp rice wine or dry sherry
½ tsp cornflour
2 eggs
salt
3–4 lettuce leaves
2 tbsp finely chopped leek
1¾ lb (800 g) cooked rice
Calories 619; protein 23.1; fat 28.5 g; sugar 64.7 g

1. Heat 1–2 tbsp oil in the wok and lightly brown both sides of the salmon. Remove the bones and skin and flake finely. Shred the chicken and sprinkle with the marinade.

2. Beat the eggs, season with salt and monosodium glutamate; cut the lettuce into ¼-in (5-mm) strips.

3. Heat 1 tbsp oil in the wok; pour in the eggs and mix with chopsticks or a fork so that the eggs will scramble into small pieces. Set aside on a plate. Wipe the wok and pour in 2 tbsp oil; stir-fry the chicken and when cooked, remove from the wok and set aside.

4. Clean the wok and heat 3 tbsp fresh oil. Stir-fry the chopped leek without allowing it to colour, add the rice and stir-fry, mixing gently but thoroughly. Add the salmon and chicken; and stir-fry. Season to taste with salt, pepper and monosodium glutamate.

5. Finally mix in the eggs and lettuce and stir-fry briefly before serving.

Curried fried rice with prawns

7 oz (200 g) shelled prawns, raw or pre-cooked
salt
Marinade for the prawns:
1 tsp rice wine or dry sherry
pinch of salt
pinch of monosodium glutamate
½ tsp cornflour
4 dried Chinese winter mushrooms, pre-soaked
1 small onion
1–2 tbsp shelled peas
5 tbsp oil
1 tbsp Chinese curry powder
1 tbsp soy sauce
1¾ lb (800 g) cooked rice
Calories 282; protein 13.2 g; fat 18 g; sugar 67.7 g

1. De-vein the prawns, soak for a short time in salted water in the proportion of 1 tsp salt to 16 fl oz (½ litre) water. Drain and pat dry and mix with the marinade.

2. Drain the mushrooms, remove the stalks and cut the caps into ½-in (1-cm) dice. Dice the onion to the same size and boil the peas in lightly salted water.

3. Heat 1 tbsp oil in the wok and stir-fry the prawns briskly, removing from the wok when just heated through.

4. Heat 1 tbsp fresh oil in the wok and stir-fry the mushrooms for a few seconds, then set aside.

5. Clean the wok, heat 3 tbsp oil and stir-fry the onion until transparent and soft; lower the heat and add the curry powder; cook, stirring for 2 minutes. Return the mushrooms to the wok and stir-fry gently. Trickle the soy sauce in down the side of the wok; once this is thoroughly warmed through, add the rice and stir-fry, stirring and turning gently but thoroughly.

6. Finally, add the prawns and peas and distribute evenly before serving.

Pai fan (boiled rice)

As with all the preceding recipes, long grain rice should be used; its low starch content means that the grains should not stick to one another.

1 lb (500g) uncooked Chinese, long grain rice
½ tsp peanut oil or corn oil (optional)
Calories 359; protein 7.5g; fat 0.8g; sugar 85.6g
Serves 4–6

1. Place the rice in a sieve and rinse under fast-running cold water.

2. Place the rice in a flame-proof casserole or saucepan and add water – 1¼ times the volume of the rice (in this case about 16 fl oz (½ litre)); ½ tsp oil may be added at this stage, which decreases the chances of the rice boiling over.

3. Bring to the boil over a medium-high heat. When the water bubbles up, stir once with a fork to distribute the rice grains and help prevent lumping. Cover and cook for 1 minute before reducing the heat to low. Simmer for 10 minutes.

4. Turn off the heat and leave to finish cooking with the retained heat for 10–12 minutes longer. The rice is done when the grains are dry and separate and if there are small holes or depressions in the surface of the rice (these are known as "fish's eyes").

Pork chops with boiled rice

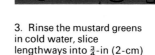

4 slices loin of pork, weighing about 3½ oz (100g) each
7 oz (200g) Chinese salted mustard greens
4 eggs
small piece root ginger
1½–1¾ lb (700–800g) hot cooked rice
4 tbsp oil
For the marinade:
4 tbsp soy sauce
2 tbsp sugar
1 tbsp rice wine or dry sherry
For the sauce:
2 tsp soy sauce
1 tsp sugar
1 tsp wine vinegar
Calories 695; protein 33g; fat 28.7g; sugar 72.2g

1. Pound the pork with the flat of the cleaver; make small cuts where there is any fat or gristle (or the meat will curl when cooked).

2. Mix the marinade ingredients, sprinkle over the pork, stir and turn to distribute evenly and leave for about 20 minutes.

3. Rinse the mustard greens in cold water, slice lengthways into ¾-in (2-cm) strips and then into small pieces.

4. Hard-boil the eggs and peel. Shred the ginger.

5. Heat 2 tbsp oil in the wok. Fry the drained pork on both sides so that it is well browned, pour in the reserved marinade and add the hard-boiled eggs. Cook, stirring and turning until the outsides of the eggs are lightly coloured. Pour in 8 fl oz (225 ml) hot water, reduce the heat to moderate and cook for about 10 minutes, mixing from time to time so that the ingredients colour evenly.

6. Heat 2 tbsp oil in another pan or skillet and stir-fry the ginger and then add the mustard greens. Stir-fry and add the sauce ingredients.

7. Arrange the boiled rice in the serving dish and top with the vegetables, pork and the halved eggs. Sprinkle with the liquid left in the wok.

Boiled rice with pork and vegetables

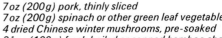

Served piping hot, this dish can provide a meal in itself; best accompanied by hot green tea or a light vegetable broth.

7oz (200g) pork, thinly sliced
7oz (200g) spinach or other green leaf vegetable
4 dried Chinese winter mushrooms, pre-soaked
3½oz (100g) fresh boiled or canned bamboo shoots
1 scant tbsp cornflour
2 tsp sugar
pinch of monosodium glutamate
pinch of pepper
4 tbsp oil
¼ tsp salt
2 tbsp soy sauce
1 tbsp rice wine or dry sherry
1½–1¾lb (700–800g) hot cooked rice
For the marinade:
2 tsp soy sauce
2 tsp rice wine or dry sherry
1 tsp sugar
1 tsp cornflour
Calories 527; protein 17.8g; fat 17.6g; sugar 73.5g

1. Cut the pork into bite-sized pieces, mix with the marinade and leave to stand. Wash the spinach, cut into pieces 2 in (5 cm) wide and leave in cold water to crisp.

2. Drain the mushrooms, remove the stalks and slice the

1

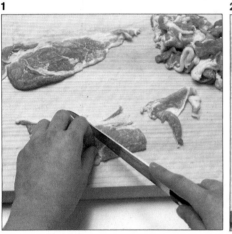

2

3

4

5

6

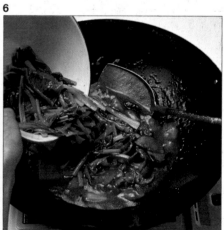

caps thinly. Slice the bamboo shoots thinly.

3. Mix 8 floz (225ml) water with the cornflour, sugar, monosodium glutamate and pepper in a bowl.

4. Heat 1½ tbsp oil in the wok, add the drained spinach with the salt and a very little water and stir-fry. Drain and set aside.

5. Heat 2½ tbsp oil in the wok and stir-fry the mushrooms. Add the pork and when the meat has changed colour, add the bamboo shoots; sprinkle with the soy sauce and rice wine.

6. Pour the mixture prepared in step 3 into the wok and when it has come to the boil add the spinach and cook, stirring and turning, until the sauce thickens; place on top of the hot boiled rice.

Rice with beef and eggs

3½oz (100g) prime lean beef, thinly sliced
6 eggs
¼ tsp salt
pinch of monosodium glutamate
pinch of pepper
1 leek
1 tbsp soy sauce
4 tbsp oil
1½–1¾lb (700–800g) hot cooked rice
¾ pint (½ litre) oil for deep frying
For the marinade:
½ tsp ginger juice
½ tsp sugar
½ tbsp rice wine or dry sherry
½ tsp baking powder or ¼ tsp dried yeast and ¼ tsp bicarbonate of
  soda
1 tbsp cornflour
Calories 676; protein 19.4g; fat 35.1g; sugar 67.7g

1. Cut the slices of beef into 1-in (2½-cm) pieces, mix with the marinade and leave to stand for about 30 minutes.

2. Beat the eggs and season with the salt, monosodium glutamate and pepper.

3. Slice the leek into ¼-in (5-mm) rings.

4. Mix the marinated meat with the soy sauce and 1 tbsp oil just before frying.

5. Heat the oil for deep-frying to 325°F (160°C). Drain the beef and add to the oil; lower the temperature and deep-fry the beef taking care that the pieces do not stick to one another. Once the beef has changed colour, remove, drain and add to the beaten egg.

6. Heat 3 tbsp oil in the wok, stir-fry the leek gently, then add the beaten eggs and meat; fry over a high heat until the bottom of the egg is set and the upper portion has thickened. Turn off the heat.

7. Place the hot rice in the serving dish and arrange the beef and egg on top.

Savoury rice

1 dried squid
1 tsp bicarbonate of soda
7oz (200g) pork, thinly sliced
4 dried Chinese winter mushrooms, pre-soaked
3 tbsp Chinese dried prawns
2oz (50g) Chinese sausage (or any dense, savoury sausage, preferably pork)
1 leek
small bunch parsley
1 egg
pinch of salt
pinch of monosodium glutamate
5 tbsp lard or oil
4 tbsp soy sauce
pinch of pepper
1¾lb (850g) uncooked long grain rice
Calories 948; protein 43.6g; fat 30g; sugar 121.7g

1. Soften the dried squid by soaking in ¾ pint (½ litre) water and the bicarbonate of soda overnight.

2. Cut the pork into ½-in (1-cm) squares; drain the mushrooms, remove the stalks and cut the caps into ½-in (1-cm) squares. Cut the squid into ½-in (1-cm) strips and then into small pieces. Rinse the prawns and drain.

3. Slice the sausage lengthways into 6–8 strips and then into small pieces; slice the leek finely and chop the parsley.

4. Beat the egg and season lightly with salt and monosodium glutamate; cook 1 or 2 thin omelettes and cut into thin strips.

5. Heat the lard in the wok; stir-fry the mushrooms for a few seconds, add the prawns and fry until they are heated through. Add the leek, pork, squid and sausage and fry, stirring and turning; sprinkle with soy sauce, monosodium glutamate and pepper.

6. Put the rice in a saucepan, add an equal volume of water and cook as directed on page 254. When nearly done top with the contents of the wok, including the liquid; continue cooking until the rice is tender. Turn off the heat, cover and leave to stand for a short while. Mix and transfer to the serving bowl, topping with the strips of omelette and the parsley.

Congee rice with taro root

This rice gruel is eaten for breakfast or as a snack at any time of day. Served with pickled and salted green vegetables, the bland rice contrasts well with their strong taste.

4 tbsp Chinese dried prawns
1 leek
4 dried Chinese winter mushrooms, pre-soaked
5 oz (150 g) pork
10 oz (300 g) taro root
3–4 tbsp peanut oil
11 oz (325 g) short grain rice
$3\frac{1}{4}$–4 pints ($1\frac{3}{4}$–$2\frac{1}{4}$ litres) stock or water
1–2 tsp salt
1 tbsp rice wine or dry sherry
pinch of pepper
$\frac{1}{2}$ tsp sesame seed oil
Calories 515; protein 13.6 g; fat 21.9 g; sugar 64.9 g

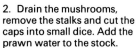

1. Wash the rice in a sieve under cold running water until the water runs clear. Drain. Wash the dried prawns and drain well. Reserve the water used. Chop the leek finely.

2. Drain the mushrooms, remove the stalks and cut the caps into small dice. Add the prawn water to the stock.

3. Peel the taro root, dice, and boil briefly to remove the stickiness. Dice the pork to the same size.

4. Heat the peanut oil in the wok, stir-fry the leek and prawns over a low heat, until both release their aroma.

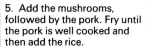

5. Add the mushrooms, followed by the pork. Fry until the pork is well cooked and then add the rice.

6. Stir and turn the rice well so that the grains are coated with oil. Transfer to a large, heavy saucepan; pour in the stock, bring to the boil, skim and then lower the heat.

7. Season with salt and rice wine; cover and cook for 20–30 minutes, stirring every now and then. Add the taro root.

8. Cook, still covered, for about 1 hour longer over a low heat, stirring every now and then, bringing the rice from the bottom of the pan up to the top. If the rice tastes too bland, add a little salt. Season with a pinch of pepper and a few drops of seasame seed oil. The rice should look rather like porridge and be thick but soft.

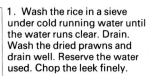

Congee rice with chicken

A complete meal or snack in itself. Congee rice is a Chinese national standby, equally popular at breakfast, midday or evening. Some eating houses specialise in various types of Congee rice, with chicken, as in this recipe, or the more choice varieties with abalone, gilt-head bream, prawns and crab.

7 oz (200 g) chicken breast
small piece root ginger
1 leek
1 dried scallop
1 lb (450 g) short grain rice
pinch of salt
pinch of monosodium glutamate
4 eggs
4 tsp soy sauce
4 tsp sesame seed oil
Calories 496; protein 22.1 g; fat 19.7 g; sugar 54.4 g

1. Bring 2 pints (1¼ litres) water to the boil; add the chicken and simmer until well done, removing any scum which forms.

2. Drain the cooked chicken and allow to cool until it can be handled; cut into ½-in (1-cm) dice and strain the stock.

3. Slice the ginger thinly and then shred; cut the leek into 2-in (5-cm) sections; slit these sections open so the layers can be opened out; cut into fine strips.

4. Soak the scallop in boiling water to allow it to soften and swell; tear into small shreds by hand; reserve the water used for soaking.

5. Wash the rice well in running water, drain and place in a heavy saucepan with the scallop and 4 pints (2¼ litres) liquid made up from the chicken stock, scallop water and, if necessary, a little more water. Bring to the boil and then reduce the heat.

6. Cook for about 30 minutes, stirring from time to time. Season with salt and monosodium glutamate, add the chicken and cook for a further 10–15 minutes. By this time the rice should be very soft.

7. Break an egg into each individual bowl and top with a few strips each of ginger and leek; add 1 tsp soy sauce and a couple of drops sesame seed oil to each bowl.

8. Ladle the boiling rice into the bowls and serve immediately, providing each person with a Chinese spoon with which to mix and eat the rice.

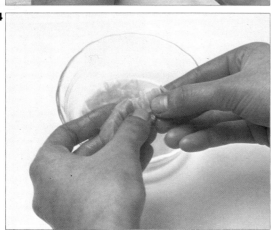

263

Fukien glutinous rice

This special round rice is creamy white and resembles seed pearls when uncooked; it has a sticky texture when cooked and is best accompanied by hot tea or a light vegetable broth.

2¼ lb (1.1 kg) glutinous rice
7 oz (200 g) fresh, unsalted, untoasted peanuts
2 oz (50 g) dried Chinese winter mushrooms
1 lb (500 g) pork
1 leek
2 oz (50 g) Chinese dried prawns
10 tablespoons oil
soy sauce
monosodium glutamate
pinch of pepper
small bunch parsley, finely chopped
sweet pickled ginger if desired
Calories 538; protein 20.5 g; fat 29.6 g; sugar 95.6 g
Serves 8–10

1. Wash the glutinous rice thoroughly and leave to soak in cold water overnight; drain. Boil the peanuts in water until tender, rinse in cold water and drain.

2. Soak the mushrooms in water for 20 minutes, remove the stalks and cut the caps into fairly wide strips approx. 1 in (2½ cm) long. Cut the meat into strips the same size. Slice the leek into thin rings. Wash the prawns and drain.

3. Heat 5 tbsp oil in the wok to medium-hot. Add the rice and fry, mixing and turning so that each grain is coated with oil. Add the peanuts.

4. Pour in 5 tbsp soy sauce and continue to fry, stirring and turning so that the rice colours evenly.

5. Set the bamboo steamer over boiling water; line it with a damp piece of cheesecloth and sprinkle the rice over the cloth, poking small holes at intervals to allow the steam to circulate freely. Cook over rapidly boiling water for about 1 hour; top up with boiling wated when necessary.

6. Heat 5 tbsp oil in the wok. Stir-fry the mushrooms for a few seconds, push to one side of the pan and stir-fry the prawns and leek in turn.

7. When the leek is lightly browned, mix in the prawns and mushrooms again, add soy sauce, and the pork, followed by a pinch each of monosodium glutamate and pepper; fry, stirring continuously.

8. Once the rice is tender, transfer to a heated serving dish, add the other ingredients and mix well; serve into individual bowls garnishing with chopped parsley and little heaps of pickled ginger.

Steamed rice in a lotus leaf

25'

6oz (175g) coarsely chopped chicken breast
4oz (125g) prawns, chopped
4–5 dried Chinese winter mushrooms, pre-soaked
generous tsp salt
1 fresh lotus leaf or dried leaf soaked overnight in cold water
5 tsp peanut oil
4oz (125g) roast duck, coarsely chopped
1 lb 6oz (625g) pre-cooked, steamed, long-grain rice (about
   9oz (275g) uncooked rice will yield this quantity)
1 carrot, cut into small dice
For the marinade:
1 tsp salt
$\frac{1}{2}$ tsp monosodium glutamate
1 tbsp cornflour
Calories 680; protein 41.5g; fat 18.2g; sugar 93.3g
Serves 12

1. Mix the chicken and prawns with the marinade and leave to stand for a few minutes. Drain the mushrooms, remove the stalks and slice the caps finely.

2. Wash the lotus leaf, pat dry and brush the inside with oil.

3. Set the bamboo steamer over boiling water. Heat 3 tbsp peanut oil in the wok and stir-fry the chicken, duck and prawns for about 1 minute. Remove and set aside.

4. In the oil remaining in the wok, stir-fry the mushrooms for 1 minute. Pour in 2 tbsp fresh oil and fry the rice until it is lightly coloured.

5. Add the chicken, duck and prawns, followed by the carrot, and stir-fry over a moderate heat for 1½ minutes.

6. Place the rice mixture in the lotus leaf and fold the leaf over the rice enclosing it in a neat package. Steam in the prepared bamboo steamer for 15 minutes. Serve very hot.

NOODLES

In those parts of China far from the main rice-growing areas, wheat and other cereal crops are sown to provide people with an alternative source of starch in their diet. Many different types of bread are eaten in China but there is a far greater variety of noodles, which are usually made with wheat flour but also with rice or soya flour.

Most Chinese noodles take the form of long straight sticks. The length is due to a tradition which remains particularly strong in the northern regions, and which maintains that they symbolise long life, for this reason they are usually included in the main dish of a birthday feast. It is supposed to be bad luck to cut the noodles before they are presented to the guests.

Noodles can be eaten as a snack, or they may form the basis of an entire meal. At banquets, dishes are not usually accompanied by rice, but the end of the meal is often signalled by the appearance of fried rice or noodles.

Chow Mein, which consists of fried noodles with vegetables and meat, is often eaten as a meal in itself. Noodles in broth are as just as popular, making a nourishing hot dish when meat or vegetables are added.

A dish of cold noodles with sliced cucumber and chicken or other ingredients is often served as a first course but can equally well appear as one of the main dishes making up the various courses of a meal.

Chicken and noodle casserole

Following the usual Chinese custom, noodles form part of a composite dish, served as a course in itself economical and simple to prepare.

½ chicken
5oz (150g) spinach
⅓ leek
small piece root ginger
2 tbsp rice wine or dry sherry
1–2 tsp salt
approx. ½lb (250g) Chinese egg noodles
Calories 464; protein 16.6g; fat 2.8g; sugar 88.9g
Serves 4–6

1. Wash the chicken, place in a large pan of boiling water and blanch. Drain.

2. Wash the spinach thoroughly and cut into

1¼–1½-in (3–4-cm) lengths. Bring the flat of the cleaver blade sharply down on the leek and ginger once or twice to bruise them.

1

2

3

4

5

6

3. Place the chicken in a large flameproof casserole, together with the leek and ginger. Add the rice wine and salt, followed by 3–4 pints (1¾–2½ litres) water to cover the chicken.

4. Place the casserole over a high heat and bring to the boil; lower the heat and skim. Cover and cook for about 1 hour, removing scum whenever necessary. Boil the noodles until tender but still firm.

5. When the chicken flesh comes away from the bones quite easily, remove the ginger and leek and discard. Add the noodles and continue cooking for a few minutes.

6. Add the spinach and cook until tender but still slightly crisp; adjust the seasoning by adding a little more salt if needed.

Chinese egg noodles in broth with meat and vegetables

1 lb (500 g) fresh Chinese egg noodles or dried noodles
3¼ pints (1¾ litres) stock (see recipe, p. 296)
12 thin slices cold roast pork
2 hard-boiled eggs
about 1 lb (500 g) spinach or other green leaf vegetable, lightly
    boiled
3½ oz (100 g) boiled fresh or canned bamboo shoots
½ leek, finely chopped
For the soy sauce flavouring:
1 tbsp peanut oil
⅓ leek, coarsely chopped
1 clove garlic, chopped
small piece root ginger, chopped
16 fl oz (½ litre) soy sauce
3 fl oz (75 ml) rice wine or dry sherry
2 tbsp rice wine or dry sherry sweetened with a little sugar
Calories 638; protein 26.4 g; fat 9.9 g; sugar 102.7 g

1. Heat the stock to boiling point in the wok or a large saucepan; shake and pull the noodles apart and boil 1–2 hanks at a time, so that they can spread out and cook more successfully.

2. Cook over high heat, stirring from time to time so that the noodles do not stick together.

3. Once the stock has returned to the boil, pour in about ⅓ pint (200ml) cold water and continue cooking.

4. Draw a strand of the noodles out of the boiling water with the chopsticks; if it does not slide back through them it is done. Drain at once. The noodles should be cooked at the last minute just before they are served.

5. While the noodles are cooking, prepare the soy sauce flavouring for the stock. Heat the peanut oil in the wok and stir-fry the coarsely chopped leek, garlic and ginger. Once these are lightly browned, add the soy sauce, rice wine and the sweetened rice wine.

6. Place 2–2½ tbsp of this flavouring in each of 4 heated serving bowls, pour about 2 fl oz (50ml) boiling hot stock into each bowl.

7. Add the well-drained, piping hot noodles to the bowls.

8. Top the noodles with 3 slices each pork and some sliced boiled bamboo shoots together with the lightly boiled spinach or other green vegetables and the hard-boiled eggs, cut into decorative flower shapes. Garnish with very finely chopped leek.

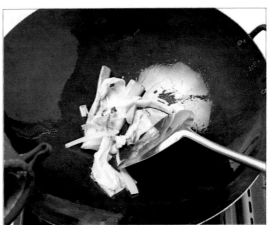

271

Noodles with pork and black bean paste

1 lb (500 g) boned and rolled shoulder of pork
2 tbsp black bean paste
3½ tbsp soy sauce
3 tbsp rice wine or dry sherry
2–3 star anise
2 oz (50 g) sugar
3 oz (75 g) boiled fresh or canned winter bamboo shoots
⅓ leek
½ lb (250 g) spinach
2 tbsp lard
pinch of salt
pinch of pepper
1 lb (500 g) Chinese egg noodles (preferably fresh)
For the sauce:
4 tbsp soy sauce
3 tbsp rice wine or dry sherry
⅔ tsp salt
2¾ pints (1½ litres) stock (see recipe, p. 296)
Calories 1019; protein 39.9 g; fat 48 g; sugar 108.5 g

1

2

3

4

1. Wipe the pork, rub all over with the black bean paste and leave to stand for 2 hours.

2. Put the soy sauce, rice wine and star anise in the wok, bring to the boil and add the pork in its covering of bean paste. Cook the pork, turning frequently, and when well moistened on all sides, pour in 1 pint (generous $\frac{1}{2}$ litre) boiling water. Reduce the heat.

3. Cover the wok and cook for about 30 minutes over a low heat.

4. Add the sugar and simmer for about 1 hour, turning the pork now and then. The pork will absorb the liquid and flavouring and turn a rich, brown colour.

5. Slice the bamboo shoots into small, diagonal pieces. Cut the leek into $1\frac{1}{2}$-in (4-cm) sections. Trim the spinach, wash well and cut in half.

6. Heat the lard in the wok; add the salt and stir-fry the spinach and leek briskly. Add the bamboo shoots and stir-fry all these vegetables together briefly; season with a little pepper and salt and turn off the heat.

7. Boil the noodles in plenty of water until tender; drain and place in a heated serving bowl, top with the savoury pork, carved into thin slices, and the spinach.

8. Combine the sauce ingredients in a saucepan, bring to the boil and pour into the serving dish.

5

6

7

8

Chinese noodles with scrambled eggs and leeks

A cheap and delicious light meal can always be prepared with the few run-of-the mill ingredients needed for this dish.

5oz (150g) prawns
salt
2½ fl oz (65ml) rice wine or dry sherry
1 tsp cornflour
2oz (50g) lard
small piece root ginger
1 leek
4 eggs, beaten
1 lb (500g) fresh Chinese egg noodles
3¼ pints (1¾ litres) stock (see recipe, p. 296)
Calories 645; protein 204g; fat 19.8g; sugar 92.3g

1. De-vein the prawns and mix with ¼ tsp salt, ½ tbsp rice wine and the cornflour.

2. Heat 2 tbsp lard in the wok; add the prawns and stir-fry briskly over a high heat for 1–2 minutes; remove from wok and set aside.

3. Chop the ginger and stir-fry in the fat remaining in the wok; cut the leek into 1¼-in (3-cm) lengths and stir-fry.

4. When the leek is soft, return the prawns to the wok, heat through and add the beaten eggs. Mix well over a high heat, combining all the ingredients in the wok. Divide the contents into 4 portions and set aside to keep warm.

5. Boil the noodles in plenty of water, drain well and divide between 4 individual heated bowls.

6. Bring the stock quickly to the boil, add 1 tbsp salt and 2fl oz (50ml) rice wine and pour the boiling stock into 4 individual bowls. Top with the four portions of prawn, leek and egg mixture.

Szechuan noodles with pork

2 tbsp peanut oil
small piece root ginger, finely chopped
7 oz (200 g) minced pork
2 tbsp soy sauce
2 tbsp rice wine or dry sherry
1 leek
1 large piece Chinese pickled, salted mustard greens (za-zai)
1 lb (500 g) fresh Chinese egg noodles
3¼ pints (1¾ litres) hot stock (see recipe, p. 296)
For the flavouring:
4 fl oz (125 ml) soy sauce
2 tbsp vinegar
2 tbsp ground sesame seeds
1¾ tsp chili oil
2 tsp sesame seed oil
Calories 714; protein 22.5 g; fat 26.7 g; sugar 94.7 g

1. Heat the peanut oil in the wok and stir-fry the ginger; as soon as it starts to release its aroma, add the minced pork, stirring and turning while frying to keep the grains separate.

2. When the pork is cooked, add the soy sauce and the rice wine.

3. Wash the leek and chop finely.

4. Wash the mustard greens thoroughly and chop.

5. Heat plenty of water in the wok or large saucepan and boil the noodles, untangling them as they cook.

7. Stir the noodles with chopsticks so that they do not stick to each other: as soon as the water boils add 8 fl oz (225 ml) cold water and then continue cooking until the noodles are tender. Drain well.

8. Mix the flavourings and pour an equal quantity into 4 china bowls, pour in the boiling stock and stir.

9. Add the noodles and top with the leek, mustard greens and the cooked minced pork.

Noodles in broth with beef and green peppers

3½oz (100g) thinly sliced beef
⅓ leek
2 green peppers
2oz (50g) boiled fresh or canned bamboo shoots
2 tbsp peanut oil
1 tsp hot black bean paste
8 floz (225ml) stock (see recipe, p. 296)
1 tbsp soy sauce
1 tbsp rice wine or dry sherry
½ tsp sugar
2 tsp cornflour
1 lb (500g) fresh Chinese egg noodles
For the marinade:
½ tsp ginger juice
1 tsp soy sauce
1 tsp cornflour
For the sauce:
2¾ pints (1½ litres) stock
6 tbsp soy sauce
4 tbsp rice wine or dry sherry
½ tsp salt
Calories 536; protein 15.8g; fat 9.2g; sugar 93.8g

1. Cut the beef into thin strips and mix with the marinade of ginger juice, soy sauce and cornflour.

2. Shred the leek, peppers and bamboo shoots the same size as the beef strips.

3. Heat the peanut oil in the wok and stir-fry the beef and leek strips. Drain and set aside.

4. In the remaining oil lightly stir-fry the peppers and bamboo shoots and then return the beef and leek to the wok.

5. Add the hot black bean paste; stir in the stock and cook rapidly over a high heat.

6. When the bean paste has dissolved in the stock, add the soy sauce, rice wine, and sugar. Stir in the cornflour mixed with 4 tsp water.

7. Boil the noodles in plenty of water, stirring so that they separate. When tender, drain and divide between 4 heated ceramic bowls.

8. Bring the sauce ingredients to the boil, pour into the bowls and top each with a quarter of the mixture from the wok.

Egg noodles with pork and black bean paste

7 oz (200g) minced pork
scant 3 fl oz (75 ml) peanut oil
1 leek, finely chopped
small piece root ginger, finely chopped
3 oz (75g) boiled fresh or canned bamboo shoots, finely
    chopped
7 oz (200g) bean sprouts
a few drops of vinegar
3 small (or 1 large) cucumbers
2 eggs
$\frac{1}{4}$ tsp salt
1 lb (500g) fresh Chinese egg noodles
a few drops of sesame seed oil
For the sauce:
3 tbsp black bean paste sweetened with a little sugar
scant 3 fl oz (75 ml) soy sauce
5 fl oz (150 ml) stock (see recipe, p. 296)
2 tbsp sugar.
Calories 786; protein 26.7g; fat 29.5g; sugar 103.3g

1. Heat the peanut oil in the wok, add the pork and stir-fry, keeping the grains separate.

2. Add the chopped leek and ginger and stir-fry until they release their aromas; add the bamboo shoots and continue frying.

3. Mix the sauce ingredients, blending them well, and add to the wok; cook over a low heat for 15–20 minutes, stirring and turning now and then.

4. Wash the bean sprouts thoroughly (remove the little black seeds if wished as these can make them a little bitter); add to a large pan of boiling water with a few drops vinegar; when still crisp refresh with cold water and drain.

5. Pare off any small bumps on the cucumber skins; shred into strips 2 in (5cm) long and soak in cold water.

6. Beat the eggs with the salt.

7. Heat a little peanut oil in the wok, pour in $\frac{1}{4}$ of the beaten egg mixture and make a small omelette, set aside and repeat three more times. Cut the omelettes into long, thin strips.

8. Boil the noodles in plenty of water until tender but firm, drain well and divide between four china bowls.

9. Top the noodles with the bean sprouts, cucumber and omelette strips and the pork mixture.

Chinese noodles with chicken and mushrooms in broth

An extremely easy recipe which is tasty and digestible.

½ small chicken
⅓ leek, crushed
small piece root ginger, crushed
scant 3 fl oz (75 ml) rice wine or dry sherry
½ bamboo shoot, boiled fresh or canned
4 fresh or dried pre-soaked Chinese winter mushrooms
1 leek
2 tbsp lard
salt
pepper
1 tbsp soy sauce
10 oz (300 g) dried Chinese egg noodles, parboiled
4 bunches Chinese greens or chard
parsley
Calories 363; protein 11.9 g; fat 7.6 g; sugar 59 g

1. Wash the chicken well. Place in a large saucepan with 4 pints (2¼ litres) water and the lightly crushed leek and ginger. Bring to the boil over a high heat.

2. Once the water has boiled, lower the heat, remove any

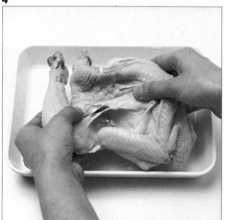

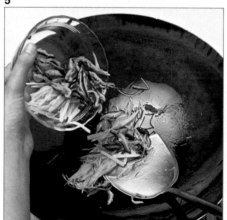

scum and boil gently for about 20 minutes; skim frequently.

3. When the stock is clear, add the rice wine and continue cooking for 20 minutes over a very low heat. Remove the chicken, set aside on a dish and strain the stock.

4. When the chicken is cool enough to handle, remove the bones and tear the flesh into small shreds by hand.

5. Cut the bamboo shoot, Chinese mushrooms and the leek into fine shreds; stir-fry in the lard and season with a little salt and pepper. Pour in 2½ pints (1½ litres) stock.

6. Season with salt and the soy sauce, add the chicken and the parboiled noodles; cook for about 5 minutes or until the noodles are tender and then transfer to a heated serving dish, topping with the Chinese greens or chard and parsley.

Crispy fried noodles

1 lb (500 g) Chinese egg noodles, steamed until tender
1 lb (500 g) lard
3 oz (75 g) carrot
3 oz (75 g) celery
2 fresh Chinese mushrooms
2 leaves Chinese cabbage
1 clove garlic
3½ oz (100 g) very fresh chicken gizzards
3 tbsp soy sauce
4 tsp rice wine or dry sherry
4 oz (125 g) raw or cooked prawns
1 tsp ginger juice
1 tsp rice wine or dry sherry
cornflour
3 oz (75 g) pork
1 small squid
4 tablespoons peanut oil
For the sauce:
1¼ pints (¾ litre) stock (see recipe, p. 296)
4 tbsp soy sauce
2 tbsp sugar
2 tbsp rice wine
pinch of salt
Calories 819; protein 33.1 g; fat 29.8 g; sugar 98.8 g

1. Place the steamed noodles in a colander and pour plenty of boiling water over them; drain well. Heat the lard in the wok and fry the noodles until crisp and golden, stirring and turning to prevent them burning. Drain. Leave the fat in the wok.

2. Cut the carrot and celery into rectangular slices; slice the mushrooms and cut the cabbage diagonally into pieces. Pound the garlic with the cleaver.

3. Wash the gizzards well; cut open, trim and score the pieces all over. Put in a bowl with 1 tbsp each soy sauce and rice wine and leave to marinate.

4. Shell the prawns, removing the heads, and de-vein. Put in a bowl with 1 tsp each ginger juice, rice wine and cornflour. Mix gently and leave to marinate.

5. Cut the pork into small, thin pieces, put in a bowl and add 2 tbsp soy sauce and 1 tsp each rice wine and cornflour. Clean the squid, remove skin and open up the body; score the inside surface with a lattice pattern and cut into bite-sized pieces. Coat with ½ tbsp cornflour.

6. Heat the fat in the wok again up to 350°F (180°C) and fry the squid, prawns, pork and gizzards, adding them to the fat in this order. Take care that they do not overcook or burn. Set aside when cooked and clean the wok.

7. Heat the peanut oil in the wok; stir-fry the garlic and when it starts to release its aroma add the carrot, celery and mushrooms followed by the fried squid, prawns, pork and gizzards. Combine the sauce ingredients, add to the wok and cook, stirring and turning over a high heat.

8. When the mixture is cooked and the vegetables are quite tender, stir in 2 tbsp cornflour dissolved in 4 tbsp water to thicken the sauce. Place the crispy noodles on a warmed serving dish and top with the contents of the wok.

Crispy noodles with chicken

5oz (150g) boneless chicken breast
1 tbsp ginger juice
1 tbsp rice wine or dry sherry
2 tsp cornflour
3 slices cooked ham
3½oz (100g) boiled fresh or canned bamboo shoots
4 dried Chinese winter mushrooms, pre-soaked
1 leek or bunch of spring onions
4 tbsp peanut oil
1lb (500g) fresh Chinese egg noodles
scant 4oz (125g) lard
For the sauce:
1¼ pints (¾ litre) stock (see recipe, p. 296)
½ tbsp salt
2 tsp sugar
2 tbsp rice wine or dry sherry
Calories 707; protein 20.8g; fat 25.1g; sugar 96g

1. Slice the chicken diagonally into thin strips and mix well with the ginger juice, rice wine and 1 tsp cornflour.

2. Cut the ham into ¼-in (5-mm) strips; slice the bamboo shoots thinly. Drain the mushrooms in water, remove the stalks and cut the caps into thin strips.

3. Cut the leek into 1¼-in (3–4-cm) lengths.

4. Heat 2 tbsp peanut oil in the wok and stir-fry the chicken; when done, drain and set aside on a plate.

5. Pour 2 tbsp fresh peanut oil into the wok and stir-fry the mushrooms, bamboo shoots and leek. Stir in the ham, add the chicken and stir-fry over a high heat.

6. Mix the sauce ingredients together and pour into the wok; cook for 1–2 minutes. Stir in 1½ tbsp cornflour mixed with an equal amount of water, to thicken.

7. Boil the noodles in plenty of water until just tender but still firm. Drain. Melt the lard in a clean wok and add the noodles. Fry over a high heat, stirring and turning, until the noodles are crisp and golden.

8. Place the noodles on a serving platter and top with the sauce and chicken mixture from the wok.

Crispy fried noodles and mixed vegetables

3½oz (100g) lean pork, sliced thinly
6 leaves Chinese cabbage
1 onion
7oz (200g) bean sprouts
½ carrot
2 green peppers
6 cloud ear mushrooms
large piece root ginger
6 tbsp lard
1 lb (500g) Chinese egg noodles, steamed
3 tbsp peanut oil
3 tbsp Worcestershire sauce
2 tbsp soy sauce
pinch of salt
pinch of pepper
Calories 627; protein 15.6g; fat 19.7g; sugar 96.8g

1. Cut the sliced pork into thin strips diagonally across the grain.

2. Cut the Chinese cabbage leaves into small pieces (ordinary cabbage may be used) and the onion into thin strips.

3. Wash the bean sprouts well and drain, remove the little black seeds and the thread-like roots.

4. Cut the carrot lengthways in half, then in pieces and finally into thin rectangular slivers. Remove the seeds, stalk and pith from the peppers and slice into narrow rings or strips.

5. Soak the mushrooms in water for 20 minutes, drain, trim off any tough sections and chop.

6. Slice the ginger into thin strips.

7. Place the noodles in a bowl, cover with boiling water and drain. Heat the lard in the wok and stir-fry the noodles over a high flame.

8. Heat the peanut oil in a frying pan, stir-fry the ginger and as soon as it starts to give off its aroma, add the pork, cabbage, onion, bean sprouts, carrot, peppers and mushrooms. Stir-fry.

9. When the ingredients are tender, season with the Worcestershire sauce, soy sauce, salt and pepper; add the noodles, mix and serve.

Fried rice noodles

1 h
30'

1 oz (25 g) Chinese dried prawns
2 dried Chinese mushrooms
10 oz (300 g) rice noodles
3½ oz (100 g) pork
2 small leeks or 1 large leek
3 oz (75 g) boiled fresh or canned bamboo shoots
⅓ carrot
2 green peppers
7 oz (200 g) bean sprouts
peanut oil
For the sauce:
4 tbsp rice wine or dry sherry
2 tsp salt
½ tsp sugar
1 tbsp soy sauce
Calories 524; protein 13.8 g; fat 16.9 g; sugar 75.5 g

1. Wash the dried prawns; soak in warm water for about 1 hour. Soak the mushrooms in water for 20 minutes. Place the rice noodles carefully in a large bowl, breaking them as little as possible. Cover with plenty of hot water, leave to stand for 10 minutes and then drain.

2. Drain the mushrooms, remove the stalks and cut the caps into thin strips. Cut the pork into bite-sized pieces.

3. Slice the leek into ¼-in (5-mm) rings; cut the bamboo shoots and carrot into rectangles; cut the peppers lengthways in half, remove the seeds and cut into strips.

4. Wash the bean sprouts; pick off the black seeds and thread-like roots and drain.

5. Drain the prawns and reserve 3 fl oz (75 ml) of the soaking water. Heat 3 tbsp peanut oil in the wok and stir-fry the drained prawns. Add the pork and continue frying over a moderate heat.

6. When the pork has changed colour, add the leek, carrot and bean sprouts and stir-fry; add the bamboo shoots, mushrooms and peppers, and cook briefly.

7. Mix the sauce ingredients with the water reserved from the prawns and pour into the wok; cook for 1–2 minutes, stirring and turning and then turn off the heat.

8. In another wok, heat 4 tbsp peanut oil; add the rice noodles and stir-fry until they are well coated with oil. Add the contents of the other wok and stir-fry briefly over a high heat before serving.

Curried egg noodles and vegetables

7oz (200g) pork, thinly sliced
salt
pepper
Chinese curry powder
cornflour
1 onion
4 fresh or canned Chinese mushrooms
7oz (200g) bean sprouts
½ carrot
small piece root ginger
6 green beans
2 tbsp lard
1 lb (500g) fresh Chinese egg noodles
2 tbsp peanut oil
For the sauce:
1¾ pints (1 litre) stock (see recipe, p. 296)
3 tbsp soy sauce
2 tbsp Worcestershire sauce
2 tbsp sugar
1 tsp salt
Calories 748; protein 21.5g; fat 26.2g; sugar 111.8g

1. Cut the pork into bite-sized pieces, add a little salt and pepper, a well rounded 1 tsp curry powder and ½ tbsp cornflour. Mix well.

2. Cut the onion in half and then into slices ¼–½ in (1 cm) wide; cut the stalks from the mushrooms and slice the caps into ½-in (1-cm) strips.

3. Wash the bean sprouts and drain well; remove the black seeds and thread-like roots.

4. Cut the carrot into strips and shred the ginger.

5. String the beans and boil fast until tender but crisp.

6. Heat the lard in the wok; add the ginger and pork and stir-fry lightly; drain and set aside on a plate.

7. Add the onion, carrot, bean sprouts and mushrooms to the wok and stir-fry quickly; return the ginger and pork to the wok with 2 tbsp curry powder. Stir and turn and when the curry is evenly distributed, pour in the sauce ingredients. Cook, mixing from time to time.

8. When the vegetables are tender, stir in 2 tbsp cornflour mixed with 4 tbsp water to thicken the sauce.

9. Boil the noodles until just tender, refresh quickly with cold water and drain. Heat the peanut oil in a skillet and stir-fry the noodles quickly.

10. Add the noodles to the other ingredients, mix and serve.

Suchow sugared noodle cake

An enjoyable dessert which is ready in a matter of minutes.

½lb (250g) dried Chinese egg noodles
4–8oz (125–225g) lard
icing sugar
Calories 309; protein 6.8g; fat 1.3g; sugar 55g

1. When buying the noodles, ensure that they are within their date-stamp time limit; if older they will have dried out too much and may be too stale for this recipe. Boil the noodles in plenty of water, drain when not quite cooked through.

2. Heat the lard in the wok and stir-fry the noodles lightly.

3. When the noodles are well coated with fat, shape and press into a firm cake, pushing them down into the wok with a wooden spatula.

4. Turn the noodle "cake" over carefully and fry on the other side until crisp and crunchy, again pressing down to shape. Transfer to a serving plate.

5. Use a fine sieve to dust the top of the cake with icing sugar and serve.

DESSERTS

Although their cuisine boasts an infinite number of sweet dishes, be they in solid form as in dim sum *and puddings or liquid, hot or cold, the Chinese rarely confine them to the end of a meal as we do in the West; they are eaten at festival time and on special occasions, as everyday snacks (*dim sum *are classified as desserts in China even though they may be savoury as well as sweet) or to provide a contrast between the courses of an elaborate meal. They may even be served as relishes.*

Soya, that ubiquitous ingredient in Chinese cookery, plays its part in the preparation of many desserts and sweetmeats, either as one of the main ingredients or in the form of jam or jelly for fillings. For instance, the Chinese make a sweet soup, which is traditionally used as a "pacer" between two of the many courses of a banquet to celebrate one of their many festivals; it involves skimming the surface of soybean milk whey (one of the many by-products extracted during the making of bean curd); this substance is then boiled and sweetened with brown sugar.

Much the same philosophy applies to fruit, of which China with her favourable climate produces a great quantity and variety. Fruit is something to be enjoyed at any time of day and is not necessarily confined to rounding off a meal as a dessert in the Western understanding of the term.

Fried sesame seed balls

It is considered lucky to serve these fried sweetmeats to guests when celebrating the Chinese New Year.

3½oz (100g) powdered red soya beans
scant 1 lb (450g) caster sugar
2 tbsp lard
rice flour
3½oz (100g) plain flour
3oz (75g) white sesame seeds
oil for frying
Calories 797; protein 14.9g; fat 26.3g; sugar 126.7g
Serves 4–6

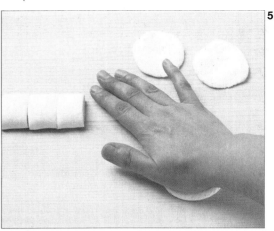

1. Place the red soya powder in a saucepan, add enough water to make a fairly thick paste and mix well over a low heat using a wooden spoon. Stir in the sugar, adding a little more water, up to 8 fl oz (225 ml) if the mixture is too thick to work with the spoon. Set aside to cool.

2. Melt the lard in a fairly large saucepan, add the cold red soya paste and cook over a low heat, mixing well with a wooden spoon.

3. Sift 5 oz (150 g) rice flour and the plain flour together into a bowl. Mix well; gradually add up to 12 fl oz (350 ml) water, working the mixture into a smooth paste or dough by hand.

4. When the mixture is firm and well blended, shape into a large ball; dust the pastry board with rice flour and gradually roll the ball into a long cylindrical sausage 1¼ in (3 cm) in diameter.

5. Cut the roll of dough into slices ¾ in (2 cm) thick (yielding about 30 portions); flatten with the heel of the palm and then, with thumbs and fingers, press out each piece into a circle.

6. Shape the cold red soya powder mixture into small balls ½ in (1 cm) in diameter. Enclose in the prepared circles of dough, seal well and roll between the hands to form smooth, round balls.

7. Put the sesame seeds in a pie plate or a shallow rimmed container and roll each ball in the seeds, covering liberally. If the seeds do not stick, moisten the surface of each ball with wet fingers before rolling.

8. Heat plenty of oil in the wok or deep fryer to about 300°F (150°C); the oil must not be too hot since the balls must cook through without burning or browning too much on the outside. Add the balls a few at a time and fry. When the balls rise to the surface of the oil, the heat may be increased slightly if they have not turned golden brown.

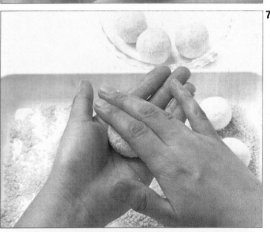

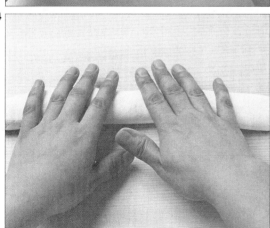

Fruit on the merry-go-round of happiness

This delicately flavoured lemon jelly is particularly refreshing in hot weather.

3oz (75g) agar-agar or 1oz (25g) gelatine
8oz (225g) sugar
juice of ½ lemon
a few drops lemon essence
1 small water melon
1 can lychees
Calories 106; protein 0.7g; fat 0.1g; sugar 28.5g
Serves 6

1. Divide the agar-agar into 2–3 pieces. Soak in cold, lightly salted water for at least 1 hour. Change the water once or twice.

2. Squeeze to remove as much water as possible. Place in a saucepan, add 1½ pints (850ml) water and bring to the boil, reduce the heat and cook gently.

3. When the agar-agar has completely dissolved, add the sugar and stir over the heat until dissolved. Remove from heat and stir in the lemon juice and essence.

4. Strain the liquid through a piece of cheesecloth or a very fine sieve.

5. Rinse an 8-in (20-cm) ring mould with cold water. Fill with the hot liquid (agar-agar sets quickly once cool and should not be stirred or disturbed when it has started to set). Leave to stand until cool and then transfer carefully to the refrigerator. (Agar-agar will set satisfactorily at room temperature.)

6. Use a melon-baller to shape the water-melon flesh (remove the seeds with a cocktail stick); drain the canned lychees.

7. Just before serving, turn the mould out onto a plate and arrange the fruit around it and in the centre of the ring.

Two-colour lake dessert

This pudding, attractively presented with the small coloured spheres bobbing on the surface can be served hot or cold.

2 tbsp white sesame seeds
5 tbsp plain flour
5 tbsp caster sugar
3 oz (75 g) rice flour
a few drops of cochineal
Calories 187; protein 3.2 g; fat 3.1 g; sugar 36.5 g

1. Toast the sesame seeds, taking care not to burn or colour them too much; place in the blender and grind fairly finely.

2. Sift the flour and place in a saucepan over a low heat; cook the flour, stirring constantly until it turns a golden, light-nut brown. Do not overcook or it will not thicken when the water is added.

3. Pour 12 fl oz (350 ml) water into the flour a very little at a time, stirring constantly over a gentle heat. Add the caster sugar and continue stirring until the mixture is quite thick.

4. Add the ground sesame seeds and stir well. Keep warm.

5. Place the rice flour in a bowl and gradually add 3 fl oz (75 ml) water; the mixture should be firm and smooth.

6. Divide this mixture in two and add a little red food colouring to one batch, turning it pale pink.

7. Shape the two batches of dough into pink and white balls, $\frac{1}{2}$ in (1 cm) in diameter. Boil in water until they rise to the surface; drain well.

8. Pour the hot custard prepared in step 3 into a heated dish, drop the coloured spheres on to the surface and serve at once.

Almond cream jelly

3 oz (75g) agar-agar or 1 oz (25g) gelatine
8 oz (225g) caster sugar
8 fl oz (225ml) milk
½ tsp almond essence
For the fruit purée topping:
¼ melon
2 tbsp caster sugar
2 canned peach halves
Calories 187; protein 1.9g; fat 1.7g; sugar 44.7g

1. Break the agar-agar into 2–3 pieces, place in a bowl of water and soak for at least 1 hour, changing the water several times.

2. Squeeze the agar-agar to get rid of all excess water. Tear into smaller pieces if wished so that it will melt more quickly. Place in a saucepan with 1¼ pints (¾ litre) water over a moderate heat.

1

2

3

4

5

6

3. Make sure that the agar-agar has completely melted, stirring with a wooden spoon as it comes to the boil Add the sugar and stir until dissolved.

4. Pour in the milk and stir; as soon as the mixture comes to the boil, turn off the heat.

5. Add the almond essence, whisk in quickly and strain through a muslin-lined sieve.

6. Rinse four glass serving dishes in cold water and pour in the agar-agar mixture (allow to cool very slightly so it will not crack the glass, but

make sure it is still quite warm, agar-agar sets at room temperature and must not be disturbed once it has started to set). The dishes should be approximately two-thirds full. Chill in the refrigerator. Remove the seeds from the

melon. Make a purée of the melon and peaches by adding 1 tbsp sugar to each and liquidizing separately in a blender for a few seconds. Pour topping over the jelly cream and serve.

Coconut snowballs

Made with glutinous rice, this sweetmeat has a pleasantly sticky consistency. In China these little cakes would be eaten in tea houses at any time of day.

8oz (250g) soya jam
6oz (175g) glutinous rice flour
1½oz (40g) desiccated coconut or freshly grated coconut
a few glacé cherries.
Calories 230; protein 4.2g; fat 3.1g; sugar 38.5g
Makes 12

1. Divide the soya jam into 12 portions.

2. Mix the rice flour with enough water to make a soft paste, divide into four portions and flatten into discs.

3. Bring 2½ pints (1½ litres) water to the boil and simmer the four discs until they rise to the surface. Drain and leave to dry out somewhat on paper towels.

4. Place the cooked rice discs in a bowl and beat hard with a wooden spoon for 5 minutes. Lightly oil the palms of the hands and shape the mixture into 12 round balls.

5. Flatten the balls, pushing them out into discs with fingers and thumbs, and place a portion of jam in the centre of each. Enclose the jam and shape into balls once more.

6. Roll the balls in the coconut and top each one with a piece of candied cherry. These little cakes can also be served hot, if they are steamed for 5 minutes, or they can be deep-fried in oil.

Cinnamon-flavoured sweet potato cakes

Fried sweet potatoes dusted with cinnamon go well with strong tea, such as the classic black tea from Yunnan called *p'u-erh.*

2–3 sweet potatoes, medium-sized
1–2 oz (25–50 g) caster sugar
$\frac{1}{2}$–3 tsp cinnamon powder
peanut oil
Calories 252; protein 1.2 g; fat 10.2 g; sugar 36.2 g
Serves 4–6

1. Wash the potatoes well, peel and cut diagonally into irregular pieces.

2. Place the potatoes in a bowl of cold water and leave to stand for a while to remove the bitter taste, drain and dry well with a clean cloth.

3. Mix the sugar with the cinnamon and sift (icing sugar can be used, if preferred).

4. Heat plenty of oil in a heavy saucepan or deep-fryer to 350°F (180°C) and lower the dried potatoes into the oil carefully. When they are golden brown on the outside, lower the heat and fry until tender and completely cooked. Drain on paper towels.

5. Place the sifted sugar and cinnamon in a large rimmed dish or bowl and roll the sweet potato pieces in the coating mixture (or shake gently). Serve hot.

Basic recipes

CHICKEN STOCK

bones and carcass of chicken
½ leek
2 small pieces root ginger
1 chicken stock cube
1 tbsp rice wine or dry sherry
Preparation time: 1½ hours
Makes 2½–3 pints (1½–1¾ litres)

1. Bring plenty of water to the boil and add the chicken bones and carcass; remove the carcass and bones after 1 minute. Crush the leek and ginger with the flat of the cleaver.

2. Pour 5 pints (3 litres) water into a large saucepan, add the chicken carcass and bones, leek and ginger, stock cube and rice wine. Bring to the boil.

3. Once the water has reached boiling point, lower the heat and skim any scum from the surface.

4. Simmer over a low heat for about 1 hour; do not cover the cooking pot if a clear stock is desired.

5. Strain the stock through a muslin-lined sieve.

GENERAL PURPOSE STOCK

carcasses from 2 chickens
approx. 5oz (150g) belly of pork with the bones left in
5–6 chicken wings
1 leek
2 small pieces root ginger
Preparation time: 2 hours 40 minutes
Makes 4 pints (2¼ litres)

1. Chop each chicken carcass in three and rinse in cold water.

2. Cut the belly pork, slicing between the bones.

3. Chop the chicken wings in half, place in a strainer and pour plenty of boiling water all over them.

4. Slice the leek in three, peel the ginger and bruise both with the flat of the cleaver blade.

5. Place the bones, wings and pork in a large, heavy saucepan, add 6 pints (3½

litres) water and bring to the boil over a high heat.

6. Once the water has boiled, turn down the heat and skim off any scum carefully. Simmer for 20 minutes.

7. Add the leek and the ginger and continue cooking for about 2 hours. If a clear stock is desired, do not cover the cooking pot and skim the surface quite frequently.

8. When the stock has reduced by about a third, turn off the heat and strain through a muslin-lined sieve.

MANDARIN PANCAKES (FOR PEKING DUCK)

8oz (250g) strong flour
sesame seed oil
Preparation time: 30 minutes
Serves 12

1. Sift the flour into a large bowl and make a well in the centre. Pour 3½ floz (100ml) boiling water into the well and work into the flour. Add 4 floz (125ml) cold water a little at a time and blend into the flour using a wooden spoon until the dough is smooth and soft. Work the dough for a further 5 minutes, cover with a damp cloth and leave for 20 minutes.

2. Roll the dough into a long, cylindrical sausage and cut into 24 pieces. Roll each piece into a small ball between the palms of the hands. Lightly

flour the pastry board and rolling pin and roll the balls out into thin, circular pancakes about 5-in (12-cm) in diameter.

3. Place a frying pan on the stove and brush it with sesame seed oil. Add one pancake and cook briefly on both sides; if brown spots appear, the pancake is overcooked.

4. Continue until all the pancakes are cooked. Fold into triangles once they are cooked and wrap in a clean linen cloth, until they are served.

PANCAKES FOR SPRING ROLLS

Shanghai spring roll skins can usually be purchased at most Chinese food stores but this recipe provides an alternative:

sifted strong flour
pinch of salt
peanut oil
Preparation time: 30 minutes

1. Mix 2 parts flour with 1 part water and a pinch of salt to make a thick mixture. Leave to stand for 1 hour.

2. Heat a griddle or frying pan and brush very lightly with peanut oil.

3. Take up a handful of the mixture, which should be quite elastic in consistency, and spread out on the griddle, shaping a pancake approx. 6in (15cm) in diameter. As the mixture cooks (the heat

should not be too high) a thin pancake will form which should be carefully peeled off the griddle.

4. Clean the griddle between pancakes with a cloth dipped in oil and repeat the procedure until the required number of pancakes or spring roll skins have been prepared. These spring roll skins can be kept in the refrigerator, covered with a damp cloth.

HSAO MAI DUMPLING CASES

8oz (250g) strong flour
pinch of salt
Preparation time: 1 hour
Makes 36

1. Sift the flour into a bowl; form a well in the centre and add 7 floz (200ml) boiling water, stirring quickly until a smooth, fairly thick dough is obtained.

2. Knead the dough for 3 minutes and then roll into a long, cylindrical sausage shape.

3. Cut the roll into 36 portions and roll each portion into a ball. Flour the pastry board lightly and, using a lightly floured rolling pin, roll each ball out into a circle about 2¾ in (7cm) in diameter.

4. The dough sheets can be kept in the refrigerator if made in advance.

IN THE KITCHEN
AND AT TABLE

In the kitchen: the ingredients

SAUCES AND FLAVOURINGS

Vinegar Chinese vinegar is made from rice and there are several types: *Black vinegar* is very strong. *Red vinegar* is best-suited to the preparation of fish dishes. *Mild vinegar* is a by-product of black vinegar and is usually included in braised dishes and stews. *White vinegar* is a delicately flavoured mild vinegar.

Monosodium glutamate (M.S.G.) A neutral salt of glutamic acid in the form of small crystals. For hundreds of years the Chinese extracted the substance from seaweed and used it to heighten the taste of food; nowadays it is derived from wheat, beets and corn. Monosodium glutamate is marketed in various countries under different names: Accent in the USA; Aji No Moto in Japan; Ve Tsin in Hong Kong. It should be used extremely sparingly and is often not necessary if very good quality, fresh ingredients are selected.

Cornflour This is the fine starch extracted from maize grains. It is valued for its lightness and for the fact that it is also very digestible. When used as a coating for foods before cooking, it gives an attractive sheen. Used for thickening sauces, it should be dissolved in a little cold water and added sparingly at the end of the cooking process. Potato flour, rice flour or wheat flour can be substituted for cornflour.

Rendered chicken fat Solid raw fat from the inside of a chicken is placed in a bowl in a steamer, covered and cooked until all the oil is released. It is then strained, all solids discarded and stored in a covered container in the refrigerator. It is usually added last to a dish to give extra flavour.

Sesame seed oil A reddish-brown oil (the more refined, light yellow oil which is also found is not a satisfactory substitute). The oil has a strong flavour and a tendency to burn and is therefore used for flavouring and not as a cooking oil.

Chili oil Powdered chili pepper is cooked in sesame seed oil to produce a hot sauce. Tabasco sauce can be substituted but does not have the same taste or consistency.

Sesame seed paste White sesame seeds are ground to make a paste which has a pleasant and distinctive flavour; it is usually sold in jars and can also be found in grocery stores under the name of *tahini*. The Chinese variety should be used whenever possible as it has the better flavour. The paste is usually diluted with stock or with soy sauce mixed with vinegar. It is often used as a sauce for boiled pork.

Sweet bean paste or sauce A mixture of fermented soya beans, white flour, sugar and spices. Hoisin sauce can be substituted.

Black bean paste A mixture of fermented black soya beans, flour, salt and a particular type of mould which aids the fermentation process. Each region of China produces its own variety. The most widely known variety is seasoned with chili peppers and may be termed "hot" black bean paste.

Shrimp sauce Made from salted shrimps. A very salty sauce, used to flavour vegetable dishes, squid, fried prawns and soups.

Soy sauce Soya beans, salt, roasted wheat and yeast mould are fermented and the resulting sauce is produced in three varieties: red soy sauce, dark or "black" soy sauce and light soy sauce. The dark, dense type *chu yow* has more colour than flavour; *shang cho* is lighter in colour and good for delicate flavouring, while *chan yow* is best suited for all-round Chinese

1. 2. 3. Soy sauce – 4. Shao Shing rice wine – 5. Sake – 6. Hoisin (barbecue) sauce – 7. Sesame oil – 8. Oyster sauce – 9. Sesame seed paste – 10. Shrimp sauce – 11. Monosodium glutamate – 12. Cornflour – 13. Fermented salted black beans – 14. Fermented black bean paste

cooking. The dark variety is used for long, slow cooking, such as red-stewed dishes.

Oyster sauce A velvety, golden brown thickish sauce made from cooked oyster liquor and salt with a decided flavour of oysters, but which marries with other tastes extremely well.

Hoisin sauce Used for marinating or as a barbecue sauce or dip for poultry, pork or duck. Made from yellow and sometimes red beans, sugar and spices, it is dark red in colour with a delicate, slightly sweet, spicy flavour.

Fermented salted black beans Small, salted beans which are used to add a distinctive flavour to fish and meat dishes. Soak in cold water for 10 minutes before use to remove excess salt.

Shao Shing This straw-coloured rice wine (sometimes known as yellow wine) tastes rather like a dry sherry or Japanese sake and is used a great deal in Chinese cooking. There is also a sweet variety. Rice wine may be replaced by dry sherry, dry vermouth or dry white wine.

SPICES

Star anise Star anise is a spice obtained by drying the six- or eight-pointed star-shaped fruit of anise. It is widely used in Chinese cooking to impart a subtle, slightly sweetish taste to slow-stewed (or red-cooked) and steamed dishes. The spice is a strong one and should be used in moderation – ½–1 piece usually suffices.

Dried mandarin peel Apart from its medicinal qualities this stimulates the appetite and is put to many other uses by Chinese herbalists; it is also added to beef dishes to mask the smell (which most Chinese find offensive). The peel can also be specially treated and eaten as a snack.

Five-spice powder Available in small packets or jars, this consists of a mixture of five ground spices: star anise, cloves, cinnamon, peppers and fennel seeds. This spice mixture is strong both in taste and aroma and should therefore be used sparingly in stews or in certain sauces. When mixed with salt it is placed on the table as a condiment and sprinkled on fried foods.

Apricot kernels Almonds are usually used by Western cooks instead of these kernels, though the taste is not quite the same. There are two kinds, one slightly sweet and the other a little bitter; the sweeter variety is used in a wide range of dishes, imparting a pleasant, distinctive flavour. Often salted and eaten as appetisers, the sweeter variety may be ground, mixed with evaporated or condensed milk and agar-agar or gelatine and made into desserts.

Chinese pepper Used as whole peppercorns when cooking meat or ground for fried foods.

Chili pepper These small, hot peppers add zest to dishes and must be used with moderation as they are very strong. They also stimulate the stomach and aid digestion. Also used as a preservative when combined with salted or pickled vegetables. Available fresh, pickled, fermented, dried or ground in oil.

Chinese parsley or coriander leaves A lacy-leafed herb with a distinctive flavour and paler colour than ordinary parsley. The plant can easily be grown indoors. The flavour is slightly bitter, it gives a good taste to soups and provides an attractive garnish.

Spring onion Young, lightly flavoured onions are widely used for flavouring and garnishing Chinese food. They can be replaced by leeks or shallots if necessary.

Gingko nuts These have a hard shell and creamy coloured flesh. Used in soups, stews and fillings. Also available dried.

Sesame seeds *White*: used for decoration, for sweets and fillings and for sesame seed paste. *Black*: impart a distinctive flavour to sweet soups, sometimes used for decoration.

Ginger Throughout this book, unless otherwise stated, fresh root ginger is to be used. At no time can powdered ginger be substituted. The fresh ginger root has a strong, distinctive taste and, together with leek and garlic, is indispensable in Chinese cooking. Its main functions are to flavour a dish, mask strong or

1. Peppercorns – 2. Five-spice powder – 3. Whole, dried chili peppers – 4. Cinnamon sticks – 5. Cloves – 6. Fennel seeds – 7. Dried mandarin peel – 8. Garlic – 9. Leek – 10. Root ginger – 11. Star anise – 12. Apricot kernels.

unpleasant odours (fish etc.) and to add an accent of extra aroma to a recipe.

For stir-fried dishes the ginger is chopped. For those which need longer cooking the ginger is bruised or pounded with the flat of the cleaver before it is added to the other ingredients. Generous amounts of ginger are used for tripe and duck dishes. Shredded or chopped ginger is also incorporated in sauces for pork or steamed fish. When cooked, ginger releases a strong but pleasant flavour and when fried imparts a sharp, lemony fragrance. Refrigerate but do not freeze.

Ginger juice Mix finely chopped or grated ginger with an equal quantity of water and place in damp muslin. Twist tightly to extract the juice. Alternatively crush in a garlic press.

BASIC AND SPECIAL INGREDIENTS

Anything edible can be included in a Chinese meal; the basic requirement remains, however, that each ingredient must be chosen and prepared with an overall aim of harmony of taste, texture, fragrance and colour in mind. The various component parts of a dish must complement each other and the freshest, best quality goods should always be chosen.

It is necessary always to choose the method of preparation which best lends itself to the particular raw material being cooked. Some ingredients are better cooked as simply as possible without any masking of their intrinsic flavour, in which case their own juices will suffice, flavoured lightly with salt and soy sauce. Some foods, however, need the contrasting and complementary presence of other ingredients. Such fish as trout, hake, bass and sole all taste their best and fullest when they are cooked in their own juices and are particularly good when steamed. Oily fish are best served with a sweet-sour sauce or braised with bamboo shoots and mushrooms; these last two ingredients belong to the category of foods whose rôle is to release their own flavour and give its savour to others. Then there are those foods which have no flavour of their own but rely totally on being impregnated with the tastes of added ingredients. Examples of these foods happen to be among the most highly prized of all Chinese delicacies, shark's fin and bird's nests, which are tasteless and have no aroma but have a gelatinous consistency. These must be subjected to long and complicated processes before they can be served as the most exotic and extravagant soups in the world.

Abalone A favourite delicacy of the Chinese, a mollusc also known as "St. Peter's ear", with firm, smooth flesh. Sold in cans or dried. The canned variety is easier to prepare and once the can is opened they will keep for several days in the refrigerator, the water changed every day. The dried variety will keep almost indefinitely, provided they are stored in a cool, dry place.

Agar-agar A natural gelatine which is extracted from various seaweeds. It is sold in the form of long, dry translucent ribbons rather like noodles, also in thin leaves and in strips about 1 ft (30 cm) long. It should be soaked in cold water for at least 30 minutes before using. Usually used for desserts (such as almond jelly cream) or for making jelly.

Seaweed The most commonly used are green seaweed (a thick, substantial variety, dried and sold in strips) which must be soaked in cold water overnight or in lukewarm water for 30 minutes before cooking, and dark purple (*nori*) seaweed (sold in dried sheets) which is also soaked and often placed on or added to the food when it is ready to serve or nearly cooked, since it loses its taste and texture if cooked for any length of time.

Chinese cabbage Long, pale green leaves with wide white ribs. There are two varieties: *pai t'sai* and the more tender *t'sai tum*. Ordinary cabbage can be substituted but will not have the same taste or texture.

Flour *Strong flour*, with a high gluten content, should be used for dough sheets for such preparations as won ton since the gluten gives the mixture greater elasticity, thus enabling it to be rolled out into extremely thin sheets. *Rice flour* is produced from ground polished rice. It is used to thicken and add body to certain sweet moulds and puddings. *Glutinous rice flour* when cooked has a sticky, elastic texture. *Plain flour*: when cooked becomes almost transparent. It is used for desserts and sweets.

Tiger lilies or lily bud stems (sometimes called golden needles). Lilies are dried and are used for flavouring vegetable dishes and steamed chicken. They must be soaked before use and will keep indefinitely in a dry place.

Lotus leaves The fresh or dried leaves of the lotus plant, used as a wrapping in which to cook foods to which they impart a distinctive flavour. If dried they must be soaked before use.

Chinese mushrooms *Straw mushrooms*: these are the best known (also called egg mushrooms). They have a rather gelatinous but pleasant texture and very little taste. They are used whole or cut in half and are available fresh or in cans. *Cloud ear mushrooms*: an edible fungus which on soaking swells to a soft brown gelatinous shape like a tiny ear. Must be carefully washed as they sometimes retain grit. Do not use water used for soaking these mushrooms for cooking. Their flavour is mild and faintly musky. Used a great deal in vegetarian dishes and stews. Soak in warm water for 20 minutes before use. *Tree ear* or *wood ear fungus* are often confused with cloud ear mushrooms, but although similar, being black and dried, the cloud ears are thinner and more delicate. *Tung-ku mushrooms* (or winter mushrooms); these must be soaked in hot or boiling water for about 30 minutes before using. They are favoured for their aroma and bouquet and are quite an expensive delicacy.

Bamboo shoots the tender shoots which appear at the base of the bamboo are gathered at the end of the rainy season. Sold fresh, canned or dried. The thick foliage on the fresh variety must be removed before use. The dried shoots must be soaked in water for 12–24 hours before cooking. The canned variety are parboiled and once the can is opened, will keep for up to a month in the refrigerator if placed in a bowl of water and the water changed every day.

Winter bamboo shoots are more difficult to come by and are therefore more expensive; they are, however, more tender and have a particularly delicate taste.

Chinese okra or gumbo, also known as the hairy melon A fuzz-covered oval vegetable of the mallow family. Inside it has a texture rather like that of courgettes, which can be used as a substitute as can cucumber.

Sea cucumbers (*bêche de mer*). Sold dried, available in varying sizes, these will keep indefinitely in a dry place. Must be soaked in water for 3 days before using.

Noodles The most commonly used varieties are: *Egg noodles* made with wheat flour. These may be fresh, home-made noodles but are also available dried. *Rice noodles* come in many different widths and lengths. *Soya or mung bean flour noodles:* (fenszu, more commonly called transparent or cellophane noodles).

These must be softened in cold water for about 30 minutes before using.

Shark's fin The main ingredient in the famous gourmet soup. Shark's fin should be bought in semi-processed form which shortens the cooking time. Possesses a very high vitamin content.

Lotus root This is a rhizome which is used in soups and vegetarian dishes. It is also crystallised and eaten as a sweet or dessert. Its crisp texture and mild, sweetish flavour and attractive appearance make it a great favourite. Available fresh, canned, sliced and dried, or crystallised. Fresh lotus root will keep well in a perforated plastic bag in the refrigerator for up to 3 weeks; once the canned variety has been opened, it will keep in water, changed daily, for a week in the refrigerator.

Rice *Chinese long-grain rice:* small, polished grains of rice with a low starch content. *Glutinous rice:* short, round, creamy white grains which become translucent and sticky when cooked. Used for puddings and fillings for sweetmeats and cakes.

Taro root An edible, starchy tuberous rhizome. Belonging to the arum lily family, it looks a little like a potato; the flesh is firm and white with red streaks and is slightly sticky. Its taste is more delicate than the ordinary potato, but the latter can be substituted.

Tofu or bean curd This product is obtained from the liquid or milk extracted from ground soya beans to which a small quantity of gypsum powder is added. Once opened, the water should be changed every day but it can be kept for up to 1 week in the refrigerator. Instant soybean curd powder is also available. *Fried bean curds:* cakes of fresh bean curd which have been fried and which keep well for several weeks in a dry place. *Dried bean curd skin:* sediment of soybean milk dried into stiff sheets. These are usually broken into pieces and soaked in tepid water for 30 minutes before cooking. Dried bean curd sheets, which are very thin and quite easily torn, are used to wrap certain ingredients and can be dissolved in warm water to produce soybean milk.

Za-zai A green leaf pickled vegetable, crisp, slightly bitter with a certain pungency. Used in soups and certain fried dishes. Also known as Chinese mustard top, or Chinese greens.

In the kitchen: cutting and chopping techniques

Chinese cookery is extremely flexible and versatile when it comes to the varying uses and quantities of ingredients. Of the total preparation time of a great many dishes, 80% is taken up in preparing the ingredients ready for cooking. Both dried and salted foods must be washed and soaked in water and what salt remains will add flavour to the other ingredients in the recipe.

Meat, pork in particular, must be trimmed carefully to remove fat and gristle. Fish are gutted and, where necessary, their scales removed although more often than not their heads and tails are left intact. Shellfish sometimes have their shells removed, sometimes not, depending on the recipe. Poultry are plucked and cleaned and usually jointed. Vegetables are washed and trimmed with great care – perhaps the most impressive example of this is when bean sprouts are painstakingly picked over to remove the thread-like root and the little black seed.

Of paramount importance is the careful cutting of all the ingredients into pieces of the same size. This helps to ensure that they will all cook evenly, and therefore have more flavour; it also gives the finished dish an attractive appearance.

SLICING

Since so many Chinese dishes undergo only brief cooking it is imperative that the ingredients should be very thinly sliced. Slicing may be lengthways, or across the grain, or diagonally. Cutting is done with a Chinese cleaver or heavy knife. The action may be a vertical, downward cut, or slicing upwards and outwards. With the knife held at an oblique (usually 45°) angle, cutting may be towards or away from the hand holding the food, or it may be horizontal, with the knife held almost parallel to the chopping board but at a slight downwards angle for safety.

One of the most common methods is of course to cut vertically down through the ingredient, into slices which are usually only $\frac{1}{10}$–$\frac{1}{8}$in (2–3mm) thick.

In order to cut ingredients into diamond-shaped pieces, cut the food diagonally into even pieces and then, holding these pieces firmly, cut downwards into $\frac{1}{10}$–$\frac{1}{8}$-in (2–3-mm) thick slices.

For even thinner slices, hold the knife almost parallel to the chopping board and cut horizontally.

STRIP AND SHRED CUTTING

Start by cutting the ingredient into 2½-in (6-cm) pieces. Then cut downwards into thin slices and cut each slice into shreds. If the ingredient is very firm or hard, cut across the fibres, if soft cut along the grain.

The ingredients are most commonly cut in strips about the size and thickness of a match; the food should therefore be sliced $\frac{1}{10}$in (2mm) thick before shredding. Stack several of these slices, overlapping them in a stepped formation, and cut off strips $\frac{1}{10}$in (2mm) wide.

When shredding such ingredients as green peppers, which are thin to start off with, simply cut downwards into thin strips.

CUTTING INTO THIN RECTANGLES

These small pieces are usually about $\frac{1}{4}-\frac{1}{2}$in (5mm–1 cm) wide and 1–2in (3–5cm) long. The technique is much the same as strip cutting. Cut into lengths and then to the desired thickness. Finally slice to the required width, to produce neat or approximate rectangles, depending on the ingredient used.

When thin ingredients such as mushrooms are to be cut into rectangles, simply cut into wide strips.

If the ingredient is of an irregular shape, the most important requirement is that the slices should be of even thickness to ensure even cooking times.

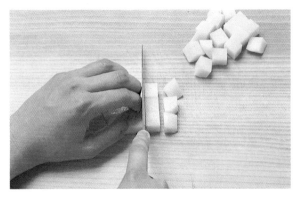

DICING OR CUBING

Dice usually measure anything from $\frac{1}{4}$ in (5 mm) to just under $\frac{1}{2}$ in (1 cm), depending on the recipe and the ingredient used. If the ingredient is an irregular shape, the pieces can follow the original shape but they must be of even thickness and size. Cut the ingredient into rectangles of the thickness required and then into dice.

For regular cubes of the most commonly used size, cut the ingredient into lengths which are $\frac{1}{2}$ in (1 cm) thick and $\frac{1}{2}$ in (1 cm) wide and then cut these lengths across into $\frac{1}{2}$-in (1-cm) cubes.

Where the ingredient used is cylindrical, such as cucumber, cut lengthways into quarters, sheer off the inner point of the triangle parallel to the outer edge and then cut the thick strips crossways or diagonally into small pieces.

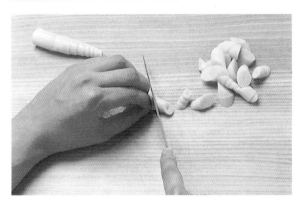

When thin cylindrical ingredients are to be cut, use the rolling cut technique: that is, cut a diagonal slice from one end of the vegetable, make a one-quarter turn of the vegetable towards you and make a diagonal slice slightly above and partly across the face of the ingredient left by slicing off the end. Continue rolling and slicing until all the vegetable is cut.

CHOPPING

This process is to reduce ingredients to very small pieces, less than $\frac{1}{8}$ in (3 mm) square. For the best appearance, cut the ingredient into thin strips and then cut across the strips at close intervals.

For example, when chopping a leek, slit it open with a knife, open the layers out flat and cut into thin strips $\frac{1}{8}$ in (3 mm) thick. Cut or chop across these strips at $\frac{1}{8}$-in (3-mm) intervals and the leek will be fairly coarsely but neatly chopped.

To chop ginger finely, slice thinly, cut the slices into needle-thin strips and then chop.

CUTTING INTO VERY SMALL CUBES

To cut ingredients into very small cubes or dice about $\frac{1}{8}$ in (3 mm) square follow the same procedure as for dicing and cubing above, simply adjusting the thickness and width of the original lengths sliced.

When irregularly shaped ingredients such as Chinese cabbage are involved (see illustration below), there will obviously be a certain uneven shape to the pieces.

ASYMETRICAL PIECES

This involves the same procedure as for dicing but on a larger scale. The ingredient should first be sliced into $\frac{3}{4}$-in (2-cm) pieces and then cut to the thickness required. The rolling cut method can also be used in this instance.

Slice the ingredient and give it a quarter-turn between each slice. Depending on the angle at which the knife is held, the pieces will vary in size.

In the kitchen: cooking methods

As many as forty different techniques are involved in Chinese cooking but only the most frequently used methods which are needed for recipes in this book are listed below.

Chu Plain boiling in water
Ch'ao General term for pan frying, quick frying and stir-frying
Cha Deep-frying
Shao Can indicate stewing or braising in some contexts and also roasting, quick-baking or barbecuing
Pao Northern-Chinese term for quick-frying whereby in the second phase the finely cut food is rapidly stir-fried over high heat, either in a thickened sauce or in flavoured oil. As a prefix it describes rapid cooking in oil or stock; literally meaning explosion, it is the last stage in any cooking process which can include steaming, shallow or deep-drying
Wei Clear-simmering. Gentle, prolonged poaching in a clear stock or flavoured sauce
Men Long, slow cooking over low heat. Braising or stewing. Food is first fried or seared in hot oil and then simmered in a little stock
Lu Soft food treatment, especially for fish or fragile foods which are cooked in a thickened soy-flavoured sauce without the usual stirring
Tun Slow steaming in a closed receptacle or double boiler
Liu Cooking in very little oil, with a minimum of movement. A thickened sauce is added during or at the end of the cooking process
Ch'eng Open or wet steaming with the food being subjected to the direct action of steam

Preparation of a dish may involve two or more of these processes. Food is often boiled before it is stir-fried or deep-fried and *vice versa*. Ingredients are often fried twice, once in their natural state and again when covered with a coating of flour, egg or some other coating. Sometimes boiling oil or water is ladled or poured over raw foods.

Certain rules must be respected for successful cooking. The ingredients must be cut to the same size. The pan must be pre-heated and the oil must reach the correct temperature given in the recipe, only then can the prepared foods be lowered into the oil, beginning with those which take longest to cook such as carrots, progressing through the ingredients and leaving such tender vegetables as bean sprouts and lettuce leaves till last.

Peanut oil is usually used for frying since it can be heated to the high temperatures required in Chinese cooking. The oil can be given extra flavour by adding a slice of ginger or a clove of garlic. Other fats used are chicken and duck fat and lard but these should not be heated to high temperatures. Many foods are marinated or mixed with seasonings, flavourings, tenderising agents or coatings when raw before cooking or between two cooking processes. Other ingredients are added at various stages, contributing to the flavour and balance of the finished dish. All these steps are clearly described in the recipes. The three most often used general cooking methods in this book can be broadly classified under three headings: stir-frying, deep or semi-deep frying and steaming.

Stir-frying This can be done in two ways. The raw ingredients are sautéed (but over a higher heat than would normally be used for sautéing) or they are first semi-deep or deep fried. In both cases the wok must be well prepared. Place it over a high heat and pour in enough oil so that it can be swirled round the hot wok or pan to cover almost all the inside surface; then pour off the oil and reserve it. The stated amount of oil listed in each recipe is then poured into the wok, heated and used for cooking. This procedure helps to ensure that the food does not stick and burn.

A few tips are worth remembering:
1. Cut the ingredients into pieces of the same size and put those which take longest to cook into the wok first. When cooking briefly over high heat, each ingredient must receive an equal and even amount of heat on all sides. If they are cut to the same size and shape the finished dish will also look much more attractive. Shredding into thin strips, thin slicing, dicing, cutting into rectangles and chopping are the most suitable methods for stir-frying.

It does not matter if the ingredients differ in consistency and texture or whether they vary in heat-resistance or change colour when exposed to heat; if the tougher, more heat-resistant foods are first to go in the pan, followed by the others, in an order which can be worked out in advance all will be well. Delicate, tender green-leaf vegetables can be added at the last minute so that they do not lose their colour and become soggy. The stir-fry-toss method should ensure that the ingredients are cooked evenly; the shape of a wok is particularly well adapted to this technique and the best heat to use is gas. Wok stands should be used with care as they can be a hazard when placed over certain types of gas burner.

2. Prepare all the ingredients and place them within easy reach before starting to cook. Watching a professional Chinese cook is an education in itself, but most fascinating is the sheer speed of progress, from the moment the oil goes into the wok until the finished dish is placed on the serving platter. The cooking process once begun, must proceed uninterruptedly over a high heat. When the ingredients are two-thirds cooked, they should be immediately transferred to a serving dish, preferably all at once to avoid the food which would otherwise be left behind in the wok being overcooked. The food finishes cooking in its own heat when already on the serving dish.

Frying With this method the aim is to cook the food evenly and to have it crisp and crunchy on the outside. This is best achieved by frying the food in two or three stages, ensuring that the oil is always at the correct temperature.

If the food is fried once and left in the hot oil until it is finally cooked through, the outside coating or batter will be over-done. When quite a large piece of meat or fish is coated, the batter will turn very brown and be far too hard.

If ingredients are twice-fried, they are first two-thirds cooked in moderately hot oil and then drained. The oil is then heated to a higher temperature and the food fried again.

The thrice-fried method consists of an initial short immersion in the hot oil, enough to achieve one-third of the cooking needed, set the batter and seal in the juices. The food is then drained and the oil allowed to return to the original temperature. The food is lowered into the oil again to fry until two-thirds done, at which point it should be very lightly coloured on the outside. Remove and drain the food once more. Finally, raise the temperature of the oil to very hot and complete the final frying. The outside of the food should be crisp and an attractive golden brown.

This method has the advantage of allowing an accurate check on the temperature of the oil each time the ingredients are removed and drained; the food is sealed quickly and what oil does penetrate will do so evenly. Any liquid released by the food can drain away when the items are removed from the fryer between stages.

Food can be fried without being dipped in batter, or it may be coated with flour or cornflour. A beaten white of egg or a few drops of oil can be added to batter to make it lighter.

Each method will produce a different effect on the appearance and texture of the food. It is usually considered that the paler and more delicate the batter, the more refined the dish; in this case the food will have been fried at a relatively low temperature. But even if frying at a low temperature is considered the proper treatment for a particular ingredient, the final touch will be rapid frying in very hot oil to seal and crisp. The same applies to foods given most of their cooking in moderately hot oil. Food cooked in very hot oil for any length of time becomes slightly bitter. Never deep-fry too many pieces of food at one time.

If oil is used for frying at low temperatures it will tend to retain odours and moisture. In order to re-use, heat to very hot, drop in one piece each of leek and ginger and once they have turned brown remove them. Turn off the heat. The oil can now be strained and re-used. Oil used for frying fish should not be re-used more than once, and then only for fish.

Steaming Fish, meat, poultry and stuffed starchy foods are steamed over a high heat. Eggs and bean curd need a more gentle heat. See pages 13 and 16 for the correct way to assemble and use the bamboo steamer.

At table: drinks and Chinese table manners

DRINKS

Everyone knows that tea is China's national drink and visitors to China find that, on every social occasion, they are offered tea in tall, beautifully decorated, lidded porcelain cups. Indeed, this refreshing and stimulating infusion has been considered an integral and indispensable part of everyday Chinese life from time immemorial and the fact that the famous Venetian traveller, Marco Polo, makes no mention of it in his writings is considered by some rather questionable authorities to be proof that he never actually set foot in China.

A description of tea is to be found in an ancient Chinese encyclopaedia written when Constantine ruled the Roman Empire; just over three centuries later the first manual on tea was compiled. Tea was already subject to tax, an indication of how popular it had become. In 1610 or thereabouts, Dutch travellers and merchants introduced tea to Europe, together with its name, *t'e* (from the dialect of the region surrounding the port of Amoy); this word survived, hardly changed, in English, French, German, Spanish and Italian, while the Japanese, Indian, Persian and Russian words for tea are all derived from the Cantonese *ch'a*.

There are three types of tea: black or fermented, green unfermented and oolong which is semi-fermented, and an infinite variety of blends, fragrances and brands. When infusing the tea-leaves the aim is to extract as much caffeine as possible and a certain amount of tannin while capturing the fugitive aroma and taste. The quality of the water used for steeping the leaves is of crucial importance; this must be boiling when added to the tea but should never be boiled for any length of time or boiled more than once or it will lose its precious oxygen content. The Chinese maintain that the kettle should always be earthenware and the teapot and cups porcelain (a Chinese invention, hence china). Tea must always be drunk while very hot and the Chinese never add sugar, milk or lemon since they adulterate the true flavour.

Westerners mistakenly believe that tea is drunk with every meal in China in the way that we drink water, wine, beer or soft drinks. The Chinese do not observe any hard and fast rules as to what goes with what, unlike Westerners who insist that certain wines accompany particular dishes, selecting a red or white, dry or sweet wine, in accordance with rigid guidelines in which each wine is allotted its proper place. This accounts for the somewhat surprising and sometimes incongruous variety of drinks one sees clustered on the tables of Chinese restaurants outside China, some patrons having chosen Chinese alcoholic beverages, some tea and others their usual beer or favourite wine – which may be excellent but are rather out of place with a Chinese meal. With the exception of some parts of China, tea plays a distinct role in the meal; it is used as a toast, as a symbol of hospitality, good-fellowship and an inseparable part of polite social intercourse. It is only served at the beginning and end of a meal and occasionally during a pause between courses to cleanse and refresh the palate, but not with the food since it does not go at all well with oil.

Instead, a light vegetable broth, which sometimes contains a few shreds of meat, is drunk as a thirst-quencher during meals. Alcoholic drinks may also be served in small delicate cups to drink the health of the other guests and generally to add to the gaiety of the occasion.

The versatile 17th-century writer Lorenzo Magalotti in his *Account of China (Relazione della Cina)*, 1672 tells of a meeting with the Jesuit priest, Johann Grueber, who had spent three years in China (1664–1666). Grueber told him that when liquid refreshment was served at certain intervals during the meal, everyone had to raise their cup to their lips at the same time with the customary toast of *zin zin zin*, after which their cup had to be seen to be empty. This little ceremony spread to the West and survived to a certain extent in the now rather dated expression "chin-chin", (*zin* was the

1. Ginseng – 2. Fen Chiew – 3. Mei Kwei Lu – 4. Chu Yeh Ching – 5. Ginseng – 6. Finest Green Tea – 7. Shao Shing rice wine – 8. Mao Tai – 9. "White" Pai Mu Tan tea – 10. Compressed tea (p'u-erh) – 11. Black Yunnan tea (p'u-erh) – 12. Medicinal tea – 13. Jasmine tea – 14. Oolong.

17th-century transcription of the Chinese expression *ch'ing*), used when clinking glasses.

Magalotti relates in his book, which revealed many aspects of China to the West (at that time almost totally ignorant of all things Chinese), that the inhabitants of that mysterious country drink "tea and rice wine, the latter in all probability being made by steeping or distilling. I say 'in all probability' since the secrets of the art are only revealed to those who swear to keep them and the lightest punishment for betrayal is death." In fact alcoholic beverages were not only distilled from rice but also from millet and sorghum (and from grapes to make wine as we in the West know it, although Magalotti states that "although they grow very fine grapes, they do not make wine from them").

The Chinese character for alcoholic drink comprises an ideogram signifying water with another which was formerly the name of the eighth month of the year (equivalent to September in the Western calendar, since the Chinese year starts in February), and refers to millet which was harvested in that month and was used to make the oldest type of "strong drink" in China. Fen Chiew, which originated in the province of Shansi, has been distilled from millet and sorghum for over 1,400 years. Another drink which comes from Shansi, Kaoliang, is also distilled from sorghum. In common with most northern Chinese spirits distilled from sorghum, Fen Chiew and Kaoliang have a high alcoholic content, whereas in southern China the alcoholic beverages made with rice – the staple crop of that area, are not so strong. The most famous Chinese spirit, Mao Tai, has much in common with Kaoliang; Mao Tai is strong, colourless and just the thing for warming people up in the freezing Peking winters; it has a rather strange smell but is sold in fascinating milky-white opaque bottles. Although it is often believed by Westerners to date back to ancient times, it is of comparatively recent origin. The story goes that at the beginning of the 18th century a merchant from Shansi settled in the city of Mao Tai in the province of Kweichow (south-eastern China) and started to distil this spirit in the same way as his native province's Kaoliang. As in the case of Fen Chiew (and, of course, Scotch whisky) the character and taste of the spirit depends on the quality of the local water.

Apart from these strong, cereal-based spirits there are many sweet liqueurs such as Chu Yeh Ching, Mei Kwei Lu and Wu Chia Pi. The first, Chu Yeh Ching, or bamboo liqueur, is made from Fen Chiew (distilled, as previously noted, from sorghum and millet) and is given added flavour and aroma by twelve different substances, including dried orange peel and bamboo leaves. The second, Mei Kwei Lu (poetically named Rose Dew) is sweeter and is made from a blend of sorghum and other cereals which are distilled and then flavoured, using aromatic herbs and rose petals; this liqueur is used a good deal for cooking as well as drinking. The third, Wu Chia Pi, is also distilled from sorghum and is given its distinctive taste and appearance (which are slightly reminiscent of Madeira) by the addition of caramelised barley sugar. In common with all alcoholic drinks, Wu Chia Pi is said to aid digestion and circulation and is used in cooking, in much the same way as Madeira and brandy, for certain gourmet meat dishes.

The wide variety of Chinese "medicinal" wines must not be forgotten. We in the West are familiar with the famous Ginseng, made from the root of *Panax ginseng* (the Latin word stems from the Greek panacea, or 'remedy for all ills'). The root grows in Manchuria and Korea and is credited with phenomenal aphrodisiac properties. This has stimulated a lucrative and colourful trade in the root, but the *Encyclopaedia Britannica* states dryly: "there is no evidence to suggest that ginseng has any value, either as a drug or as an aphrodisiac". There are countless other medicinal wines, including a liqueur distilled from snakes and another from tiger bones.

Although many of the alcoholic drinks we have mentioned are called wines and are served during Chinese meals, none of them really matches the Western conception of a table wine (although they marry well with food; Mao Tai, for example, is the perfect accompaniment to Peking Duck). The nearest equivalent of our table wines would be what the Chinese call "yellow wine". To quote Magalotti again: "their rice wine is pale and clear with amber glints, a very beautiful golden-yellow in colour: it has a very delicate taste and is sometimes so strong that we Europeans would mistake it for a Spanish wine. The common people drink from earthenware receptacles, the nobles from very curiously engraved gold and silver cups, while important dignitaries drink from polished and carved rhinoceros horns with richly jewelled gold mountings." This description conjures up the exotic and luxurious life-style of Imperial China and the rice wine to which Magalotti refers is Shao Shing, which originated from the city of the same name in the province of Chekiang and is still considered the best of the "yellow wines" to this day. It can be as strong as 18° and is made from glutinous rice, millet and ordinary rice; it resembles the Japanese rice wine, saké, and is usually drunk in the same way – warmed and served in delicate little porcelain cups. It is usually aged for 10 years but sometimes for over 40 years to produce a very rare wine of exceptional quality. It used to be the custom to put aside some Shao Shing when a baby girl was born, to be opened and drunk on her wedding day.

Lastly, we come to wine made from grapes. Today, vines are grown in various parts of China, but the total area given over to viticulture is only one forty-fifth of the total area devoted to growing vines in Italy. Very little wine is produced from grapes in China, the white wine normally being too acid and the red too sweet for Western tastes. Indigenous vines are known to have been cultivated 4,000 years ago and the wine was used for medicinal purposes. The European vine was introduced to China via the Silk Road under the Han dynasty in 130 BC, and Marco Polo referred to wine made from European grapes. Towards the end of the Ming dynasty in the 17th century new varieties of vine were introduced from Turkestan. Later, however, viticulture declined. Nevertheless, Chinese wine is celebrated in Chinese classical literature in the works of Li Po, who is considered the greatest Chinese lyric poet and who belonged to a group of poets called "The Six Idlers of the Bamboo Stream". Li Po was admitted to the Imperial academy by the Emperor Hsuan-tsung of the Tang dynasty and enjoyed a certain favour despite his tendency to drunkenness. He wrote a great deal of poetry, some of which survives, and from which the following lines are taken:

Amidst the flowers a jug of wine
I pour alone lacking companionship,
So raising the cup I invite the moon,
Then turn to my shadow which makes three of us.
Because the moon does not know how to drink
My shadow merely follows my body.
The moon has brought the shadow to keep me company a while,
The practice of mirth should keep pace with spring.

(*Anthology of Chinese Literature*, compiled and edited by Cyril Birch)

SERVING A MEAL: CHINESE TABLE MANNERS AND ETIQUETTE

There is no rigid system of etiquette to be observed when being entertained in China; the main thing is to relax and savour the food with obvious enjoyment. Usually the table is round and the food will be arranged on serving dishes in the centre.

The guest should always sit in the place indicated by the host, to decline the place of honour or to wish to change might appear ill-mannered. It is considered good etiquette to wait until the host invites everyone to start the meal before eating.

The seat farthest away from and facing the entrance is the place of honour, while those on either side are the least important; this is the basis on which the table seating is planned. If eating informally, with friends, people sit down without ceremony as they arrive.

The use of a circular revolving food-tray in the middle of the table enables everyone to reach dishes and serve himself without stretching over or getting up which would be thought impolite. As in the West, excessive deference or reluctance to accept delicacies pressed upon one would become irritating and a guest can therefore feel free to go ahead and help himself to a reasonable amount of his chosen dishes, with a simple word of thanks. The dishes are served first to important guests and after that it matters little whether the revolving centrepiece is turned from left to right or vice versa.

It is also a mistake to try to be too finicky and "refined" when eating foods on the bone or in their shells; anything that is too difficult to cope with using chopsticks is best eaten with both hands. When prawns have to be removed from their shells at table, a finger bowl is usually provided and the shells can be peeled off using both hands or using chopsticks and one hand. When meat has been chopped into small, bite-sized pieces on the bone, simply place the morsel in your mouth and as the meat is eaten, remove the bones; usually the meat is so well-cooked and tender that it falls off the bones once in the mouth, so there is no problem. The expert removes the bones from his mouth with chopsticks.

In Hong Kong it is customary to drop the bones and shells on to the tablecloth, since the dirtier the tablecloth after the meal, the more relaxed and enjoyable the meat is thought to have been. Often, however, plates are provided for this purpose, or scraps can always be pushed to the side of one's plate and will be removed before the next course.

In China plates are not necessarily changed for each course, but only when someone's bowl or plate is full of bones or other leftovers. When helping yourself to a dish with plenty of sauce, hold your bowl very close to the serving dish to avoid spills.

Some people might consider it unhygienic for everyone to help themselves with their own chopsticks but this is a result of the underlying philosophy that everyone is gathered together round the table and the bonds of fellowship make this consideration of secondary importance, or irrelevant. Indeed, it is considered good form and a friendly gesture for a host to select a particularly choice morsel and to place it in his guest's bowl with his own chopsticks. On formal occasions each serving dish has its own set of utensils, so that each guest can transfer the food to his bowl and then eat with his or her own chopsticks.

SELECTING A CHINESE MENU

It is best to start the meal with light and delicate dishes, progressing towards full-flavoured, richer fare or the palate will be blunted by stronger tastes and fail to appreciate the more subtle flavours.

The Chinese maintain that a menu should start with Yang foods – solid yet light – and finish with Yin foods – dishes with sauces, and liquids. By beginning the meal with the accent on Yang, the stomach is suitably prepared for all the food which is to follow and will be better able to absorb it, avoiding sudden contrasts of hot and cold. The meal will end with tea, since liquid is the epitome of the Yin form of nourishment. The menu should include a variety of foods cooked by different methods, such as stir-fried, fried, stewed or braised dishes, and should incorporate a wide range of ingredients, tastes and textures.

The age and sex of those present must also be borne in mind: if there is a preponderance of elderly people, then the food should be light and not too strongly or richly flavoured. The menu could include a starter of some kind, shark's fin soup, one or two stir-fried dishes with fairly delicate ingredients such as prawns or seafood; a dish of bean curd and minced pork and a more strongly flavoured dish of prawns in chili sauce. This could be followed by Cantonese rice or fried noodles, but only if the preceding dishes were not accompanied by boiled rice; a dessert would then round the meal off suitably.

An old Chinese saying should be remembered when planning a meal: "There is no need to strive for perfection in combining the five tastes, or to take inordinate pains to mingle the aromas, or to go to great lengths to seek out rare ingredients from far-off lands".

Drawing on the wide selection of recipes given in this book, it should be easy, using a little flair and imagination, to plan some delicious Chinese meals. The following menus are merely suggestions:

Southern Chinese menu
Steamed chicken salad with noodles pp. 40–41; Sweet and sour pork pp. 72–73; Stir-fried prawns with broad beans p. 153; Ch'ao tou ya (stir-fried bean sprouts) p. 204; Pai fan (boiled rice) p. 254.

Light meal
Steamed fish pp. 136–137; Bean curd with black beans Szechuan style pp. 206–207; Fried eggs, tomatoes and mushrooms p. 186; Stir-fried green beans with mushrooms pp. 190–191; Fish balls in broth p. 242; Pai fan (boiled rice) p. 254.

Vegetarian meal
Green bean salad p. 44; Bean curd and prawn salad p. 53; Fried aubergines with sweet and sour sauce p. 203; Mushroom soup p. 216; Pai fan (boiled rice) p. 254; Suchow sugared noodle cake p. 286.

Rich, full-flavoured menu
Piquant cucumber salad p. 45; Stir-fried beef and onions p. 101; Chili fried scampi pp. 160–161; Pai fan (boiled rice) p. 254; Bamboo shoot soup p. 229.

Summer menu
Steamed chicken with mild garlic dressing pp. 38–39; Bean curd and turnip tops with thousand year old eggs pp. 54–55; Chinese chicken and ham salad with noodles pp. 56–57; Lettuce and fillets of fish in broth p. 222; Almond cream jelly p. 293.

Winter dinner
Crispy fried prawn snacks pp. 28–29; Peking bean curd soup p. 228; Casseroled shizitou (braised pork balls) pp. 84–85; Stir-fried mange-tout with black bean paste p. 192; Congee rice with chicken pp. 262–263.

An appetising meal for children
Won ton soup p. 213; Fried eggs, tomatoes and

mushrooms p. 186; Fried fish with peanuts p. 152; Sweet and sour chicken legs p. 115; Five-colour fried rice pp. 250–251; Two-colour lake dessert p. 291.

Elaborate dinner party menu
Seven-colour hors d'oeuvre pp. 20–22; Yu Ch'i (shark's fin soup) p. 212; Hsiang su fei ya (classic spiced duck) p. 130; Steamed bean curd and white of egg pp. 208–209; Cantonese fried scampi pp. 156–157; Cucumbers and scallops with mushrooms p. 194; Yangchow fried rice pp. 248–249; Fruit on the merry-go-round of happiness p. 290.

Reception or party menu
Spring rolls p. 24; Bean sprout and noodle salad pp. 46–47; Chiao tzu (steamed or boiled stuffed dumplings) pp. 60–62; Five-colour hsao mai (steamed dumplings) pp. 64–65; Cha shao (roast pork) p. 67; Tea eggs p. 187; Fried rice noodles p. 284; Coconut snowballs p. 294.

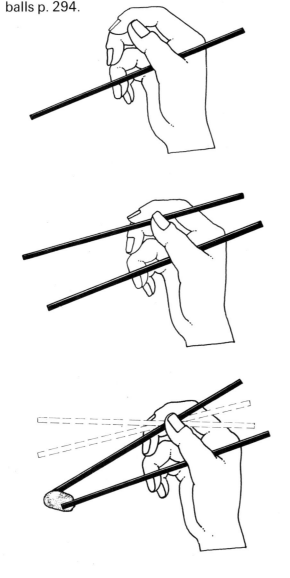

HOW TO USE CHOPSTICKS

The use of chopsticks dates back to the Shang dynasty (1766–1123 B.C.) but nobody knows when they began to take over from fingers, of which they can be considered an extension. They are a symbol of man's progressively more civilised eating habits, rather like the introduction of chairs to enable the diners to sit comfortably round the table.

Chopsticks used to be known by the name of *chu*, a word which stems from the concept of "helping"; since however this word sounded a little like the word "finish" – an inauspicious word, this led to a gradual change in favour of the expression *k'uai-tzu* meaning "that which is quick". One is most likely to hear chopsticks referred to as *faai-tsi*, their name in Cantonese. This is another example of the Chinese people's superstitious attitude to those words in common use which sound like other words and acquire their significance by association. The ideograms which represent the word *k'uai-tzu* are pronounced in the same way as the good wish to newly married couples for "children soon" and ivory chopsticks are often given as a wedding present.

There is no strict rule as to how to hold chopsticks so long as they grasp the food firmly so that it can be carried safely from bowl to mouth. A few hints may be helpful:
1) The first chopstick should rest in the crook of the hand between thumb and forefinger, resting on the ring finger; this chopstick remains in a fixed position.
2) The second chopstick is gripped between the tip of the thumb and the tip of the index and the middle finger, moving freely.
3) It should be easy to close the tips of the chopsticks together so that they touch.

The perceptive and imaginative Chinese have acquired a metaphor for man's progress through life and the pattern of his growth from infancy to maturity; a child is taught to hold his chopsticks very close to their tips, so that his fingers almost touch the food, but gradually as he grows older, so his fingers move up the chopsticks towards the other end as he attains adulthood, a progression which is repeated over and over again as it was with his forefathers.

List of recipes

Picture sources

Roberto Circià, Giorgio Perego, 14–15, 301, 311; Sun Tzi Hsi, 24, 66, 67, 68, 128–129, 130, 204, 212, 213, 254, 266, 294; Michael Hancock, 299.
Additional illustrations © Shogakukan Publishing Co. Ltd., Tokyo.